W0246634

From Hagiographies to Biographies

From Hagiographies to Biographies

Rāmānuja in Tradition and History

RANJEETA DUTTA

OXFORD
UNIVERSITY PRESS

Oxford University Press is a department of the University of Oxford. It furthers the University's objective of excellence in research, scholarship, and education by publishing worldwide. Oxford is a registered trademark of Oxford University Press in the UK and in certain other countries

Published in India by
Oxford University Press
YMCA Library Building, 1 Jai Singh Road, New Delhi 110001, India

First Edition published in 2014

ISBN-13: 978-0-19-809229-2
ISBN-10: 0-19-809229-6

Typeset in Adobe Garamond Pro 10.5/13
by The Graphics Solution, New Delhi 110 092
Printed and bound in India at Repro India Ltd., Mumbai

For Ma and Baba

CONTENTS

FOREWORD

The collective memory of a community grows through a process that selectively archives what it considers the most important elements of its historical or believed past. This archiving of information about a person, event, or an experience is not a one-time act. On the contrary, it is an ongoing practice that requires social memories to be periodically recalled and rejuvenated. Such acts of recall and rejuvenation occur at different points of time in a society's history and each such act introduces new elements. The sheer passage of time, the force of circumstances and, not the least, the aspirations of a changing community coalesce to transform older memories so as to make them useful for a different purpose. Even as collective memories seek legitimacy through the pretence of being truthful registers of the past, they are, even more importantly, a means of creating an appropriate past that complements contemporary objectives. Remembering is a selective procedure. In the life of communities, it is one where choices are made by each succeeding generation at significant historical junctures. This results in a layering of memories that blend and permeate into each other and are almost impossible to peel apart. Belief and history, thus merged, pose an enormous challenge to historians who despite the recent theoretical expansions that have occurred in the discipline are still expected to engage in reasonably sound empirical research.

This book traces the trajectory of several long-term trends that enable us to situate Ramanuja within the tradition of the Srivaisnava community as well as in the empirical historical situation. Early hagiographies initially represented the identity of Ramanuja in several different ways. Yet, certain elements of continuity in these hagiographies enabled his community of followers to further create a distinct identity for itself. A close connection existed between the perceived actions of Ramanuja, his image as an *acarya*, and the manner in which Srivaisnava beliefs came to be projected. The significance and contribution of the historical context within which all this happened has been perceptively elaborated by the author. Hagiographers and biographers—whatever the case may be—were nurtured by the particular milieu in which they lived and worked and this resulted in their divergence of perspectives. Some central questions, such as the one attempting to deal with the reality of social hierarchies, were indeed common to both genres. They transgressed the limitations imposed by the existential conditions of the authors and forged a bond between narratives produced during different historic periods. Nevertheless, the diversity both in hagiographical and biographical works persisted. In short, the core academic concern of the author is to elucidate the intricate interplay between religious convictions, social processes, and historical situations, and to reveal how this contributed to the processes of writing about, and representing, Ramanuja to his followers and to those beyond.

It is always a matter of great satisfaction to see research supported by the Indian Institute of Advanced Study appear in the form of an important publication. I am inclined to believe that this book by Ranjeeta Dutta is the result not simply of financial support extended by the Institute, but also of the environment of fellowship and constructive debate that it creates for scholars in residence.

Chetan Singh
Director
Indian Institute of Advanced Study, Shimla

ACKNOWLEDGEMENTS

This work would not have been possible if I had not been awarded a Fellowship at the Indian Institute of Advanced Study, Shimla. I wish to thank the Director of the Institute, Professor Peter Ronald D'Souza for providing me with this opportunity. The interactions in the conferences and the study weeks held over two years at the Institute helped me to shape my ideas. The workshop on 'Philosophy in Colonial India', held in October 2009, made me realize that the history of ideas cannot be ignored while dealing with a study on Rāmānuja. Subsequently, this made me a reluctant initiate into the area of intellectual traditions in the pre-colonial period of Indian history. However, since this work focuses on the hagiographical representations of Rāmānuja, this aspect though somewhat marginalized has not gone completely unattended in the monograph. The international conference on 'History and Memory', held in April 2010, contributed to the shaping of several arguments regarding memory and historical consciousness, some of which I have tried to incorporate here. Both these areas—the history of ideas, and history and memory—have reoriented my academic perspectives and will hopefully inform my future research.

The interactions with some of my fellow colleagues at the Institute were indeed helpful in conceptualizing this work. I am grateful to Sanjay Palshikar and Pramod Kumar for patiently listening to my ideas and offering valuable suggestions at the expense of their own time. I have no words to thank my friends, Kanchana Natarajan, Anita Cherian, and Queeny Singh at the Institute and Biswamoy Pati in Delhi. Notwithstanding their academic engagements, they have unfailingly stood by me, their encouragement a crucial antidote to my frequent phases of self-doubt. I am indebted to Shri Premchand, Librarian, IIAS, and the library staff, all of whom went beyond the call of duty to help me as much as possible. I am also indebted to Shri S.P. Thakur, Secretary, IIAS, Debarshi Sen, Ashok Sharma, and Shashank Thakur for efficiently sorting out nagging administrative issues. Heartfelt thanks are due to the Institute staff, especially Kesar, Om Prakash, Barud Ram, Chandrakala, Jeet Ram, Thomas, and Rakesh, who cheerfully and willingly fulfilled the demands I made upon them.

I am grateful to Jamia Millia Islamia for granting me leave for two years without which undertaking the exercise of writing this monograph would have been impossible. I am especially indebted to Narayani Gupta for her unflinching support. There are no words to express my gratitude to Vaijanthi Raghunathan, who despite her professional and personal commitments helped me to grapple with the nuances of the texts which were often beyond my understanding.

I am grateful to the editors at Oxford University Press for their patience, flexibility, and complete faith in my project. I also thank Smriti Vohra for assistance during the later stages of manuscript preparation.

As with other aspects of my life, throughout the writing of this book, my parents, my sister, and my teacher, Professor R. Champakalakshmi, steadily believed in my efforts, shared my disappointments, rejoiced in my progress, and inspired me to continue when I faltered. They make it all possible. I hope I have made a beginning somewhere and will not disappoint them. Lastly, I am solely responsible for any errors that remain in this monograph.

CHAPTER ONE

Encountering Rāmānuja

Some Preliminaries

THE BEGINNING

In April 2009, along with a friend I took a trip to Vṛndāvan, approximately 144 kilometres southeast of Delhi.[1] The purpose of the trip was to visit the library at the Sri Caitanya Prem Samsthan (SCPS) for consulting the *Journal of Vaishnava Studies* that had been unavailable in any of the libraries of Delhi as well as online. The journal, founded in 1992 by Stephen J. Rosen, had articles dealing with various aspects of Vaiṣṇavism that were of particular relevance for our respective research on the history of the Śrīvaiṣṇava community of South India.[2] While

[1] I am grateful to Bharati Jagnnathan for persuading me to take this trip with her. It is because of her enthusiasm that I saw several interesting facets of Vṛndāvan, which otherwise would have been missed.

[2] Steven J. Rosen, also known as Satyaraja Dasa, is an American. He is a member of International Society of Krishna Consciousness (ISKCON) and has written several books on Vaiṣṇavism.

meandering in a rickshaw through the narrow lanes of Vṛndāvan, we stumbled upon a spectacle of colour, crowd, and festivity—the *Rath kā Melā* (festival of the chariot), a grand ten-day festival that the people of Vṛndāvan eagerly wait for each year. Caught between the fervour of people, heat, and dust, we saw a huge chariot-car with an image of Viṣṇu being pulled forward with thick ropes by excited devotees. The chariot, manned by priests who looked every bit like the Śrīvaiṣṇava priests in the temples of Tamil Nadu, Andhra Pradesh, and Karnataka, was an amazing sight, as we never had imagined the presence and influence of a south Indian/Tamil tradition in a north Indian sacred centre. For the histories taught at colleges and universities usually treat 'north India' as distinct from 'south India' on the basis of the latter's assumed characteristic polity, economy, kinship, and caste structures. While unravelling mentally the binaries of north and south, we followed the chariot-car, encountering a gamut of cultural situations that further questioned not only the notion of discrete historical trajectories, but also the exceptionalism of the south influenced by the 'dominant north' with the latter's supposed pan-Indian appeal.[3]

The chariot reached its final destination—the gardens adjoining the famous Raṅgājī Temple. The temple, built in 1851 and dedicated to Śrī Gōdā Raṅgamaṉṉār, that is Gōdā or Āṇṭāḷ, the only woman Āḻvār (the early Vaiṣṇava saints in the Tamil region) and her lord, Raṅgamaṉṉār, had predominantly a Dravidian style of architecture with tall *gopuram*s (gateways), *dhvajastamba* (flag staff), and a tank.[4] Raṅgamaṉṉār is none

[3] Nair (2006), 'Beyond Exceptionalism. South India and the Modern Historical Imagination', *Indian Economic and Social History Review*, 43, 3, pp. 323 and 325. Also see Champakalakshmi (2000 [1955, 1958, 1966, 1975]), 'Introduction', in Nilakanta Sastri, *A History of South India: From Prehistoric Times to the Fall of Vijayanagar*, pp. xv–xvi.

[4] According to the Śrīvaiṣṇava tradition, Bhūmidevī, consort of Viṣṇu, appeared as a baby girl under a basil plant in a temple at Śrīvilliputtūr, located near Madurai, the capital of the Pāṇṭiyas. The infant was discovered by the priest Viṣṇucitta (Periyāḻvār), who was a devotee of Viṣṇu (Viṣṇucitta is revered as one of the twelve Āḻvārs by the Śrīvaiṣṇavas). He raised her as his daughter and named her Gōdā. As she grew up, Gōdā's devotion to Kṛṣṇa took the form of passionate love and she wished to marry him. Everyday she would wear the garland meant for the Lord and then offer it to Him. When Viṣṇucitta came to know of this, he reprimanded her, only to be told by the Lord in his dream

other than Raṅganātha, the form of Viṣṇu revered by most Śrīvaiṣṇavas of south India and—as we had so suddenly come to know—also seemingly a popular god in Vṛndāvan. We were also informed by the priests that the temple was modelled on the Raṅganāthasvāmī temple at Śrīraṅgam or perhaps on the Āṇṭāḷ temple of Śrīvilliputtūr, both in Tamil Nadu. Further, the priests told us that this temple belonged to the Rāmānujīs, or the followers of Rāmānuja. The priests of the Raṅgājī temple, despite wearing external body marks of the Teṉkaḷai affiliation of the Śrīvaiṣṇava community, claimed that they had little association with that community, except for acknowledging Rāmānuja (eleventh–twelfth century) as its founder.[5] The Teṉkaḷai group of the Śrīvaiṣṇava community is known for its proclivity to Tamil hymns of the Āḻvārs and hence is considered broad-based in its approach, as compared to the Vaṭakaḷai group that gives precedence to the Sanskrit Vedas and is considered more brāhmaṇical in its orientation.

Such a different perception of Rāmānuja, that acknowledged him more as an individual religious leader, somewhat distinguished from the Śrīvaiṣṇava community, made one realize that he had another context that went beyond Vṛndāvan. He seems to have been the fulcrum of the spiritual genealogies of the Rāmānandīs, one of the largest ascetic sects that developed in north India in the fifteenth and sixteenth centuries. According to the Rāmānandī tradition, the community was founded by Rāmānand who lived in Benares in the fourteenth century and was a

---

that the Lord had happily accepted Gōdā's offering. When she reached the marriageable age, Gōdā refused to marry any mortal man. The anxious father was assured in his dream by the Lord that he would marry her at Śrīraṅgam. On reaching Śrīraṅgam with her father Viṣṇucitta, Gōdā merged into the image of Lord Raṅganātha, symbolizing a cosmic union. Known in the tradition as Āṇṭāḷ (one who rules the Lord) and Sūḍikkoḍutta Nācciyār (the bright creeper-like girl who gave her garlands after wearing them) Gōdā has been canonized as an Āḻvār and her compositions, *Tiruppāvai* and *Nācciyār Tirumoḻi*, are sung widely in the Śrīvaiṣṇava temples.

[5] The dates traditionally cited for Rāmānuja are from c. 1017 to 1137 CE. However, John B.Carman is of the opinion that possibly Rāmānuja's time period is from c. 1077–1157 CE. For details, see Carman (1981). *The Theology of Rāmānuja: An Essay in Interreligious Understanding*, pp. 44–7. Since both the sets of dates correspond to years between eleventh and twelfth centuries, I will henceforth mention this broad chronological span.

follower of Rāmānuja. Rāmānand's teachings considered to be diatribe against the caste hierarchies presumably inspired 'a minor social revolution in the Ganges basin' by admitting women, *śūdras*, and untouchables as ascetics within the Rāmānandī fold, who would otherwise be denied access to asceticism by the brāhmaṇical normative tradition.[6] In fact, Rāmānandī's social programme is said to have motivated the devotional poetic compositions of Tulsī Dās, Mīrā Bāi, and Kabīr, which form a significant part of the Hindi literature and school textbooks, and have captured the imagination of films and literary works.[7] That a *brāhmaṇa*, articulating in Sanskrit, affiliated to an intellectual tradition of Vedānta, could be a part of the historical memory of an eclectic religious group that rejected brāhmaṇical hierarchy made me look at the diverse ways in which Rāmānuja was received outside the Śrīvaiṣṇava milieu.[8]

The Rāmānandī hagiographies and the researches based on them have diverse opinions about the nature of Rāmānand's association with the Śrīvaiṣṇava community, also known as the Śrī Sampradāya community.[9] Some feel that Rāmānand was an ascetic, a follower of Rāma, who lived amongst the Śrīvaiṣṇavas in the Tamil region and was

[6] Burghart (2004 [1978]), 'The Founding of the Ramanandi Sect', pp. 227–29.

[7] See, for instance, some of the documentary films made by Shabnam Virmani, Drishti Media, and Human Rights Collective, Bangalore, under Kabir Project: *Had-Anhad* (Bounded-Boundless), *Chalo Hamare Des* (Come to My Country), *Koi Sunta Hai* (Someone Is Listening), *Kabira Khada Bazaar Mein* (In the Market Stands Kabir).

[8] The word *Vedānta* means the end of the Vedas and refers to the *Upaniṣads*, the last portion of the Vedic literature. The first explanation of the *Upaniṣads* was the *Vedāntasūtras* or the *Brahmasūtra*, written by Bādarāyana, and this became the accepted basis of the Vedānta philosophy. The interpretations on the *Vedāntasūtras* or the *Brahmasūtra* considered a part of the Vedānta philosophy include: Advaita Vedānta, Viśiṣṭādvaita Vedānta, and Dvaita Vedānta.

[9] Burghart (2004 [1978]), 'The Founding of the Ramanandi Sect', pp. 228–30; Pinch (1996a), 'Reinventing Ramanand: Caste and History in Gangetic India', *Modern Asian Studies* 30: 3 (July): pp. 549–71; Pinch (1996b), *Peasants and Monks in British India*; Van der Veer (1987), 'Taming the Ascetic: Devotionalism in a Hindu Monastic Order', *Man* 22 (4): 680–95; Aggarwal (2011 [2010]), 'The Impact of Sectarian Lobbyism on Hindi Literary Historiography: The Fascinating Story of Bhagavacharya Ramanandi', in Hans Harder (ed.), *Literature and Nationalist Ideology*, pp. 209–58.

influenced by Rāmānuja's theology. He is supposed to have accompanied the Śrīvaiṣṇavas on a pilgrimage to Benares around 1430 CE to preach the *Ādhyātma Rāmāyaṇa* and Rāmānuja's *Śrībhāṣya* and settled there permanently.[10] Another opinion assigns Prayāga as Rāmānand's birthplace and Swāmī Rāghavanand the head of the Śrī monastery at Benares as his *guru*, who initiated him as a *tridaṇḍin sanyāsī* (*sanyāsī* with three pointed staff, the hallmark of Śrīvaiṣṇava ascetisism).[11] There is another view that Rāmānand was born after 1400 CE and became a follower of the Śrīvaiṣṇava community founded by Rāmānuja. He is supposed to have undertaken a pilgrimage and on his return was denied the privilege of eating with his fellow disciples due to his alleged transgression of caste rules of commensality during his travels. Upset with this exclusivistic attitude, Rāmānand is said to have left the Śrīvaiṣṇava community and established his own religious community.[12] Some scholars differ and feel that it was Rāmānand's *guru*, Rāghavanand, who had to leave the Śrīvaiṣṇavas on the ground of breaking the rules of commensality and this incident did not lead to the formation of a separate community. Further, during his pilgrimage, Rāmānand was influenced by Tāntricism and thus left the Śrīvaiṣṇavas that followed the *saguṇa* (devotion to a personalized God with attributes) *bhakti* of Rāmānuja. Thereafter, he migrated to the north to learn the Tāntric doctrines from the *nirguṇa* (devotion to God without attributes) ascetics residing in the Gangetic belt.[13] Lastly, a group of scholars feel that Rāmānand went to Ayodhya with a mission of reconverting those Hindus who were forced to embrace Islam at some point in time. Thereafter, all of them joined the Śrī Sampradāya of Rāmānuja. According to this opinion, the conservative element within the Śrī Sampradāya resented the presence

[10] Farquhar (1967 [1920]), *An Outline of the Religious Literature of India*, Delhi, in Burghart (2004 [1978]), pp. 229–30; Pinch (1996a), pp. 552–53.

[11] Ghurye (1964), *Indian Sadhus*, Bombay, in Burghart: (2004 [1978]), p. 230.

[12] Wilson (1846), *Sketch of the Religious Sects of the Hindus*, Calcutta, in Burghart (2004 [1978]), p. 230. This story of excommunication can be found in an article by Grierson, under the entry 'Ramanandi, Ramawat' in *Encyclopaedia of Religion and Ethics*, in Pinch (1996a), p. 552.

[13] Sinha, 1957, *Ram Bhakti men Rasik Sampradaya*, Balrampur, in Burghart (2004 [1978]), p. 230.

of Rāmānand and the reconverted Hindus. Finally Rāmānand with his followers left the Sampradāya and founded a new religious community called the Rāmānandīs.[14] Richard Burghart feels that Rāmānand never founded the Rāmānandī community as the biographical information on Rāmānand in various Rāmānandī literature is ambiguous and contradictory, unlike the definite information available on the life of Śaṅkarācārya, Gorakhanātha, and Caitanya, the founders of Advaita, Nāthpanthī, and the Gauḍiya traditions respectively.[15]

Whatever may be the various views on the origin of the Rāmānandīs and Rāmānand's role in it, these stories identify Rāmānand as a Śrīvaiṣṇava; acknowledge the influence of Rāmānuja's ideas on him; highlight his interaction with the Śrīvaiṣṇavas in the Tamil or the Dravida region; and most significantly, inform us about the knowledge of synonymity of Śrīvaiṣṇavism with Rāmānuja by the fourteenth century outside the southern boundaries. The spiritual genealogies of Rāmānand, in the early fifteenth and late sixteenth centuries, viz., *Rāmarcaṇapaddhiti* and Nābhā Jī's *Bhaktamāl* respectively included, in addition to Rāmānuja, the Śrīvaiṣṇava personalities that appeared in the Śrīvaiṣṇava hagiographies too, viz., Viśvakasena, Ṣaṭhagōpa (Nammāḻvār), Pundarikākṣa, Rāmamiśra, Yāmunācārya, Mahāpūrnācārya, and Kūreśa and Rāmānand was identified as the spiritual descendant of Rāmānuja.[16] The Vaiṣṇava *ācaryā* from Karnataka, Madhavācārya (fourteenth century) also figures in these genealogies. It appears that the Śrī Sampradāya had powerful monastic establishments in north India and that amongst the four Vaiṣṇava orders or *catuh sampradāya*, one was founded by Rāmānuja and the other three established by Nimbāraka, Viṣṇuswāmī, and Madhvācārya. The scholars feel that this association with the Śrī Sampradāya, despite its preference for the initiation of twice born males into the ascetic order, was '...to profit from the established reputation of the Sri sect and Sri monastic facilities at the pilgrimage centre than to abrogate this link and to fend for themselves in the competition with other ascetic sects'.[17] Interestingly, the sixteenth-century *Bhaktamāl* also identifies a weaver (Kabīr), a cobbler (Rāidās), a farmer (Dhana), a

[14] Barthwal (1936), *The Nirguna School of Hindi Poetry*, Benares, in Burghart, p. 230.

[15] Burghart (2004 [1978]), pp. 227–32, 246–47.

[16] Ibid., pp. 234–39.

[17] Ibid., pp. 242–43.

barber (Sena), a woman (Padmāvatī), a *kṣatriya* (Pīpa), and *brāhmaṇas* (Sursurānand and Sursurī, Anantānand, Sabhānand, Narharyānand, and Bhāvanand) as disciples of Rāmānanda.[18]

However, it is in the early eighteenth century and finally in early nineteenth century that the association between Rāmānuja and Śrī Sampradāya became controversial. One section amongst the Rāmānandis found Ramanuja's canonization irrelevant on the grounds that Rāmānuja's teachings and the Śrīvaiṣṇava community had a Sanskritic/Vedic theological orientation. Thus, an independent role was assigned to Rāmānanda in the spread of Vaiṣṇavism, making him the sole founder of the Rāmānandī sect, due to divine inspiration.[19] Those followers who continued to identify Rāmānanda as a part of the lineage of Rāmānuja were called Rāmānujīs and this temple that we visited on our research trip was their sacred institutional centre.[20]

The influential figure of Rāmānuja was yet another threshold where the line between northern and southern devotional traditions collapsed in the popular religious imagination. Thus began my journey into a world of devotees inhabiting Vṛndāvan, where Rāmānuja was perceived as the most important *ācārya* of the Śrīvaiṣṇava community and a philosopher of Viśiṣṭādvaita Vedānta, but most significantly, the Rāmānujīs' primordial *guru* who inspired several generations of their own *gurus* and caused a collapsing of the regional binaries.

Interestingly, the Rāmānujīs we spoke with were reluctant to discuss their association with the Śrīvaiṣṇavas. However, the official history of the temple clearly establishes the link of the founder of the temple, Śrī Raṅgadeśika Swāmījī, with the Śrīvaiṣṇavas at Kāñcīpuram:

> One night in a dream he (Swamiji) was chased by a mad bull and wherever he went the bull kept chasing, when he turned towards North the bull stopped. Taking this as a divine sign, he joined Swami Sri Anantacharya of Kanchipuram who was going to North on a pilgrimage. When they

[18] Ibid., p. 229.

[19] Pinch (1996a), p. 557.

[20] For details on the controversy that took place amongst the Rāmānandīs in the nineteenth and twentieth century over their *guru* Rāmānanda's association with Rāmānuja, see Burghart (2004 [1978]), pp. 238–47; Pinch (1996a), pp. 549–71; Pinch (1996b), Chapter 2, 'Ramanand and Ramanandis, ca. 1900–1940', pp. 48–80.

reached Sri Goverdhanji, he met Swami Srinivasacharyaji, the head of Goverdhan Peeth of Sri Vaishnav sect, who was a very learned scholar. Sri Rangadeshik Swamiji became his disciple and very soon established himself as a brilliant scholar. Finding him suitable to carry forward the torch of Sri Vaishanvavism, Swami Srinivasacharyaji asked Sri Rangadeshik Swamiji to take over the reins of Sri Goverdhan Peeth.

In a very short period of time Swamiji's name and reputation as a great Vaishnava scholar had spread all over India. Inspired by his knowledge and devotion the brothers Seth Sri Radhakrishnaji and Sri Govind Dasji of Mathura approached Swamiji for discipleship and offered all their wealth at Swamiji's feet. Once when Swamiji was explaining about the greatness of the South Indian temples, then the brothers expressed their wish for establishing Sri Goda-Rangamannar at Vrindavan. Swamiji had always thought about the unfulfilled wish of Andal where she expresses her desire to spend her life at Vrindavan. Taking the wish of (the) brothers as divine indication, Swamiji immediately went to Sri Rangam and expressed this desire to the divine couple Sri Goda-Rangamannar and sought their permission for starting the construction of the temple. Skilled labourers were hired from Sri Rangam and brought to Vrindavan and the construction work for the temple commenced in the year 1845. The brothers contributed whole heartedly and with their effort and Sri Goda Rangamannar's grace the temple was completed in the year 1851 A.D.[21]

This official history documents the interaction and transmission between the Śrīvaiṣṇavas and Rāmānujīs in the nineteenth century. However, the historical process of transmission and diffusion of the image of Rāmānuja as an iconic religious symbol outside the southern boundaries before this period requires a detailed analysis, which is beyond the scope of this monograph.

While attempting to analyse the various perceptions of Rāmānuja, I realized that such an analysis would be justified only if one first explored the ways in he was perceived in his original context, the Tamil milieu and the Śrīvaiṣṇava community. These perspectives influenced the development of some of the enduring images of Rāmānuja that not only circulated within the south Indian context but also became the basis of undertsanding and perceiving him at the pan-Indian level. The Rāmānandī tradition delineated Rāmānuja as a great intellectual

[21] About the Rangaji Temple Vrindāvan, http://blessingsonthenet.com/indian-temple/article/1045/history-of-sri-rangaji-temple.

philosopher, but in the nineteenth century found him and the Śrīvaiṣṇava community conservative and Sankritic in their approach. Within the southern context, the memories of Rāmānuja today evoke an image of a benign saint who was not only a great exegete, but also a champion of the oppressed and the poor. His philosophy of the Viśiṣṭādvaita has been percieved to have had a seminal impact on the medieval *bhakti*, for it made the act of *prapatti* or spiritual salvation through surrender to God accessible to everybody, irrespective of the individual's caste status. This idea has been considered revolutionary, and modern biographers of Rāmānuja have asserted that such a radical position was singular in the environment of devotional movements in medieval South India. Further, focusing on devotion to Viṣṇu and his various forms through an intensely personal relationship with him, Rāmānuja is understood as the proponent of *saguṇa bhakti* that was comprehensible to an average *bhakta* or devotee. This was in sharp contrast to Śaṅkara's Advaita that has been considered to be highly intellectual and abstract. The larger frame of reference today is that Rāmānuja was a 'social reformer', a point that will be taken up in the next section.

An early analysis revealed that it was not so much Rāmānuja's Viśiṣṭādvaita and his intellectual writings as his image as an *ācārya* and a *guru* that was the basis of such perceptions. This image of an *ācārya* and a *guru* was originally crafted at an early stage in the Śrīvaiṣṇava textual tradition, primarily through the *guruparamparā*s (hagiographies), the *stotra*s (praise-poems), and *vyākhyāna*s (commentaries). These particular images that evolved and developed between the twelfth and fifteenth centuries were subsequently institutionalized in the temple festivals and rituals that became crucial in the history of representations of Rāmānuja. These early depictions of Rāmānuja as an exemplar not only set the tone for subsequent imaging of the saint in the Śrīvaiṣṇava hagiographies after the fifteenth century, but also formed the template of modern delineations of Rāmānuja in the popular domains of cinema, theatre, children's books, biographies, and academic researches, thus highlighting the different ways in which Rāmānuja has been remembered.[22] While concentrating on the

[22] Some of the well-known modern biographies on Ramanuja are Narasimhachary (2007 [2004]), *Sri Ramanuja*; Seshadri (1998), *Srivaishnavism and Social Change*; Swami Ramakrishnananda (1986), *Life of Sri Ramanuja*. For further references on academic researches of this kind, see Lakshamma

delineations of Rāmānuja, this study will also attempt to describe their influence on modern print and visual productions of the *ācārya*, for these have been crucial in popularizing his image and may even be said to be the link between the Śrīvaiṣṇava community and the larger world. This study asserts that the modern representations, while using the textual sources, especially the *guruparamparā*s and the *stotra*s, often ignored the variations in these narratives and the complexities arising from them. Therefore, the memories of Rāmānuja circulating in the secular public domains of cinema, theatre, children's books, biographies and researches often ignored, and still continue to ignore, the complexities that a biographical, in this case, hagiographical, process in history involves. Also these modern biographies overlook the fact that the received image of any historical personality is a result of a historical accretion of motifs that memorialize him or her for posterity. In order to fully comprehend the process of imaging Rāmānuja as an *ācārya*, the layers of historical encrustations have to be removed and the early hagiographcial representations that became the bedrock of subesquent delineations need to be analysed in a separate study.

The aim of this monograph will be to examine the hagiographical delineations of Rāmānuja within a particular historical context, that is, between the twelfth and fifteenth centuries when the image of Rāmānuja as both a popular *bhakti* saint and an important philosopher was crystallized through processes of canonization. Such processes appeared for the first time in the the *guruparamparā* texts of the Śrīvaiṣṇava community of south India. Other textual genres such as *stotra*s and the *vyākhyāna*s also depict Rāmānuja in this way, but the exaltation of him as the most important *ācārya* or the preceptor of the community is particularly graphic in the *guruparamparā*s. This era was important, for during this period, the Śrīvaiṣṇavas developed a community consciousness that generated a textual tradition and institutional networks imparting a cohesiveness to the community structure that was otherwise missing. Embedded within the process of early renderings of Rāmānuja were issues of caste, identities, community consciousness, and notions of a

---

(1990). *The Impact of Rāmānuja's Teachings on Life and Conditions in Society*. For children's books, see *Rāmānuja: A Great Vaishnava Saint* (1974): Amar Chitra Katha 715. For theatre and films, see Indira Parthasarathy (2008), *Ramanujar: The Life and Ideas of Ramanuja*, and *Rāmānuja* directed by Iyer.

devotional tradition that became integral to the history of the Śrīvaisnava community.

Interestingly, three hagiographies associated with the Vaṭakaḷai and Teṉkaḷai affiliations were also written in the fourteenth and fifteenth centuries. The Teṉkaḷai text *Āṟāyirappaṭi Guruparamparāprabhāvam* and the Vaṭakaḷai texts *Pannīrāyirappaṭi Guruparamparāprabhāvam* and *Muāyirappaṭi Guruparamparāprabhāvam* were written within their respective ideological contexts and delineated Rāmānuja accordingly. Both the Vaṭakaḷai and Teṉkaḷai groups claimed direct descent from Rāmānuja through two different sets of lineage but had theological differences, especially related to the issues of *prapatti*, position of the goddess Śrī, the role of the *guru*, and relative precedence of the Tamil hymns over the Sanskrit Vedas and vice-versa. These theological differences coupled with variant social practices became the basis of irreconciliable differences that ultimately ossified into two sub-sects. The Vaṭakaḷais consider Vedāntadeśika (traditional dates: c. 1268–1369 CE) as their preceptor and and the Teṉkaḷais consider Maṇavāḷamāmuṉi (traditional dates: c. 1370–1443 CE) as their *guru*. Both of them believe that the lineage of their respective *ācārya*s is the direct 'legitimate' line of descent from Rāmānuja. The *guruparamparā*s and the *stotra*s after the fourteenth or fifteenth century, especially within the Vaṭakaḷai–Teṉkaḷai hagiographical frame, based their delineations on the early representations, and further encrusted the narratives within their respective contexts and worldviews.

While analysisng the *guruparamparā*s from the twelfth and fifteenth centuries, this study will also engage with various moments of interactions in history when the notion of a remembered past was structured resulting in the historical memory or memories through which the past would become a received tradition. Such a construction of cultural memories filtering through the layers of historical time did have an enduring influence on the modern biographies of Rāmānuja that used these hagiographical reserves as historical reality to craft his life history. Ensconced within the modern political worldview of 'social protest' and 'social reform', Rāmānuja, as stated earlier, was exemplified by his biographers as a 'rebel saint' who dissented against the brāhmaṇical conventions, caste hierarchies, and political order of the day. Simultaneously, his biographies also depicted his efforts at evolving the Viśiṣṭādvaita exegesis that negated the significance of caste status in religious practice and foregrounded the principle of direct accessibility to the divine.

HAGIOGRAPHIES AND BIOGRAPHIES: TRADITION, MEMORY, AND PERCEPTIONS

The Śrīvaiṣṇavas are a distinct Vaiṣṇava community in south India, confined primarily to the present Tamil Nadu and southern parts of Andhra Pradesh and Karnataka. The community considers Viṣṇu and his consort Lakṣmī as their supreme gods, accepts Rāmānuja as its most important religious and spiritual leader, and regards the Sanskrit Vedas and the *Nālāyira Divya Prabandham* (a collection of 4,000 Tamil hymns of the Āḻvārs, the early Vaiṣṇava saints) as its main scriptures. The prefix 'Śrī' in Śrīvaiṣṇavism has two meanings. One, it is an honorary prefix, which sets the community apart from other religious traditions. Two, it denotes an important exegetical concept, that is, the role of Śrī or Lakṣmī as the mediatrix between Viṣṇu and his devotees. It is believed that by helping the devotees achieve *prapatti* or complete self-surrender to God, Śrī also enhances the *saulabhya* (accessibility) of the divine.

As stated before, the present-day Śrīvaiṣṇavas are divided into two main sects: the Vaṭakaḷais and the Teṉkaḷais. The Vaṭakaḷai represent the Sanskritic tradition, give preference to the Sanskrit Vedas over the Dravida Vedas, and are considered to be brāhmaṇical and conservative in their outlook. Kāñcīpuram in Tamil Nadu is their institutional centre, and Vedāntadeśika their spiritual preceptor. The Teṉkaḷais, on the other hand, represent the Tamil tradition, regard the Dravida Vedas as their scriptures and therefore, they are considered to be more broad-based than the Vaṭakaḷais and have had a large non-brāhmaṇa following. Śrīrangam in Tamil Nadu is their centre and Maṇavāḷamāmuṉi their religious leader. Today the entire Śrīvaiṣṇava tradition, its texts and institutional structure, viz. temples and *maṭha*s, are aligned as the Vaṭakaḷai or Teṉkaḷai. However, despite their distinct identities, both acknowledge their affiliation to the larger Śrīviaṣṇava community.

Rāmānuja, more popularly known for his philosophy of Viśiṣṭādvaita outside the Tamil region, was born, probably in 1017 AD, to a *brāhmaṇa* family in Śrīperumbudūr. The narratives go to great lengths in describing the intellectual expertise of the *brāhmaṇa*s of Pūtūr or Bhūtapuri, present-day Śrīperumbudūr. Rāmānuja was born into the *āsūri kula*, supposedly an erudite and elite *brāhmaṇa* lineage. His father, Keśavācārya Sōmayaji, was an expert in performing *yajñas*. Rāmānuja's early years were spent in Kāñcīpuram, then an important religious and trading centre. His later years were spent in Śrīraṅgam, an emerging urban centre with a rich rural hinterland, currently in Tiruchchirapalli district in Tamil Nadu, where he died, probably in 1137 AD, at the age of one hundred and twenty. This unusually long historical period of one hundred and twenty years of Rāmānuja's life saw the propsering of the Cōḷa dynasty, its subsequent weakening, the rising influence of Śaivism in the Tamil region (where Śaivism was also the royal cult), the increasing importance of temples, and the gradual marginalization of those *brāhmaṇas* who had settled in the *brahmadeyas*. These villages, based on royal land grants to the *brāhmaṇas*, were intended to nurture and dissmeniate the royal ideology and bring as much area as possible under cultivation, thus efficiently integrating the local population within the parameters of the state. In this context, dominated by the *brāhmaṇas* economically and ideologically, the *brahmadeyas* emerged as the centres of brāhmaṇical culture and knowledge. According to the hagiographies, Śrīperumbudūr, the birthplace of Rāmānuja, was one such *brāhmaṇa* settlement in the Toṇḍaimaṇḍalam region. We have no autobiographical references in Rāmānuja's works. His works, written in Sanskrit, deal with the metaphysics of religion, existence, and salvation. Neither are there any biographical accounts written during his lifetime. We know about him mostly from the Śrīvaiṣṇava hagiographies or *guruparamparās* and *caritas* and other poetic compositions like the *stotras* and *taṉiyaṉs*. The latter two are usually verses in praise and are sung or recited almost everyday in Śrīvaiṣṇava households.

On the basis of Rāmānuja's works, it can be concluded that he was formulating a coherent philosophy and was engaged in constant dialogue with the Advaita philosophy of Śaṅkarācārya, whose subsequent followers were probably in touch with Rāmānuja. It should be noted that Śaṅkara lived in the eighth century in Kerala and thus could not possibly have met Rāmānuja. Hence there must have been an environment of debates and discussions, circulation and diffusion of ideas, and perpetuation of intellectual traditions of which Rāmānuja was a part. Rāmānuja's ideas, termed as Viśiṣṭādvaita much after him, included commentaries on the Vedānta, the *Gītā*, and the *Upaniṣads*. He evolved a coherent structure of ideas that focused on the direct experience of God and placed Śrīvaiṣṇavism on an equal footing with other religious traditions with already extant textual traditions. Although articulated in Sanskrit, Rāmānuja's interpretations of the Vedānta differed from Śaṅkara's monistic interpretations (Advaita, i.e. non-dualism) and presented an alternative model for the perception of divinity based on 'qualified' monism (i.e. Viśiṣṭādvaita). According to the Advaita Vedānta of Śaṅkara, 'Brahman or the ultimate reality is identified with the Self as pure consciousness and as such the material world is ultimately real, being the product of ignorance, i.e. *avidyā* or *māyā*'.[23] For Śaṅkara, *karma* identified with ritual was not only in contradiction with *jñāna* or knowledge, but also an obstacle in *jñāna*'s realization. Śaṅkara rejected *karma* as it 'pre-supposed duality in many ways—the body and the world' and he advocated non-dualism and exclusive attainment of *jñāna* as a means of salvation and 'freedom from ignorance'.[24] Rāmānuja's interpretation of the Upaniṣadic Vedāntic tradition based on theism considered the Brahman as God—in this case, Viṣṇu. He agreed with the doctrine of monism (*advaita*), 'but it was qualified monism (*viśiṣṭādvaita*) inasmuch as there was also room in it for reality of the individual souls and the external or material world'.[25] Thus according to Rāmānuja, 'The highest reality is God, endowed with all desirable qualities not consisting of knowledge alone, but having knowledge as an attribute, all powerful, all pervading and all-merciful.'[26] In Rāmānuja's view devotion or *bhakti* to God and God's grace were the only ways of attaining salvation. Further, Rāmānuja felt that rituals were *yajña*s for propitiating deities, the performance of which led to 'awarding of rewards by the Supreme Person'.[27] These ideas must have met with acceptance and considerable intellectual success as is evident in the subsequent following of the Śrīvaiṣṇava community.

Modern writings are full of comparisons between Rāmānuja and Śaṅkara. Often these analogies, which label Rāmānuja's ideas as 'theology' in contrast to Śaṅkara's ideas that are labelled as 'philosophy', give

[23] Chattopadhyaya (1975 [1964]), *Indian Philosophy*, pp. 68–9.

[24] Ibid., p. 93 and p. 71.

[25] Ibid., p. 71.

[26] Keith, *Encyclopeadia of Religion and Ethics*, Vol. 10, 572, quoted in Chattopadhyaya (1975 [1964]), p. 71.

[27] Chattopadhyaya (1975 [1964]), pp. 56–7.

an impression that the two thinkers were contemporaries. As stated earlier, with a difference of three centuries between these philosophers, Śaṅkara's Vedantic ideas would have been available to Rāmānuja through a filtered received tradition. These ideological differences embedded in the categories of 'theology' and 'philosophy' have accquired a social dimension that associates the theology of Viśiṣṭādvaita with *saguṇa* Brahman, which is easily comprehensible to the common people, and the philosophy of Advaita with the concept of *nirguṇa* Brahman, which addresses an exclusive intellectually motivated audience. Such a social interpretation of ideas have become the basis of understanding the personality of Rāmānuja as a liberal and democratic religious figure. This impression is further underscored in the modern works on the basis of certain hagiographical accounts. For instance, Rāmānuja is said to have shouted out the *Dvaya mantra*, exclusively meant for *brāhmaṇa*s, from the top of the temple tower at Tirukōṭṭiyūr so that everyone, irrespective of caste status, could hear, learn, and recite it.[28] Though censured by the Śrīvaiṣṇava *brāhmaṇa* community, which included his own *guru*, Rāmānuja was undeterred.[29] This account, along with such other narratives accepted as historical reality, has been documented as a radical step taken by Rāmānuja, who the writings have felt deserve to be upheld as a 'social reformer'—a point that is overstressed considering that this narrative was not so dramatic as the modern representations would like us to believe. Interestingly, in two of the hagiographies, viz., the *Divyasūricaritam*, which has two long chapters on Rāmānuja, and the *Yatirāja Vaibhavam*, which deals exclusively with Rāmānuja's life, it is not the *Dvaya mantra*, but the *Carama śloka* that Rāmānuja learnt from his *guru* and revealed to everybody. Further, the *stotra*s dedicated to him and the *Rāmānuja Nūṟṟandādi*, a hymnal composition that

[28] Garuḍa Vāhana Paṇḍita. *Divyasūricaritam*. (trans. from Hindi by Pandita Madhavacharya) Sampathakumaracharya and Venkatachari (eds). 1978. Bombay: Ananthacharya Research Institute, Chapter 18, *śloka 2*; *The Yatirājavaibhavam of Āndhrapūrṇa (Life of Rāmānuja)* in *The Indian Antiquary, A Journal of Oriental Research* (1909 [1985]), Vol. XXXVII, Sir Richard Carnac Temple (ed.), 1872–1933, Delhi: Swati Publication, *śloka* 58.

[29] Piṉbaḷagiya Perumāḷ Jīyar. *Āṟāyirappaṭi Guruparamparāprabhāvam*. Tiru Krishnaswami Ayyangar (ed.), (1968), pp. 192–8; *Muāyirappaṭi Guruparamparāprabhāvam* (Vaṭakaḷai) of Tritīya Brahmatantrasvatantra Parkāla Svāmī, 1968, pp. 95–6.

forms a part of the *Nālāyira Divya Prabandham*, do not mention this famous incident.

Therefore, it becomes crucial to understand the ways Rāmānuja has been received in modern times. Clearly, the variations in the hagiographies have been ignored and a fixed image of Rāmānuja as a social reformer has been presented. Such an orientation can be traced back to the discursive domain of nineteenth-century India in which the discussions on social reforms influenced by the nationalist perspective was a response to the perceptions of religion, in this case, what came to be regarded as Hinduism.[30] Ranging from a critique of the Indian past to a sympathetic approach towards it, the writings of the Christian missionaries, Orientalists, Utilitarian, and Evangelicals generated a debate amongst the middle-class Indian intelligentsia on the question of Hindu-self identity and an Indian 'self' against the background of colonialism. Consequently, a conservative attitude emerged that advocated reforms of the brāhmaṇical beliefs, but defining reform as 'controlled change' 'based on "class consensus" and not "class war"'.[31] Further, this nineteenth-century reformist discourse assigned the agency of change to the 'western–educated, upper caste males' and focussed on the *brāhmaṇa* religious figures, especially Śaṅkara and Rāmānuja, along with Caitanya and Maharashtrian saint-poets.[32] On one hand, it was maintained that 'the customs and institutions with which the social reformer proposes to deal are common to the higher classes of Hindu society from which the lower classes take their standard'.[33] On the other hand, men like

[30] Dalmia (1997), *The Nationalization of Hindu Traditions*, pp. 338–429; Dalmia, 'The Only Real Religion of the Hindus', in *The Oxford India Hinduism Reader*, Dalmia and Stietencron (eds) (2007), pp. 90–128; Sen (ed.) (2008 [2005, 2003], *Social and Religious Reform: The Hindus of British India*, pp. 3–63; Sen, 'The Idea of Social Reform and Its Critique among Hindus of Nineteenth-Century India', in *Development of Modern Indian Thought and the Social Sciences*, Sabyasachi Bhattacharya (ed.) (2007), *History of Science, Philosophy and Culture in Indian Civilization*, Vol. X, Part 5, pp. 107–37.

[31] Sen in *Development of Modern Indian Thought and the Social Sciences*, Bhattacharya (ed.) (2007), p. 108.

[32] Ibid., pp. 108–9.

[33] Sir Chandravarkar in Sen in *Development of Modern Indian Thought and the Social Sciences*, Bhattacharya (ed.) (2007), p. 109.

Swami Vivekananda felt that without the stirring of mass consciousness, the reforms had no relevance.[34] It is in this context that the image of Rāmānuja as a compassionate social reformer was juxtaposed with that of Śaṅkara, who was depicted as an intellectual philosopher.

> The movement of Sankara forced its way through its high intellectuality, but it could be of little service to the masses, because of its adherence to strict caste laws, very small scope for ordinary emotion and making Sanskrit the only vehicle of communication. Ramanuja, on the other hand, with a most practical philosophy, a great appeal to the emotions, an entire denial of birthrights before spiritual attainments and appeals through popular tongue, completely succeeded in bringing the masses back to the Vedic religion.[35]

In the early twentieth century, conservative attitudes in the discourse of social reform persisted, but 'the idealisation of the past was based less on comprehending on Indian reality and more on what was considered appropriate from a twentieth century perspective'.[36] Situated in the context of E.V. Ramaswamy Naicker's ideas and anti-brāhmaṇa sentiment, it became crucial for the upper caste Tamil intelligentsic to attribute the epithet of 'the Great Reformer and Religionist of the 12th Century' to Rāmānuja.[37] However, an analysis of the theme of dissent in Chapter Five of this monograph demonstrates that the discourse on caste was far more complex to be simplistically squeezed into the frame of rejection or adherence.

As the above example of the hagiographical narrative of Rāmānuja reciting aloud the *Dvaya mantra* from the top of the temple tower indicates, the hagiographical delineations of Rāmānuja were never monolithic, homogeneous, and seamless. Each of these narratives, located in a specific context, reflected differing notions of history and community/community identities revolving around the image or images of Rāmānuja. The narratives negotiating with diverse historical processes produced varied versions. These versions were transmitted through several layers of historical time. Such a complex process of production and

34 Ibid.

35 Swami Vivekananda, *The Historical Evolution of India*, in Swami Ramakrishnananda, *Life of Sri Ramanuja*, Preface, p. i.

36 Thapar (1999), *Śakuntalā. Texts, Readings, Histories*, p. 241.

37 Gōvindāchārya (1906), *The Life of Rāmānujāchārya* p. 28.

transmission appeared to have been completely marginalized by the nineteenth century. Within the topical discourse of social reforms, analysts of this period ignored the fact that the same narratives that reinforced Rāmānuja's status as a 'social reformer' were either absent from the hagiographies or were at variance with one another. The detailed analyses of the texts show that the accounts of Rāmānuja, especially those focusing on his activities of 'social reform' invariably foregrounded in the modern works, appeared only from the fourteenth century onwards.

The nineteenth and twentieth century delineation of Rāmānuja as a reformer has persisted and has become relevant within the contemporary framework of polarized caste identities and politics. The cultural expressions in the public domain, such as theatre, popular biographies, the *Amar Chitra Katha* comics series on Indian mythology and history, films, newspaper articles, and even academic research in the twentieth and twenty-first centuries, have in their presentation of religion and philosophy unquestioningly reiterated the hagiographic exaltations of Rāmānuja. In most of these works, there invariable comparison with Śaṅkara and his philosophy, and inevitably Śaṅkara's Advaita is always is a considered as more intellectual and abstract while Rāmānuja's Viśiṣṭādvaita is perceived as accessible/comprehensible to an average devotee. Above all, there is a blanket acceptance and projection of Rāmānuja as a 'social reformer'.

The famous Tamil playwright Indira Parthasarathy's award-winning play *Ramanujar* has the distinction of emphasizing that Rāmānuja, despite being located in the medieval period, continues to have significant relevance in modern times.[38] When asked in an interview whether Rāmānuja was an appropriate subject for theatre, he replied:

> Ramanujar's life was full of drama. He was a 12th century saint and he was perhaps the first social revolutionary in Tamil religious history. He differed from Sankara. Sankara's god was not a personal god, but Ramanujar explained it in a personal way. Ramanujar felt that a personal god was necessary, like even if there was no god, create him. Every man needs his personal god. At the same time, he did not like the caste hierarchy that existed. He felt that personal salvation was a right for everyone. So, he protested against the caste system. His earliest guru was not a brahmin. Ramanujar was a brahmin, and his guru, Thirukachchi Nambi, was a vaisya. He was born an activist. He was the first religious teacher to give

[38] Parthasarathy (2008), *Ramanujar: The Life and Ideas of Ramanuja.*

> the management of a temple to the untouchables, as they were called in those days. He called them the 'blessed tribe', in Thamizh *'thiruk kulath-thaar'*. Gandhiji was greatly influenced by Ramanujar. If you study the life of Gandhi, you will find that he followed the entire social engineering structure that Ramanujar followed. Whom Ramanujar called as *thiruk kulaththaar*, Gandhiji called them *Harijans*.[39]

Parthasarathy is known for historical plays in which his characterization of the protagonist is often a departure from the dominant historical projections. For instance, his play *Aurangzeb* written in 1973 delineated a radically different emperor from the typically rendered ruthless bigot of Mughal history. Similarly, his critically acclaimed play *Nandan Kathai* (The Legend of Nandan), written in 1978, reinterpreted the story of an untouchable agricultural labourer pining to enter the temple of Śiva. This play raised uncomfortable issues about caste privileges and brāhmaṇical domination within the framework of *bhakti*, thus questioning the popular perception of *bhakti* as a protest against the established social hierarchies. Interestingly, in the case of *Ramanujar*, Parthasarathy does not reinvent or reinterpret the character of Rāmānuja. Rather, his treatment of Rāmānuja is in conformity with a specific medieval hagiographical interpretation that became dominant in the nineteenth century. In this work Parthasarathy, otherwise known for radical political views that have influenced his literary compositions and have been also significant in the political context of Dalit or anti-caste movements in Tamil Nadu, has unquestioningly accepted the received tradition and incorporated it in the modern playwriting.

Such an understanding, while claiming to recast a medieval religious and spiritual leader, also conforms to and reifies a received tradition that continues to be an active part of the cultural memory of the Śrīvaiṣṇavas today. However, this reception is not merely a linear transmission of the past to the present, but it is the present acting on the past. Thus, 'the past is modelled, invented, reinvented, and reconstructed by the present' selecting from the range of memories on Rāmānuja codified in the various versions of the hagiographies.[40] The hagiographies while

[39] 'An Interview with Indira Parthasarathy', by Balalji. Part I and II. Its Different KZSU Stanford 90.1 FM. http://www.itsdiff.com/.

[40] Assmann (1997), *Moses the Egyptian*, p. 9.

revering Rāmānuja as their most important spiritual and religious leader, an *ācārya*, presented an image of a philosopher engaged intensely in intellectual debates, a compassionate man questioning the *varṇa* hierarchies, an astute administrator, and above all a true devotee of Viṣṇu. The modern biographies while documenting these aspects primarily acclaimed him as a rebel saint and memorialized him as someone who dissented against the brāhmaṇical conventions, caste hierarchy, and the political order of the day.

Crucially, the figure of Rāmānuja as 'reformer' needs to be understood in relation to the figure of him as a 'saint'. The hagiographies cannot be seen as mere panegyric accounts eulogizing the lives of their respective subjects, who were the holy 'saints' of the respective religious communites, represented by *guruparamparās*. The term 'saint' that has had a specific association with the formation of the scriptural canon was not a pre-given category used by the hagiographers, but was presented in a teleogical manner: through various tropes the narratives gradually progressed towards the delineation of an *ācārya* or a 'saint'—in this case, Rāmānuja—and constructed a valorized and cherished image that was memorialized and reiterated over centuries of dissemination.[41] Such a cultural memory was further institutionalized in ritual forms and festivals that commemorated Rāmānuja and other religious personalities as *ācārya*s (preceptors) or 'saints'. Indeed, this has been the main purpose of these life histories that over time assumed scriptural proportions. But this intent and status does not warrant the dismissal of hagiographies as ahistorical or unhistorical. Often striding across the binaries between myth and history, these texts, while articulating the worldviews of particular religious communities, also described the larger historical context, 'which often became the bedrock of shaping the lives of their subjects'.[42] Thus these life stories, shaped by the context, the vision of hagiographers, and community ideas and ideals, became an exemplar for devotees. Seen from this perspective, these texts function as 'multiple lenses through

[41] Also see Novetzke (2008), *History, Bhakti and Public Memory*; Assmann (1997), *Moses the Egyptian*, pp. 1–22.

[42] Arnold and Blackburn, (eds) (2004), *Telling Lives in India: Biography, Autobiography, and Life History*, pp. 1–23.

which a particular historical time and the larger attitudes of the period towards the past and present of that period could be seen'.[43]

The Śrīvaiṣṇava response to the historical context and the subsequent textual articulation from the twelfth to the fifteenth century interpreted within exegetical and religious value systems did have a crucial role to play in the shaping of the life-stories, just as the life-stories influenced community ideals. Hence these life stories were in a real sense the history of the community. Located in a particular context, through their narratives about Rāmānuja's attitude of dissent and devotion, his hagiographers were putting forward a certain vision for the Śrīvaiṣṇavas and attempting to create a particular kind of collective consciousness. Thus in many ways, they were deeply invested in constructing the social aspect of an individual whose contribution to the development of ideas, as reflected in his novel interpretation of the Vedānta, was already recognized as seminal.

Therefore, the hagiographies simultaneously delineated the history of Śrīvaiṣṇavism, issues of community consciousness and solidarity, caste, identities, and a notion of a tradition—all of which were heavily influenced by the contemporary socio-political context. Along with their multiple and layered tellings of Rāmānuja's life in the hagiographies, the perceptions of the Śrīvaiṣṇava community and Rāmānuja also emerged in the texts of other religious traditions. As in the sixteenth-century text *Saravdarśanasaṅgraha*, Rāmānuja was understood as the exponent of the Viśiṣṭādvaita *darśana*.[44] In the hagiographies of Rāmānanda as discussed in the previous section, Rāmānuja was presented as the founder of the Śrīvaiṣṇava community (Śrī Samapradāya), whose growing orthodoxy caused some of its followers to break away and start new *sampradāyas*. According to these texts, Rāmānanda left the Śrī Samapradāya because of its inherent conservatism; he inspired several popular sects, including that of the Rāmānandīs with whom Kabīr is associated.

Thus, the contradictions between memory and history, in which memory stands for orality and subjectivity and history for literacy and objectivity, so often highlighted in memory studies in the case of

[43] Ibid.

[44] Madhava Acharya (1961), *The Sarva-Darśana Saṃgraha* (Review of the Different Systems of Hindu Philosophy), pp. 64–86.

hagiographies is not always tenable.[45] The Śrīvaiṣṇava hagiographies during the period of study must be selecting from a stock of oral narratives. This process of selection gave preference to those accounts that seemed appropriate to the community ideology. This was followed by writing it down—a process of memorializing for posterity. Perhaps the variations present in these texts represented those narratives left out by one *guruparamparā* but included by another depending on their respective orientations. This subjectivity in selecting the past was a continuous process, an 'ongoing work of reconstructive imagination', and therefore always to be 'processed' and 'mediated'.[46]

Histories based upon inscriptions have frequently been regarded as objective, and the analysis of the hagiographies are subordinated to it or marginalized as too subjective for the writing of a larger general history. This may have some relevance, but cannot be overstated. One should not forget that the inscriptions also reflect a point of view of their patrons or donors, who may be rulers, merchants, agriculturists, and so on. The argument is not for giving precedence to one form of historical evidence over the other. Rather, it is emphasized here that a proper historical analysis of a context within a specified chronological span should be based on multiple sources and not a single group of sources prioritized over the others. Seen from this perspective, the Śrīvaiṣṇava hagiographies were not discrete texts. Rather, they reflected the larger discursive environment of that particular period, comprising political biographies, literature, scripture, and other works, hence reflecting, borrowing, and influencing the cultural and social ethos of the period in which they were situated. One may conclude that the Śrīvaiṣṇava hagiographical ideas would have circulated in secular domains as well as the religious domains of other communties. The Tulukka Nācciyār myth discussed in Chapter 3 clearly shows an interaction and mutual flow between the hagiographies and political biographies, manifesting in a strong intertextuality that helped in the circulation of ideas outside their respective domains.[47] This discursive exchange (of which inscriptions

[45] Novetzke (2008), pp. 27–41.

[46] Jan Assmann (1997), p. 14.

[47] See also, for a discussion on the narratives as history, Stone (1979), 'The Revival of Narrative: Reflections on a New Old History', *Past and Present*, 85 (November), pp. 3–24; Hobsbawm (1980), 'The Revival of Narratives: Some Comments', *Past and Present*, 86 (February), pp. 3–8.

were also a part), contributed to the total historical vision of that time, blurring the demarcation between the sacred and the secular, history and myth, subjectivity, and objectivity.

Hagiographies were certainly a mode of articulating history that may not have coincided with the modern style of history writing. Contemporary scholars note that

> history in South India has been written in many genres and that writing history is not a matter of strict adherence to formal characteristics and types. In this respect, the comparison with the emerging Western historiography of the modern period is important. In Western Europe, history did emerge as a relatively fixed and stable genre, even before the positivist turn of the nineteenth century. This genre had clear formal features, a characteristic frame, and a relatively clear cut method; sources relating to the past were collected, sifted through and organized, ranked for their reliability, and eventually set out in prose narratives. The choice of prose was thematized; from the time of Hegel onwards, Western historians insisted that no other medium was suited to a history claiming to embody truth… in South India, history was not itself a genre, and no single genre was allotted to historical writing.[48]

Thus, this brings us to the question of whether hagiographies and biographies are dichotomous categories or closely allied to each other. The modern genre of biographies or life histories—in this case, of great men—that claim to be secular, objective, and scientific in their approach have in fact often been based on hagiographical narratives that are considered to be in contradiction to modern biographical methods. Seen to be representing the social concerns of the groups that composed them, hagiographies are seen as a mode of literary myth-making within a particular historical context that aimed to represent the religious and spiritual leaders of specific communities as exemplars with special qualities that made them extraordinary and charismatic. However, such a dichotomous perception between biographies and hagiographies are not always tenable as the latter have always remained a part of the subconscious and conscious arenas of modernity where tradition, history, and received memory coalesce, blurring the distinction between the sacred and the secular. Therefore, it may be concluded that the modern

[48] Rao, Shulman, and Subrahmanyam (2001), *Textures of Time*, p. 3.

biographies of Rāmānuja, addressed to the secular public domain, have themselves been hagiographic in nature.

FRAMEWORK OF THE STUDY

When I undertook this project at the Indian Institute of Advanced Study, my colleagues were of the opinion that I was either working on the philosophy of Rāmānuja, or attempting to write his biography—such is the popular academic perception of research on Rāmānuja. At the outset, I take this opportunity to clarify that my study is not an attempt to analyse the ideas of Rāmānuja within the epistemological discourse of Indian philosophy. Such an exercise requires a prolonged engagement with his works and the metaphysics of Viśiṣṭādvaita, as well as sustained interaction with the disciplines of philosophy and Indology, in which I have no formal training. Nor do I attempt to reconstruct the historical biography of Rāmānuja. With virtually no autobiographical details available, and given the ambiguous nature of the historical references, writing a comprehensive and historically objective life-history would be far too ambitious a project. I attempt to analyse what Rāmānuja's hagiographies from the twelfth to the fifteenth century tell us about him and his activities; how these, in the course of their narration, project him in a particular manner as a religious and spiritual leader; and how the received image of Rāmānuja manifests in different cultural modes in the modern era. Thus, this journey from the sacred world of hagiographies to the secular world of biographies is also an attempt to describe how the past enters and is received and assimilated into the present. The translations attempted for this work and presented in the text are not exact but approximate. However, I have tried my best to keep the original sense in these translations.

Chapter 2 discusses the nature of the Śrīvaiṣṇava hagiographies, their relation to the larger textual tradition of the community, the notion of a canon and its relation to the community identity, and finally the structure of the narratives within the larger textual framework of the hagiographies. While discussing the similarities of themes in the hagiographical texts, it has been pointed out that there were differences in their internal structures, presenting us with diverse representations of Rāmānuja's life. Analysing the structure of the hagiographical tradition and the context in which this textual tradition developed, this chapter also discusses the role of these texts in generating historical consciousness and constructing historical memory or memories. Chapter 3 focuses on the general historical context that influenced the narrative structure and the context within these texts and subsequently the representations of Rāmānuja in the hagiographical narratives. It is emphasized here that even in the early representations of Rāmānuja there was no one single voice. Variations were always present and reflected the complex orientations of the respective texts. The context discussed here focuses on the rise of *brāhmaṇa* villages, that is, the *brahmadeyas*, temples, and networks of control involving the ruling dynasties, especially of the Cōḷas and the Vijayanagara Empire. The response of the hagiographies to the context is discussed by analysing the narratives that appear in them. All this influenced the social base that registered the inclusion of different social groups into the community. There is also a discussion on the rise of Śrīraṅgam as an important institutional centre. Its importance is registered in the narratives that make Śrīraṅgam the focus of Rāmānuja's activities. Chapter 4 analyses the themes in the *guruparamparās* that evolved the image of Rāmānuja as an exemplar *ācārya* of the Śrīvaiṣṇava community. The hagiographical narratives discussed in this chapter focuses on the issues of polemics and sectarianism that demarcated an exclusive Śrīvaiṣṇava metaphysical space by projecting Rāmānuja to be an intellectually superior exegete; by portraying the entire Śrīvaiṣṇava tradition as embodied in the representations of Rāmānuja; by highlighting his activities regarding the spread of the community networks; and finally, through the memorializing process of Rāmānuja as an *ācārya* in the *stotras* that have always been a part of the everyday domestic as well as liturgical practices. Chapter 5 discusses the ways in which the Śrīvaiṣṇava hagiographical narratives on Rāmānuja treated the issues of social hierarchy that travelled through many layers of history to enter the modern biographical domain, thus collapsing the distinction between the two. Though the biographies eulogized him as a 'social reformer', it needs to be pointed out that the tropes on Rāmānuja and the social system have never been unanimous in their representations. Even during the twelfth and thirteenth centuries, following closely upon Rāmānuja's death, the oral as well as the written forms varied and were influenced by the particular genre of religious literature and the intentions of the authors and the social groups they were representing. It seems that these different versions not only registered the diverse perceptions of

Rāmānuja's attitude towards the *varṇāśramadharma* but also reflected the varying social attitudes of the hagiographers and authors and the frameworks within which they operated. Chapter 6 concludes with a discussion on how a subject of a specific religious concern became universal example of toleration and broadmindedness. This chapter will raise certain questions: Are there no hagiographies written on Rāmānuja anymore? Did they belong only to the past? Was it that once they constructed and encrusted the story of Rāmānuja, the themes froze and stabilized as the tradition? An overview of the Rāmānuja theme and its circulation in public performances like theatre, films, and comics will be undertaken.

CHAPTER TWO

Texts, Tradition, and the Śrīvaiṣṇava Community

I bow to Lakṣmī and Nārāyaṇa who are together like the sun and its rays protecting the three worlds and banishing fear from this world.

O the glory of the *divyasūris* and me a dimwit! My courage in writing about their lives is as shallow as the strength of the lotus creeper used in tying an elephant.

Divyasūricaritam, Chapter 1: *śloka* 1–2

Salutations to the great *yogin* Rāmānujācārya, who removed the internal contradictions between the *śrutis*, *smṛtis* and *sūtras* (*Vedānta-sūtras*)

Salutations to you, Āndhrapūrṇa of respectable qualities, devoted to serve the eminent sage, Rāmānuja, by offering milk to him.

Yatirāja Vaibhavam[1]

[1] This text was composed by Āndhrapūrṇa (Vaṭuka Nambi). The first two lines of invocation to Rāmānuja are omitted in the current edition. However, the editor confirms that they are included in other palm leaf manuscripts. For details, see *Yatirāja Vaibhavam of Āndhrapūrṇa* (*Vaṭuka Nambi*), Varadachariar (ed.), 1978, p. 27, note 2.

SITUATING THE TEXTS: IDEOLOGIES AND LEGACIES

These two sets of invocatory verses belong to two different *guruparamparās*, viz., the *Divyasūricaritam* and the *Yatirāja Vaibhavam* respectively.[2] The former comprises the biographies, *carita*, of the holy wise men, in which the last two chapters (seventeen and eighteen), are dedicated to Rāmānuja. The latter is exclusively devoted to Rāmānuja. While the *Divyasūricaritam* places Rāmānuja in the direct line of the Āḻvārs and *ācāryas*, creating a cohort of religious leaders dedicated to Viṣṇu, the *Yatirāja Vaibhavam* aims to project Rāmānuja as the singularly important religious leader of the Śrīvaiṣṇava community. Written in Sanskrit somewhere probably between the twelfth and thirteenth centuries, both these *guruparamparā* texts belong to the Śrīvaiṣṇava hagiographical tradition and have also been used extensively to write about Rāmānuja in recent times.[3] However, despite belonging to approximately the same time and written in the same language, Sanskrit, these two texts show marked differences in their internal structures, as manifested in the two sets of benedictory verses that form the epigraph of this chapter.

Around the fourteenth and fifteenth centuries CE, three Śrīvaiṣṇava hagiographies were composed, viz., *Āṟāyirappaṭi Guruparamparāprabhāvam* (*Splendour of the Guru Lineage according to 6,000*) by Piṉpaḷakiyaperumāḷ Jīyar, *Pannīrāyirappaṭi Guruparamparāprabhāvam* (*Splendour of the Guru Lineage according to 12,000*) by Dvitīya (second) Brahmatantrasvatantra Parkālaswāmī Jīyar, and *Muāyirappaṭi Guruparamparāprabhāvam* (*Splendour of the Guru Lineage according to 3000*) by Tritīya (third)

[2] The editions used in this work are: Garuḍa Vāhana Paṇḍita, *Divyasūricaritam* (trans. from Hindi by Pandita Madhavacharya), Sampathakumaracharya and Venkatachari (eds), 1978, Bombay: Ananthacharya Research Institute; *Yatirāja Vaibhavam of Āndhrapūrṇa (Vaṭuka Nambi)*, Varadachariar (ed.), 1978, Madras: M.C. Krishnan; Krishnaswami Aiyangar, *The Yatirājavaibhavam of Āndhrapūrṇa (Life of Rāmānuja)* in *The Indian Antiquary, A Journal of Oriental Research* (1909[1985]), Vol. XXXVII, Sir Richard Carnac Temple (ed.), 1872–1933, Delhi: Swati Publication, pp. 129–44. Unless specified, the edition of the *Yatirājavaibhavam* cited in this chapter will be that of Varadachariar (ed.), 1978.

[3] Gōvindāchārya (1906), *The Life of Rāmānujāchārya*; Aiyengar (1908), *The Life and Teachings of Sri Ramanujacharya*; Krishnaswami Aiyangar, Chariar and Rangacharya (1911), *Sri Ramanujacharya*; Nagaswamy (2008), *Rāmānuja. Myth and Reality*; Parthasarathy (2008), *Ramanujar*.

Brahmatantrasvatantra Parkālaswāmī Jīyar.[4] Written in a language that was a combination of Tamil and Sanskrit (identified as Maṇipravāḷa by modern scholars), these hagiographies not only wrote about the Āḻvārs and *ācāryas*, but went beyond Rāmānuja's life and narrated the lives of the *ācāryas* after Rāmānuja, thus documenting the history of the Śrīvaiṣṇava community after the twelfth century. Interestingly, these texts were at variance about the names of the *ācāryas* succeeding Rāmānuja and provided different succession lists. The *Āṟāyirappaṭi Guruparamparāprabhāvam* (henceforth, *Āṟāyirappaṭi*) considered Embār, followed by Parāśara Bhaṭṭar and Nañjīyar, to be the direct descendants of Rāmānuja. The text ended with the life of Nampiḷḷai (traditional dates: c.1207–1321 CE). The author, Piṉpaḷakiyaperumāḷ Jīyar, was supposed to be the disciple of Nampiḷḷai.[5] However, latter Teṉkaḷai hagiographies extended this line of descent to Piḷḷai Lokācārya (traditional dates: c.1264–1327 CE) and Maṇavāḷamāmuṉi (traditional dates: c.1337–1443 CE). The *Muāyirappaṭi Guruparamparāprabhāvam* (henceforth, *Muāyirappaṭi*), considered Piḷḷāṉ to be the direct disciple of Rāmānuja, with the succession extending to Vedāntadeśika (traditional dates: c.1268–1369 CE) and Brahmantantrasvatantra Jīyar (traditional dates: c.1286–1386 CE), the founder of the Parkāla *maṭha* in the fourteenth century. Maṇavāḷamāmuṉi and Vedāntadeśika are considered to be the founders of the Vaṭakaḷai and Teṉkaḷai sub-groups respectively in Śrīvaiṣṇavism and till today the *Āṟāyirappaṭi* is considered sacred by the Teṉkaḷais, and the *Pannīrāyirappaṭi* and *Muāyirappaṭi* are revered as the cardinal *guruparamparā* texts of the Vaṭakaḷais.[6]

[4] The editions used in this work are: Piṉpaḷakiyaperumāḷ Jīyar, *Āṟāyirappaṭi Guruparamparāprabhāvam*, Ayyangar (ed.), 1968, Tirucci: Puttur Agraharam; *Muāyirappaṭi Guruparamparāprabhāvam (Vaṭakaḷai) of Tritiya Brahmatantrasvatantra Parkālaswāmī Jīyar*, 1968, Chennai: Lifco. I could not obtain *Pannīrāyirappaṭi Guruparamparāprabhāvam* (henceforth, *Pannīrāyirappaṭi*) as it is probably lost and hence unavailable.

[5] Krishnaswami Ayyangar (ed.), 1968, p. ii.

[6] The modern edition clearly acknowledges the Parkāla *maṭha* and benedictions of the modern 42nd and 43rd *jīyar*s of the Ahobila *maṭha* (Ahobilam in Andhra Pradesh) and Āṇḍavan *maṭha* (Śrīraṅgam in Tamil Nadu), both powerful Śrīvaiṣṇava monastic institutions of Vaṭakaḷai lineage, thus clearly expressing the sectarian Vaṭakaḷai affiliation. It seems from the foreword to the text that Parkāla *maṭha* had also published a Telugu and Tamil version some fifty-five years ago from the date of publication of this edition.

The Śrīvaiṣṇava textual tradition to which the doctrinal works of Vedāntadeśika, Maṇavāḷamāmuṉi, and other *ācāryas* belong did not register any knowledge of the two distinct groups of Vaṭakaḷai and Teṉkaḷai, and therefore, neither professed any affiliation to them.[7] But their respective works undoubtedly reflected ideological differences that, following their time, became the basis of two different schools of thought. Each of these schools while indexing the notional distinctions claimed themselves as the valid channel for transmission of the tradition through presumably correct interpretations of the Tamil hymns and the Viśiṣṭādvaita doctrine of Rāmānuja. The basis of these two schools was their respective ācāryic lineages or the *guruparamparās* in which Vedāntadeśika and Maṇavāḷamāmuṉi were central. Thus entrenched within their own lineages, the schools with their respective theological orientations asserted themselves as the legitimate successors of Rāmānuja, and therefore claimed to be the rightful representatives of the Śrīvaiṣṇava community around the fourteenth and fifteenth centuries. These ācāryic lineages or *guruparamparās* were subsequently documented in the hagiographies of this period. Thus, the hagiographies became the legitimizing mechanism providing an unbroken lineage, from the Āḻvārs to the *ācāryas*, including Rāmānuja and the respective *ācāryas* after him. The narratives in the *Āṟāyirappaṭi*, *Pannīrāyirappaṭi*, and *Muāyirappaṭi* justified their particular ācāryic lineage or *guruparamparā* and registered an orientation in congruence with that lineage—all of which predated the formation of the Vaṭakaḷai and Teṉkaḷai Śrīvaiṣṇava groups.

Thus, the differences in the succession list registered in the hagiographies were not merely empirical. Such a development was located in the historical context of this period. The decline of the Cōḷas in the thirteenth century, the emergence of several new dynasties, and finally the establishment of the Vijayanagar Empire in the fourteenth century, along with the rise of new warrior and mercantile groups with non-*brāhmaṇa* social identities, influenced the religious discourse within the Śrīvaiṣṇava community. Perspectives on social hierarchy and institutional accessibility to temples were some of the crucial issues that informed contemporary theological debates. By the fourteenth century, notional differences on the interpretations of core issues of the Śrīvaiṣṇava

[7] Mumme (1997), 'Śrīvaiṣṇava Hagiography: Lessons from Biblical Scholarship', *Journal of Vaishnava Studies*, 5 (2): 179–200.

theology, mainly, the nature of god and soul, *prapatti* (salvation), and the role of Śrī developed. These differing orientations further influenced the textual tradition of the Śrīvaiṣṇavas. This was especially reflected in the language of these texts, which was a fusion of Sanskrit and Tamil. Such a language was not a mere linguistic innovation but indicated the community's effort to broaden its social base by incorporating different cultural and linguistic elements.[8] This combination reflected an important ideological position that posited the existence of two Vedāntas: the Sanskrit Vedānta and the Tamil Vedānta (the hymns of the Āḻvārs). (The implications of this ideological difference will be discussed more fully in the next section of this chapter.)

Thus, in an environment of active intellectual discussions and growing patronage, two different schools of theology emerged, each of which acquired a considerable following after the fourteenth century that subsequently crystallized into the Vaṭakaḷai and Teṉkaḷai groups. While a discussion on the schism is currently beyond the scope of this work, it needs to be reiterated that during the period taken up for study, the hagiographies do not chronicle the evolution of the Vaṭakaḷai and Teṉkaḷai groups, but undoubtedly record the ideological differences and two sets of lineages that were the precursors of the schism.

Since the *guruparamparās*, or the lineages, registered contesting claims and were becoming an integral part of the Śrīvaiṣṇava identity, the hagiographies in the post-fourteenth century record *taṉiyaṉs* or invocatory verses dedicated to Vedāntadeśika or Maṇavāḷamāmuṉi—an expression of unflinching loyalty to their respective ācāryic lineage. The editions consulted here along with the commentaries and other genre of Śrīvaiṣṇava texts begin with these *taṉiyaṉs* underscoring the significance of the lineage. Thus, the *taṉiyaṉ* in the *Āṟāyirappaṭi* states:

> I bow down to Śrī Maṇavāḷamāmuṉi
> Who is the recipient of the grace of Śrīśailesa
> He is the ocean of knowledge, devotion and detachment (*vairāgya)*
> He is forever immersed in his devotion to the king of ascetics (Rāmānuja)[9]

[8] See Venkatachari (1978), *The Maṇipravāḷa Literature of the Śrīvaiṣṇava Ācāryas.*

[9] *Āṟāyirappaṭi Guruparamparāprabhāvam*, p. 1. Śrīśailesa, also Tiruvāymoḻipiḷḷai in Tamil, was the teacher of Maṇavāḷamāmuṉi.

The *Yatindrapravanaprabhāvam*—a later hagiography, tentatively dated to late fifteenth or early sixteenth century—records that when Maṇavāḷamāmuṉi was discussing the *Prabhandham* in front of Lord Raṅganātha in the temple at Śrīraṅgam, a boy stepped out and recited this Sanskrit verse. On being asked to repeat the *taṉiyaṉ*, the boy was unable to do so as he did not know Sanskrit. Then it was taken to have been divinely inspired by Raṅganātha himself, who is supposed to have further taught this verse to the priests at Veṅkateśvara temple at Tirupati and Aḻagarkōyil at Tirumāliruñcōḷai.[10]

The importance of the *guruparamparā* is further accentuated in another *taṉiyaṉ* of the Teṉkaḷai affiliation:

> I pay my respect to the line of *gurus* commencing with the consort of Lakṣmī (Viṣṇu), with Nāthamuni and Yāmunācārya in the middle and extending as far as my own *guru.*[11]

Similarly, the *Muāyirappaṭi* narrates that Brahmantantrasvatantra Jīyar composed a *taṉiyaṉ* in honour of Vedāntadeśika and enjoined that it should be recited before and after the recital of the *Prabandhams*:

> I bow down to Śrī Veṅkaṭanātha who is also Vedāntācārya
> Who is the crest jewel of knowledge *(jñāna)* and detachment *(vairāgya)*
> And who is the recipient of the grace of Rāmānuja[12]

The *Muāyirappaṭi* also tells us that one day Vedāntadeśika went to Lord Raṅganātha at Śrīraṅgam. The Lord in order to honour him commanded that this *taṉiyaṉ* should be recited before and after the recitation of the Āḻvār hymns.[13] The *taṉiyaṉs* are now prefixed to almost all the Śrīvaiṣṇava texts. Benedictory in nature, *taṉiyaṉs* are recited or expected to be recited in the everyday domestic and liturgical sphere of Śrīvaiṣṇava life, and are therefore significant mnemonic devices utilized in the transmission of the tradition.

[10] Mumme (1997), 'Śrīvaiṣṇava Hagiography: Lessons from Biblical Scholarship', *Journal of Vaishnava Studies*, 5(2): 181, fn. 10.

[11] *Ārāyirappaṭi Guruparamparāprabhāvam*, p. 1.

[12] *Muāyirappaṭi Guruparamparāprabhāvam*, p. 43.

[13] Mumme (1997), 'Śrīvaiṣṇava Hagiography: Lessons from Biblical Scholarship', p. 181, fn. 10.

Thus, despite belonging to the same genre of texts, the hagiographies were informed by their respective orientations. Embedded in these differences is the dynamism of the hagiographical tradition. Fluctuating between the fluidity and fixity of the tradition and the Śrīvaiṣṇava community, the hagiographies with their variations offer us diverse representations of Rāmānuja's life. This chapter sets out to examine the hagiographical tradition that represented Rāmānuja as an exemplar in varied ways. This tradition had a unitary aim in projecting Rāmānuja as the most important *ācārya* of the community: as an important philosopher with a new interpretation of the Vedānta to his credit; as an organizer, spreading the community network through innovations in the temple organization and consolidation of the pilgrimage complex; and finally, creating an organization for the perpetuation of the Śrīvaiṣṇava community.

However, intersecting with this hagiographic portrayal of Rāmānuja were issues of community consciousness, the notion of a tradition, multiple identities within the Śrīvaiṣṇava community, disciples, and patronage, and, finally, articulation in relation to the other religious traditions. While documenting Rāmānuja's life, the *guruparamparā*s also delineated the history of Śrīvaiṣṇavism and its community, reinforcing a normative paradigm that emerged as a reference point for the self-definition of the Śrīvaiṣṇava identity. Thus providing their own as well as the Śrīvaiṣṇava worldview, the hagiographies interpreted and preserved the ideas, becoming an important vehicle of transmission and dissemination of the history and tradition of the Śrīvaiṣṇava community.

The first section of this chapter analyses the structure of the hagiographical tradition and is divided into two parts. The first part discusses the intent of these texts and the knotty issue of authorship. The second part focusses on the equally complex problem of the chronology of these texts. The next section discusses the context in which this textual tradition developed. The third section discusses the Śrīvaiṣṇava textual tradition in general as the *guruparamparā*s were a part of the larger Śrīvaiṣṇava textual tradition and along with other genres of texts represented a canonical structure. The last section discusses the role of these texts in generating historical consciousness and constructing historical memory or memories.

TEXTS: STRUCTURE AND MEANING

a) Purpose and Authorship:

The word *carita* literally means 'deeds', 'behaviour' or 'conducts', and 'life', 'biography', and 'history'.[14] In the latter set of meanings, *carita* also connotes legends in the biographical narration, with an emphasis on recounting or narration. The *Divyasūricaritam* or the biography of the holy sages was written with this aim. The colophon at the end of the first chapter states that the author of *Divyasūricaritam* was Garuḍavāhana Śrīnivāsa and he was the son of a *brāhmaṇa* couple, Sarvajñacūdāmaṇi and Bhuvanādhipā. The colophon also informs us that Sarvajñacūdāmaṇi was the *adhipati* (chief or in-charge) of an *ārogyaśālā* (hospital/health centre) in the temple of Raṅganāthasvāmī at Śrīraṅgam and the author seems to have inherited this office from his father. The colophon at the end of the eighteenth (last) chapter states that the author belonged to the Kāśyapa *gotra (kāśyapakulatilakasya)*, was in-charge of the *ārogyaśālā* at the Raṅganātha temple (*ārogyaśālāvallabha*), and Garuḍavāhana Paṇḍita and *Kavivaidyapurandara* were probably his title.

Ślokas 86 and 87 in Chapter 17 provide an account of Rāmānuja instituting this *ārogyaśālā* and entrusting Garuḍavāhana Bhaṭṭa (Paṇḍita) with the responsibility of its upkeep, thus establishing and legitimizing the status of the author within the Śrīvaiṣṇava community:

> One day, Yatirāja (Rāmānuja) overheard a conversation of one of his disciple who admitted that he was offering god milk and *jāmun* together, knowing well that the combination was toxic. Rāmānuja was upset and punished this *śiṣya*. Thereafter, in order to cure Lord Raṅganātha who was like a king, Rāmānuja prepared a *kāśāya* (medicinal concoction) and offered it to Him, thereby serving the Lord. In addition, he installed a *ārogyaśalā* and made it the shrine of Lord Dhanvantri. From that day onwards, Garuḍavāhana Bhaṭṭa offered the *kāśāya* everyday to Lord Raṅganātha.[15]

Interestingly, an inscription dated c.1256 CE records the founding of a *śālai* on the 'west side of the *gopura* enshrining the god Eḍuttakai-Aḻagiya

[14] See lexical entry *carita* in Apte (1957–59), 3 vols, p. 699, entry 11, Nos 2 and 3 and in Macdonell (1929), *A Practical Sanskrit Dictionary with Transliteration, Accentuation, and Etymological Analysis Throughout*, p. 92.

[15] Divyasūricaritam, Ch. 17, *ślokas* 86 and 87.

Nāyaṉār in the Raṅganātha temple' at Śrīraṅgam.[16] According to the inscription, Chiṅgadeva Singaṇṇa Daṇḍanāyaka, a *pradhāna* of the Hoysala king Rāmanātha, made a donation for the upkeep of this *śālai*. Further, the inscription reports that the care of the *śālai* was entrusted to Garuḍavāhana Paṉḍita, referred in the epigraph as '*rakṣaka*' (protector) of the donor.[17] Therefore, service to the god and to the community especially of a system started by Rāmānuja was the basis of legitimacy of the hagiographical exercise undertaken by Garuḍavāhana Paṉḍita.

Disclaiming any original contribution, Garuḍavāhana Paṉḍita stated in a typical mode of self-abnegation that he was merely attempting to repeat on a modest scale what his preceding *ācārya*s had already done extensively, that is, recounting the lives of the *divyasūri*s.[18] Clearly, reference to a pre-existing tradition of writing or discussing the sacred biographies of the twelve Āḻvārs and three Śrīvaiṣṇava *ācārya*s (Nāthamuni, Yāmuna, and Rāmānuja) was revoked in this *guruparamparā* in order to validate its content. This legitimacy was intended to enhance the credibility of the text to the audience, who would then be in no doubt about the veracity of the narratives that were to follow.

The relevance of this hagiographic exercise was further highlighted through an association with Viṣṇu. The text narrates that Viṣṇu, the creator of the Vedas, sent his *avatāra*s or incarnations to the earth to reinstate the revered status of the holy texts (probably the Vedas) which were being disrespected. These *avatāra*s were also supposed to win over those who were not following the scriptural codes as laid down by Viṣṇu. However, evil persisted, and Viṣṇu decided to descend, along with his consorts Śrī, Bhūdevī, and Nīladevī, to Śrīraṅgam to deliver people from their ignorance. As mentioned earlier, Śrīraṅgam was the centre of the Śrīvaiṣṇava activities and the site of the important temple of Raṅganāthasvāmī. Further, the text (i.e., the *Divyasūricaritam*) tells us that Viṣṇu ordered his companions to take birth on earth in different *varṇa*s and in various places.[19] Thus, Ādiśeṣa, the thousand-hooded cosmic serpent on which Viṣṇu reclines, Viśvakasena, his minister, and

[16] Archaeological Survey of India, *South Indian Inscriptions*, Vol. XXIV, No. 226.

[17] Ibid.

[18] *Divyasūricaritam*, Ch. 1, *śloka*s 4–20.

[19] Ibid, *nānāvarṇasamutpannā nānādeśeṣu vasina*: Ch. 1, *śloka* 85.

Viṣṇu's divine weapons—conch, discus, and so on—took birth as the *divyasūris* that were the Āḻvārs and *ācāryas*. In this context Rāmānuja was considered to be the incarnation of Ādiśeṣa. The text introduces the notion of cyclical time in which Viṣṇu repeated his act of incarnation and each incarnation was supposed to have marked the beginning of a new age. This frame of *avatāra* presents a Śrīvaiṣṇava alternative in the text implying that the previous *avatāras* were limited in achieving their aims as sin and suffering persisted.[20] Further, we are told that Viṣṇu, who had already informed his consort Lakṣmī about his designs, also explained that the *Vedāntaśāstras* that sing his glory and emphasize the rules of the hymns of *varṇāśramadharma* have been translated into Tamil by the *Prabandhams* (the hymns of the Āḻvārs). Viṣṇu emphasized that these *Prabandhams* would dispel the incorrect *śāstras* (philosophy), deliver the people from the darkness of their ignorance that was a consequence of not following the Vedas, and gradually bring them on to the right path of *bhakti* (devotion) and *śarṇāgati* (taking refuge in the lord). Thus, the *Divyasūricaritam* in its first chapter used the Vaiṣṇava motifs of *avatāra*, and the immanence and transcendence of God within a distinct Śrīvaiṣṇava framework. It further indicated the fallaciousness of preexisting ideas, and introduced the crucial Śrīvaiṣṇava theological concepts of *bhakti* and *śarṇāgati*. The chapter also highlighted a textual tradition comprising the Vedic and the Tamil hymns and the significance of Śrīraṅgam as the sacred centre. The *Divyasūricaritam* also has a certain literary texture, as its form and structure seems to have been inspired from the Sanskrit *mahākāvya* style, reminiscent of Kālidāsa's compositions.[21] After narrating the life story of Āṇṭāḷ and her marriage in lyrical detail, the text has a long chapter describing the four seasons, commencing with spring. This was probably intended to provide the reader some relief before the next presentation, a detailed account of the lives of the *ācāryas*, including Rāmānuja. Alternately, this textual device might have been aimed at fuelling the curiosity of readers eager for the biography of Rāmānuja that was placed at the end of the text.

As indicated by the title, the *Yatirāja Vaibhavam* was dedicated exclusively to the recounting of the *vaibhava* (glory) of Rāmānuja as

[20] Ibid, Ch. 1, *ślokas* 80–3.

[21] Ramanujam (1973), *History of Vaishnavism in South India up to Ramanuja*, p. 13; Hardy (1992), 'The Śrī Vaiṣṇava Hagiography of Parkāla', in Shackle and Snell (eds), p. 84.

yatirāja (the king of ascetics). This Sanskrit text comprising 114 *śloka*s is attributed to Āndhra Pūrṇa (Tamil: Vaṭuka Nambi), an immediate disciple of Rāmānuja. The subsequent *guruparamparās*, the *Āṟāyirappaṭi* and *Muāyirappaṭi*, refer to Vaṭuka Nambi as one of the closest disciples of Rāmānuja. These two hagiographies delineated Vaṭuka Nambi as a steadfast disciple of Rāmānuja and recounted episodes of his unflinching devotion to his *guru*, whose status he considered higher than that of the Lord. Vaṭuka Nambi is said to have composed verses and taught everybody that an '*ācārya's* feet was the only refuge'.[22] Although the *Āṟāyirappaṭi* did not cite the *Yatirāja Vaibhavam*, the *Muāyirappaṭi* cited three verses in Sanskrit about Rāmānuja fulfilling his preceptor Yāmuna's three wishes (to be discussed subsequently) and reported that these verses were condensed in Vaṭuka Nambi's *Yatirāja Vaibhavam*.[23]

The pithy style of this text suggests that the author was addressing an audience already familiar with the narrative, or that he was highlighting only those aspects of the narrative that were already in circulation, or were indispensable for the delineation of Rāmānuja, in accordance with community mores. Āndhra Pūrṇa declared unflinching loyalty and devotion to Rāmānuja as the basis of his claim to the privilege of being the *guru*'s close associate:

> May he, the illustrious lord of the ascetics, who assigned some work to some of his close disciples as restricted to each one of them, and to me the servant, most undeserving, and restricted to him alone, the work of preparing milk for him who made me the servant of the servants bend before his feet, as his ardent devotee, as if I was the source of his welfare—may he be protecting me forever.[24]

In all probability, his intention was to seek out or strengthen his place within the community organization.

Like all the Śrīvaiṣṇava texts, the editions of the *Yatirāja Vaibhavam* used here begin with a *taṉiyaṉ* or an invocatory verse that situates the text within the tradition and validates its status as sacred . The *taṉiyaṉ*s cited as epigraphs of this chapter highlight the author's claim to be a

[22] *Āṟāyirappaṭi*, pp. 272–74 and p. 288.

[23] *Muāyirappaṭi*, p.111.

[24] *Yatirāja Vaibhavam*, p. 113.

disciple *par excellence* on the basis of his service to his *guru*, Rāmānuja, the *yatirāja* or the great king of ascetics. Further, in some of the palm leaf manuscripts, a *taṉiyaṉ* dedicated to Rāmānuja precedes the *taṉiyaṉ* devoted to Āndhra Pūrṇa.[25] Such an arrangement accentuated Āndhra Pūrṇa's status and endorsed the *guru–śiṣya* (preceptor–disciple) relationship, emphasizing that devotion to one's preceptor was analogous to devotion to God. Clearly it was a model of an ideal *guru–śiṣya paramparā* for the community to emulate. These two *taṉiyaṉs* are also crucial for they tell us the manner in which the community wanted to remember Rāmānuja and Āndhra Pūrṇa, and how this method and process was reinforced by the tradition. Rāmānuja is depicted as a *yogī* or a *yati* and a philosopher who interpreted the Vedas, the *smṛtis*, and the *Vedānta-sūtras* in a correct manner, removing the contradictions surrounding the corpus of metaphysical knowledge, implying that the previous interpretations were incorrect and problematic, and Āndhra Pūrṇa as a disciple-servitor committed to his *guru*. Embedded within this frame of devotion and obedience to the *guru* was the dominant idea of *bhakti* that infused the *Yatirāja Vaibhavam* with spiritual significance.[26]

Just as the *Divyasūricaritam* situated Rāmānuja as a part of a *guruparamparā*, both the *Āṟāyirappaṭi* and *Muāyirappaṭi* treated the narratives as a part of the unbroken sequence of religious and spiritual leaders preceding and succeeding him. They also provided similar accounts of Viṣṇu's decision to redeem the world through his various incarnations, whose role would be to propagate the *Dravida Vedas* or the *Prabandhams*.[27] The *Āṟāyirappaṭi* provided a context for the mythical incarnations by locating the *avatāras* in the fertile river valleys. It specified that these *avatāras* were weapons and ornaments of Viṣṇu. They took birth in different *varṇas* near the different rivers, namely, *Tāmbraparaṇi*, Kāvēri, Pāyasvini, Mahābhāga, Praticī, and Saraswatī, in

[25] Ibid., p. 27.

[26] Krishnaswami Aiyangar in his 'Introduction' to the *Yatirāja Vaibhavam* says, 'We find his name, however, among those of the 74 successors of Rāmānuja in the propagation of the Vaishṇava Gospel', and the author of the *Prapannāmṛitam*, who lived a contemporary of Venkaṭapatirāya (died 1614 A.D.) claims to be a descendant of Āndhrapūrṇa (or Vaḍuganambi as he is called in Tamil). For details, see, Krishnaswami Aiyangar; *The Yatirājavaibhavam of Āndhrapūrṇa* (*Life of Rāmānuja*), p.129.

[27] *Āṟāyirappaṭi*, pp. 6–7; *Muāyirappaṭi*, pp. 5–6.

the *Dravida* country (*bhūbhāga*).[28] Interestingly, in several editions of the *Āṟāyirappaṭi*, the *Divyasūricaritam* has been often acknowledged as a source, though the authenticity of this acknowledgement has been a matter of dispute among scholars.[29]

Unlike the *Divyasūricaritam* and *Yatirāja Vaibhavam*, which derived their respective legitimacy from the service to Rāmānuja, the *Āṟāyirappaṭi* and *Muāyirappaṭi* established their reputation on the basis of their adherence to the *ācāryas* of their individual lineages. Needless to say that Rāmānuja was most prominent in these hagiographies and these texts dedicated the lengthiest section to his life.

The *Muāyirappaṭi* emphasized the imperativeness of knowing the *guruparamparās* for certain reasons: imparting the right knowledge of the *mantras*; to acquire scholarship; the transmission of this knowledge and tradition by an *ācārya*, who should be sanctioned by the *śāstras* and possess good conduct and devotion; to dispel the *ācaryāvrittānta* (interpretations by exegetes) that were false and did not have the sanction of the *śāstras*; to correct the dissenters (*bāhayantra virodhīs*); know the teachings of previous *ācaryās*, and; finally, perform eternal service to them.[30] While highlighting the notion of tradition, transmission, and lineage, the repeated reference to 'dissenters' shows that there were conflicting opinions by the fourteenth century, when this text was composed. Some scholars hold that it was a Vaṭakaḷai reaction to the Teṉkaḷai ideas.[31] However, the contents of the text do not indicate this. Rather, without any specific references, the hagiography generally refers to the contesting ideas as illegitimate. This proves the point that one has been making, which is, that by the fifteenth century, undoubtedly notional differences and two schools of thought were present, but they were not grouped as binaries that were the Vaṭakaḷai and Teṉkaḷai.

Further, by claiming that it was derived from the *śāstras*, the *Muāyirappaṭi* attempted to establish its veracity and authority. Reference to Vedāntadeśika and his works in the introductory portion reflects that a clear sectarian lineage had emerged and the author was positioning

[28] *Āṟāyirappaṭi*, p. 7.

[29] Ramanujam (1973), pp. 39–44; Venkatachari (1978) in *Divyasūricaritam*, p. vii; Hardy (1992), p. 85.

[30] *Muāyirappaṭi Guruparamparāprabhāvam*, pp. 4–6.

[31] Mumme (1997), p. 162.

himself clearly within a particular lineage and this hagiography became the medium to assert this lineage. The author, Tritīya (third) Bramatantrasvatantra Parkālaswāmī Jīyar, also acknowledged certain preexistent hagiographies that, according to him, were supposed to have had authority and relevance for the Śrīvaiṣṇava tradition. These hagiographies were the *Divyasūricaritam* written by Garuḍavāhana Paṇḍita and the *Pannīrāyirappaṭi* and *Prabandhanirvāha* written by Tirumalai Śrīnivāsācārya. Like the author of the *Divyasūricaritam*, the author of the *Muāyirappaṭi* stated that he was commissioned by his *ācārya*, the Dvitīya (second) Bramatantrasvatantra Parkālaswāmī Jīyar, the author of the *Pannīrāyirappaṭi*, to compose this text. Thus, the *guru–śiṣya* relationship and service to the *guru* (not Rāmānuja) became the legitimizing basis of the composition and transmission of the hagiography and the lineage.

These different texts of the hagiographical tradition drew upon a common stock of narratives, especially where Rāmānuja was concerned. Indicating the widely existent cultural circulation and transmission of such accounts from one generation to another, the hagiographies received and reworked upon these narrative, thus augmenting the tradition. On one hand, the hagiographies put forth the existence of a unified Śrīvaiṣṇava community by mythologizing the biographical accounts of the Āḻvārs and the *ācāryas*. On the other hand, these texts reflected 'the social location and ideology' of the different groups they were representing or aimed to represent.[32] They provided legitimacy to multiple identities during the contest over power and control of resources in the temples. Nonetheless, they also asserted their affiliation to the larger Śrīvaiṣṇava community.

However, omissions and additions were common for these narratives and reflected the worldview of the hagiographers. For instance, the life of Rāmānuja in these texts represented the concerns of the hagiographers themselves. Establishing Rāmānuja as an important *ācārya* of the community through generic styles, anecdotes, and motifs, the authors were expressing their respective anxieties regarding the larger Śrīvaiṣṇava community in general, as well as specific concerns regarding their own status within it.

[32] Ramanujan (1992), 'Three Hundred *Rāmayāṇas*: Five Examples and Three Thoughts on Translation', in Richman (ed.), *Many Rāmayāṇas: The Diversity of a Narrative Tradition in South Asia*, pp. 22–49.

It would be appropriate here to briefly discuss the notion of an 'author' within the Śrīvaiṣṇava hagiographic tradition. Within the overarching community framework there was a complex relationship between the 'author' and the text. Neither Garuḍavāhana Paṇḍita nor Āndhra Pūrṇa, Piṉpaḷakiyaperumāḷ Jīyar, and Tritīya Brahmatantra Parkālaswāmī Jīyar can be considered 'authors' in the modern sense of the term; nor can they claim any 'authority' over their texts by virtue of having composed them. The presence of their names 'says less about the authorship side of the "author" than about the author's authority...'[33] In this case, 'the authority of the authors' came from the subjects being narrated, that is, the Āḻvārs and *ācārya*s in the case of Garuḍavāhana Paṇḍita, Piṉpaḷakiyaperumāḷ Jīyar, and Tritīya Brahmatantra Parkālaswāmī Jīyar, and Rāmānuja in the case of Āndhra Pūrṇa. Further, the hagiographers' identity as Śrīvaiṣṇava *brāhmaṇa*s, their association with Rāmānuja (based directly or indirectly upon the Śrīvaiṣṇava ethics of service, loyalty and lineage affiliations), and the textual transmission of the tradition through the *guruparamparā*s that acquired scriptural status were the actual roots of their 'authorship'. Divested of Śrīvaiṣṇava affiliation, any hagiographer's claim to an independent identity as a producer of the text would have no relevance or credibility either within or outside the community. In the *Muāyirappaṭi*, the concept of the authorship acquires an additional dimension with the status of the author being based on his *maṭha* affiliation, the Brahmatantra Parakāla *maṭha*, which had emerged as a significant Śrīvaiṣṇava institution by the fourteenth century. Therefore, it is not surprising that his individual name is not known to us and we know his title that has a *jīyar* suffix indicating that, in all likelihood, he was the head of the *maṭha*. Similarly, the Piṉpaḷakiyaperumāḷ Jīyar, author of the *Āṟāyirappaṭi*, could have been affiliated to a *maṭha* as indicated by the *jīyar* suffix to his name. Though we have no information with regard to this, we are told by the modern editor that Piṉpaḷakiyaperumāḷ Jīyar's

[33] See Hawley (1988), 'Author and Authority in the Bhakti Poetry of North India', *Journal of Asian Studies*, 47(2): 270. Also see Novetzke (2003), 'Divining an Author: The Idea of Authorship in an Indian Religious Tradition', *History of Religion*, 42 (3): 213–42; Pollock (2008), 'Is There an Indian Intellectual History? Introduction to "Theory and Method in Indian Intellectual History"', *Journal of Indian Philosophy* 36(5–6): 533–42; and Jonardon Ganeri (2008), 'Contextualism in the Study of Indian Intellectual Cultures', *Journal of Indian Philosophy*, 36(5–6): 551–62.

disciples recorded his discourses and subsequently systematized them into a *gururparamparā* and popularized it.[34]

It is thus clear that the author was not 'individualized' and the texts were not subjective productions.[35] The *Divyasūricaritam* does not claim to initiate a new hagiographic trajectory. Garuḍavāhana Paṉḍita unequivocally situated himself within the tradition and stated that he was following the path of the *pūrvācāryas* (previous *ācāryas*) in extolling the *divyasūris*. Similarly, the Tritīya Bramatantrasvatantra Parkālaswāmī Jīyar also acknowledged the preexistent hagiographies and clearly stated that he was commissioned by his predecessor, the Dvitīya Bramatantrasvatantra Parkālaswāmī Jīyar. This mode of textual allegiance and acknowledgement is alien to the modern concept of an author and particularly authorship that legitimizes itself by the assertion of attempting something different and new, the authorial exercise being completely individualized. Nevertheless, both Garuḍavāhana Paṉḍita and Āndhra Pūrṇa presented facets of their individuality through inserting (primarily at the beginning or end of a chapter or of the work itself) their name, genealogy, family background, and occupation, a strategy that definitely indicated a wish to be memorialized for posterity. Tritīya Bramatantrasvatantra Parkālaswāmī Jīyar derived his individuality from his institutional affiliation. But the authors of the *Āṟāyirappaṭi* and *Muāyirappaṭi*, despite their association with respective ācāryic lineage, did not transgress the Śrīvaiṣṇava boundaries, an indication that these texts intended their own lineages to represent the community identity and tradition.

In relation to this, it is important to note that with regard to Śrīvaiṣṇava commentaries or explanatory treatises, the individual author was an important figure, since in many cases he was an *ācārya* of the community and his works presented important exegetical logic and arguments that frequently became the basis of various polemical debates. In this sense the works of Yāmuna, Rāmānuja, Vedāntadeśika, and Maṇavāḷamāmuṉi were indeed 'individualized', and their individual authority—not as an independent author but as a religious leader with a certain orientation—determined the status of the texts.

[34] *Āṟāyirappaṭi*, p. iii.

[35] Foucault (1984 [1969]), 'What Is an Author?', in Paul Rabinow (ed.), *The Foucault Reader*, p. 118. Also see, Barthes (1977 [1968]), 'The Death of the Author', in Heath (trans./ed.), *Image, Music, Text*, pp. 142–8.

Associated with this concept of author and the text has been the problem of actual authorship of the hagiographies as available in their present editions. Some scholars feel that, with time, the Śrīvaiṣṇava hagiographies have undergone several additions and interpolations and the editions available to us are the redacted versions of the originals.[36] Therefore, they contend that while these authors may have originally written these texts, they were in all likelihood not the authors of the present versions available to us. This has been especially pointed out in the case of the *Āṟāyirappaṭi* and its author, Piṉpaḷakiyaperumāḷ Jīyar.[37] The scholars are of the opinion that Piṉpaḷakiyaperumāḷ Jīyar was a disciple of Nampiḷḷai, he was very old at the time of Nampiḷḷai's death, and could not have outlived his *ācārya* for long. He wrote this text towards the end of his life and being a traditionalist, out of respect, did not document the lives of his contemporaries like Nampiḷḷai and Nañjīyar, who were also his *ācāryas*. Therefore, in all possibility, he ended his narrative with the account of Rāmānuja. Thereafter, the accounts of the *ācāryas* after Rāmānuja were penned down by later authors with a distinct Teṉkaḷai bias. It has been held that the *Āṟāyirappaṭi* was composed in the thirteenth century and was the first *guruparamparāprabhāvaṁ* (an issue to be taken up for discussion shortly). Therefore, the experts feel that between the seventeenth and nineteenth centuries, when disputes between Vaṭakaḷais and Teṉkaḷais over the control of temple resources became frequent, then in order to provide legitimacy, the original *Āṟāyirappaṭi* was embellished with the post-Rāmānuja narratives. The scholars also point out that during this period, most of the Śrīvaiṣṇava hagiographies, like *Yatindrapravanaprabhāvam*, *Periya Tirumuṭai Aṭaivu*, *Prapannāmṛtam*, and interestingly even *Muāyirappaṭi* were composed.[38]

The premise that Piṉpaḷakiyaperumāḷ Jīyar stopped with the account of Rāmānuja may be correct. But the reasons cited by the scholars that the Jīyar out of reverence would never write about his own *ācāryas* is not convincing.[39] Perhaps one may surmise that he was commissioned to write or it was entirely his own decision to compose the hagiography in order

[36] Ramanujam (1973), *History of Vansnavism*, pp. 4–59; Mumme (1997), *The Theology of Maṇavāḷamāmuṉi*, pp. 159–64.

[37] Ramanujam (1973), *History of Vansnavism*, pp. 50–1.

[38] Mumme (1997), *The Theology of Maṇavāḷamāmuṉi*, pp. 162–3.

[39] Ramanujam (1973), *History of Vansnavism*, p. 51.

to establish the lineage of preceptors or the *ācārya parapamparā* to which he was associated and provide a credible context for assertion of temple rights to them. However, the argument that the examples from subsequent versions of the *Āṟāyirappaṭi* containing stories of *ācārya*s who came much after Piṉpaḻakiyaperumāḷ Jīyar were later additions, can be taken as valid.[40]

At the risk of repetition, it needs to be emphasized that the differences in the Śrīvaiṣṇava community before the sixteenth century existed but did not ossify into two distinct groups. Epigraphical sources between the thirteenth and fifteenth centuries point towards competition between different Śrīvaiṣṇava religious leaders over the control of patronage, pilgrimage, and temple resources. The emergence of the *maṭha*s as significant institutions with the powerful Śrīvaiṣṇava leaders controlling or attempting to control them should be seen in this context. Therefore, the hagiographies used in this study in all possibility were composed during this period to provide a reference point for the claims made by the various *ācārya*s, who by this time had notional doctrinal differences amongst themselves too. For instance, the context of composing the *Muāyirappaṭi* by Tritīya Bramatantrasvatantra Parkālaswāmī Jīyar was situated within the Parkāla *maṭha*. There is a possibility that he was the head of the *maṭha* and may had probably commissioned the composition of the hagiography in order to establish the reputation of the *maṭha* and thereby attract patronage. Therefore, as a sacred text of the community, it was befitting that the authorship of the *Muāyirappaṭi* was attributed to a person in a position of authority.

The history of the Parkāla *maṭha* shows that the composition of a hagiography would have been significant for this institution as it constantly shifted its base from one place to another, evidently for patronage. The epigraphical evidence refers to the establishment of the *maṭha* in Varadarājasvāmī temple at Kāñcīpuram around 1359 CE when a certain Bramatantrasvatantra *jīyar* was granted a *maṭha* and some lands on the representation of the supervisor of the temple, Perumāḷ Tāḍan, to the Lord. The inscription further refers to an order issued by the deity of the temple, Varadarājasvāmī himself, stating the purpose of establishing the *maṭha*. 'It would contain the books that he had accumulated and propagate here, "Rāmānuja—*darśanam*" or the philosophy of Rāmānuja, after him the disciples in succession would

[40] Ibid., pp. 54–5.

take the possession of the *matha* and continue the work.'[41] From Kāñcīpuram, the *maṭha* shifted its base to Tirupati and after sometime established the base finally in Mysore.[42]

However, considering the fluid nature of the Indian textual tradition, the fixity of the author with regard to a particular text should not be overemphasized. There is no internal evidence within the text like in the case of *Āṟāyirappaṭi* that tells us that Piṉpaḷakiyaperumāḷ Jīyar was the author. Perhaps, it can be concluded that the Śrīvaiṣṇava tradition attributed the composition to him. The editor's note on the *Āṟāyirappaṭi* discussed a short while ago points towards oral discourses being codified into a written text by Jīyar's disciples. Fortunately, for the purpose of this study, the narratives on the life of Rāmānuja form the core of the analysis, which the scholars anyway feel was written in the *Āṟāyirappaṭi* by Piṉpaḷakiyaperumāḷ Jīyar.

The central focus of the *guruparamparā* texts was the notion of a Śrīvaiṣṇava spiritual genealogy and therefore individual authorship becomes secondary. The succession of religious leaders implied continuity in the line of the Āḻvārs and *ācāryas* themselves, as well as a lineage that established apparently credible connections (however historically invalid) between them. The primary basis of this lineage was the devotion to Viṣṇu, followed by knowledge of the Vedas (especially in the case of the *ācāryas*), knowledge of the Tamil hymns of the Āḻvārs, and finally an interaction amongst this community of religious leaders, especially between those who came immediately before and after the particular subject of the hagiography. This interaction formed the crucial link in the concatenate of the lineage, and the hagiographies provided a context through their descriptions.

In his *Gītābhāṣya*, Rāmānuja acknowledged Yāmuna as his preceptor.[43] Further, in his *Śrībhāṣya*, a commentary on the *Brahmasūtra*, Rāmānuja emphasized that he was following the views of his previous *ācāryas*, 'The Predecessors-teachers abridged the voluminous exposition of the "*Brahmasutras*" made by his reverence Baudhyayana; [and] in

[41] Annual Report on Indian Epigraphy (1919), No. 574; Rangacharya (1949), *The Origin and Growth of the Parakala Matha*, pp. xiv–xv.

[42] Rangacharya (1949), *The Origin and Growth of the Parakala Matha*, p. 13

[43] Rāmānuja, *Gitābhāṣya* (translated from Sanskrit by Sampatkumaran) (1985), p. 1.

accordance with their views, the words of the "*Sutras*" would be commented upon by us.'[44]

Therefore, it is not surprising that the 'authors' of the *Divyasūricaritam* and *Muāyirappaṭi* also acknowledged a pre-existing tradition of praise of the *divyasūri*s by the *purvācārya*s (previous *ācārya*s), and included themselves as a part of this tradition. Such acknowledgements seem to have emerged as a style or norm in the composition of the individual Śrīvaiṣṇava texts, validating them within the overall scriptural tradition.[45] A philosophical lineage imparted legitimacy, and invoking it before the commencement of the actual composition was an accepted practice to gain textual credibility and authority.

Chronology of the Hagiographies: A Note

Modern scholars have been preoccupied with the possible dating of these hagiographies—an exercise ridden with tentativeness and controversy. On the basis of the information regarding Rāmānuja entrusting the responsibility of the *śālai* to Garuḍavāhana Paṇḍita and the latter's biographical details, one may conclude that the author of the *Divyasūricaritam* was a contemporary or lived a little later than Rāmānuja and this text was written during the twelfth century. But B.V. Ramanujam warns against such a conclusion.[46] According to him, there is a verse colophon that states Garuḍavāhana Paṇḍita's *gotra* as Vādhūla, his father's name as Varada, *guru*'s name as Varavarādhīśa, and his mother's name as Lōkēśa.[47]

[44] *Śrībhāṣya of Rāmānuja* (trans. from Sanskrit/ed. by Raghunath Damodar Karmakar) (1959), p. 2, *sūtra* 2. According to Venkatachari (1978, p. 13), this practice by commentators of claiming to be part of the genealogy of previous teachers is specific to Śrīvaiṣṇava theologians; no such assertion is made by Śaṅkara.

[45] Ibid.

[46] Ramanujam (1973), *History of Vaisnavism*, pp. 13–44.

[47] Ibid., pp. 13–14. The edition used in this work, however, informs that a manuscript procured from the Government Oriental Manuscript Library, Chennai, documents Garuḍavāhana Paṇḍita's *gotra* as Vādhūla, his father's name as Varada and *guru*'s name as Varavarādhīśa. The same edition also informs that in the version published by Mysore Vidyatarangini Press, the mother's name was 'Lōkēśvarī' and the *guru* and the father had the same name, with the latter referred to as 'Vādhūlavarada' and designated the *adhipati* of the *ārogyaśāla* at the Raṅganātha temple at Śrīraṅgam. See *Divyasūricaritam*, p. 22.

Convinced about the veracity of this verse colophon, Ramanujam concludes that Varavarādhīśa was Maṇavāḷamāmuṉi, Varada was one of his main disciples (*aśtadiggagaja*), and Garuḍavāhana Paṉḍita was either the latter's son or grandson and thus lived in the last quarter of the fifteenth century or the first quarter of the sixteenth century. Further, Ramanujam also informs us that Varada and Garuḍavāhana Paṉḍita belonged to the powerful Kōyil Kanḍāḍāiaṉṉāṉ family of Śrīvaiṣṇava *brāhmaṇas* whose *gotra*, incidentally, was Vādhūla.[48]

While one agrees with Ramanujam that Garuḍavāhana Paṉḍita was a title bestowed upon those who were in charge of the Dhanvantri shrine (*ārogyaśālā*), the basis on which he considers the verse colophon to be genuine and the prose colophon (discussed in Section I) to be an interpolation is not convincing. According to him, 'The prose colophon must in all probability have been a later introduction by persons who were misled into thinking that the author of the Kāvya was original Garuḍavāhana Paṉḍita of the Kāśyapa Gotra.... It is unusual and not quite in the fitness of things that a Kāvya writer should write the colophon to his work in prose.'[49] However, Ramanujam does not provide us any information about the identity of these 'persons' and the reasons for their introducing the prose colophon.

If the author, Garuḍavāhana Paṉḍita, belonged to the ācāryic lineage of Maṇavāḷamāmuṉi, as Ramanujam claims, then one is puzzled about the absence of any acknowledgement of the *ācārya* by the author. As stated before, during the fifteenth and sixteenth centuries, notional differences within the community along with the textual tradition were gradually getting aligned along the Sanskritic and Tamil orientations. Therefore, according to the conventions of that period, the author, Garuḍavāhana Paṉḍita, should have stated his allegiance to Maṇavāḷamāmuṉi. The lack of recognition of this particular lineage can be taken as evidence in support of the prose colophon that mentions the *kāśyapa gotra* and other family details of the author. If one accepts Ramanujam's premise that the ancestor of Garuḍavāhana Paṉḍita was affiliated to Maṇavāḷamāmuṉi, could it be then that this affiliation in the verse colophon was contrived? Could it be that since the proximity of the author to Rāmānuja already endorsed the status of this text, became the basis of its appropriation by

[48] Ramanujam (1973), *History of Vaisnavism*, pp. 24–5.

[49] Ibid., pp. 23–4.

the Teṉkaḷai tradition? If that is so, the verse colophon that Ramanujam relies upon could be a later introduction by the Teṉkaḷai tradition.

Further, Ramanujam points out that in the edition of the *Divyasūricaritam* he has consulted, *śloka*s 7 in Chapter 17 refers to Garuḍavāhana Paṇḍita 'in third person' and does not indicate that it is the author himself.[50] However, the structure of the narratives in Chapter 17 shows that these two *śloka*s are a part of the documentation of Rāmānuja's introduction of reforms in the Raṅganāthasvāmī temple at Śrīraṅgam, which included the institution of 'ten services', for the *brāhmaṇa*s and *śūdra*s, respectively.[51] Therefore, the reference to Garuḍavāhana Paṇḍita as the individual author of the text in these *śloka*s would be irrelevant and incongruent with the tenor of the narratives.

With regard to the evidence from the textual tradition, Ramanujam points out that while the *Āṟāyirappaṭi* does not mention Rāmānuja instituting the services of Garuḍavāhana Paṇḍita, the *Kōil Oḻugu* (Chronicle of the Śrīraṅgam temple) and the *Rāmānujārya Divyacaritam* by Piḷḷailokam Jīyar (sixteenth century) refer to it, but do not mention that Garuḍavāhana Paṇḍita was the author of the *Divyasūricaritam*.[52] This may be true, but do any of these texts acknowledge each other? The inter-textual references within the hagiographical tradition are only evident when a prior hagiography is acknowledged or a dissent is registered from the previous tradition as in the case of the *Muāyirappaṭi* cited above. In fact, the *Muāyirappaṭi* written in the fourteenth century mentions the *Divyasūricaritam* as one of the authoritative hagiographies, which indicates that by this time the *Divyasūricaritam* was written and already circulating amongst the Śrīvaiṣṇava audience.

Further, Ramanujam points out that just because the author of the *Divyasūricaritam* concludes the text without mentioning the demise of Rāmānuja, this cannot be taken as sufficient evidence for author's contemporariness with Rāmānuja. According to him, the accounts of the Āḻvārs also conclude in a similar manner; and such a treatment was in congruence with the tradition of immortalizing the *divyasūri*s, thus expressing reverence for them.[53] It seems that Ramanujam has applied

50 Ibid., p.19. In the edition consulted in this monograph, the *śloka*s are 86 and 87 in Chapter 17.

51 *Divyasūricaritam*, Ch. 17, *śloka*s 84 and 85.

52 Ramanujam (1973), *History of Vaisnavism*, pp. 14–19.

53 Ibid., pp. 14–15.

his personal worldview of deference to these texts. Both the *Āṟāyirappaṭi* and *Muāyirappaṭi* give a detailed account of Rāmānuja preparing for his end, his funeral procession, and the ensuing sadness that descended upon his followers thereafter.[54] The *Āṟāyirappaṭi* provides details about Rāmānuja's funeral procession that enables one to know the composition of the Śrīvaiṣṇava community at that point of time:

> As in the case of Ālavandār, Uḍaiyavar was given the *samskāra* [last rites] according to the *brahmaveda* by Tirukurugai Pirān Piḷḷāṉ. With all instruments playing, he was laid on the *pītha* of the *divyavimāna* with all the paraphernalia. At that time, Villi Jīyar, Yativara Jīyar, 700 *jīyars* chanted various portions of the *Upaniṣads*. Bhaṭṭar, Kanḍāḍaiāṇḍāṉ, Naḍādūrāḻvān and other *mudalis* [disciples] wearing the symbols of a Śrīvaiṣṇava, accompanied the procession. Also there were 9000 Śrīvaiṣṇava *upavitadhārīs* [those who did not have the thread], 12,000 *tatapāvaran* Śrīvaiṣṇavas both in front and back accompanied the body, chanting the *Tiruvāymoḻi* with the *tāla* [tune], sung by 700 *tampirāns* who included Tiruvāymoḻi Araiyar.... Streets were decorated with puffed rice and flowers scattered all over. Married women carried lamps in their hands and went with sugarcane and pots of water. The body was being fanned on both the sides and conches were sounded announcing that Uḍaiyavar had gone to Paramapada. His body was taken all through the streets ... [and] was very privately laid in the interior section of the temple. According to the rules of *yatisamskāra* [last rites of an ascetic], he was laid to rest.[55]

The narratives prior to and during the demise of Rāmānuja became an occasion to introduce the transmission of the tradition and highlight the organization of the community, a theme that will be taken up in Chapter 4. Interestingly, there is no mention of Rāmānuja's demise in *Yatirāja Vaibhavam*, whose author was also supposed to be the contemporary or one of the closest disciples of Rāmānuja. Therefore, the lack of mention of Rāmānuja's demise in the *Divyasūricaritam* clearly supports twelfth or thirteenth century as the date of its composition.

Ramanujam does not take into account the context associated with these texts. A fifteenth or a sixteenth century hagiography, according to the conventions of that period, was bound to acknowledge the school

[54] *Āṟāyirappaṭi*, pp. 303–24; *Muāyirappaṭi*, pp. 130–3.

[55] *Āṟāyirappaṭi*, pp. 321–2. This is an approximate translation.

of thought it identified with and therefore would include history of its *ācāryic* lineage after Rāmānuja. Since the *Divyasūricaritam* neither mentions the demise of Rāmānuja nor the post-Rāmānuja period, would it then not be reasonable to conclude that it was situated in a context when such issues had not assumed significance? Ramanujam is dismissive about the schism and feels that '...with Ramanuja ended a definite epoch in the history of Vaisnavism in South India.... Evidently, the author believed that the schismatic period of post-Ramanuja Vaisnavism was not a fit subject for Kavya delineation'.[56] His bias about the schism is evident in his comment on this period as the most unproductive one in the history of Śrīvaiṣṇavism—clearly a viewpoint that endorses homogeneity and unity as the essence of religion, and diversity and multiplicity as chaotic and divisive.[57] Further, Ramanujam underscores the passages from the *Divyasūricaritam* in the *Āṟāyirappaṭi* as interpolations and on the contrary points out the *Divyasūricaritam* was a Sanskrit translation of the *Āṟāyirappaṭi* as evident in several textual borrowings from the latter by the former.[58] One may ask then, was there not a similar likelihood of interpolations in the *Divyasūricaritam* ? In Ramanujam's opinion, the *Āṟāyirappaṭi* was a 'purely historical' work and the *Divyasūricaritam* was a 'non-historical' work.[59] Ascribing an earlier period to *Āṟāyirappaṭi*, Ramanujam's estimation that this was the first *guruparamparā* and the *Divyasūricaritam* was based on it appears problematic, in the light of the sectarian character of *Āṟāyirappaṭi* in affiliating with a specific lineage that became the basis of the Teṉkaḷai identity. Besides, the thematic treatment in *Āṟāyirappaṭi* is detailed and varied compared to the themes in the *Divyasūricaritam* and *Yatirāja Vaibhavam*. Narratives on caste, reforms, and the community organization—especially into 74 *simhāsanapatis* or seats of discipleship—are treated in an elaborate fashion in the *Āṟāyirappaṭi* and *Muāyirappaṭi*. One tends to agree with Friedhelm Hardy, in whose opinion:

56 Ramanujam (1973), *The History of Vaisnavism*, p. 17.

57 Ibid., pp. 25–31. Ramanujam also provides a detailed interpretation of an unpublished manuscript to prove that Garuḍavāhana Paṇḍita belonged to a later period.

58 Ibid., pp. 31–44.

59 Ibid., p. 13.

> The first major work dealing with the 'lives' of the Āḻvārs is a *mahakāvya*, the *Divyasūricaritam* by Garuḍavāhana (12th century).... Later works which deal with the 'life-stories' of the Āḻvārs like the Teṉkaḷai (6000–) *Guruparamparāprabhāvam*, the *Periyatirumuṭiyaṭaivu*, the Vaṭakaḷai (12,000, 3000–) *Guruparamparāprabhāvam*, the very late Teṉkaḷai *Prapannāmrtam* (17th century) and small didactic poems like Vēṅkaṭanātha's *Prabandhasāram* and Maṇavāḷa Māmuṉi's *Upadeśaratnamālai* are not only based consecutively on each other but ultimately seem to derive information from the *Divyasūricaritam*.[60]

Thus, even if one finds the twelfth century to be too early for the composition of the *Divyasūricaritam*, the thirteenth century in all likelihood can be assumed as the time period of this hagiography. Whether the *Divyasūricaritam* was based upon the *Āṟāyirappaṭi* or vice versa is an issue that will require a longer discussion. However, instead of focusing too much on the vertical line of succession amongst the texts, it is important to realize that the readings of the hagiographies show that the inter-textuality involved not merely acknowledging each other, but also having common themes, a certain literary style, and sharing common concerns, of course with individual variations. As Assmann points out, such a textual and thematic dimension was related to the notion of 'discourse', which meant a 'concatenation of texts which are based on each other, and treat or negotiate a common subject matter'.[61] Hence, there was a 'textual conversation' between the Śrīvaiṣṇava hagiographies and a corresponding hagiographical discourse 'that created stronger affinity between the texts' and made the notion of authorship secondary.[62]

CONTEXT: IDEAS AND TRANSMISSION

This section discusses the religious context in which the Śrīvaiṣṇava textual tradition evolved and was codified into a canon from the tenth to the fifteenth century. Beginning from the oral transmission and

[60] Hardy (1983), *Viraha-Bhakti: The Early History of Kṛṣṇa Devotion in South India*, p. 243.

[61] Assmann (1997), *Moses the Egyptian*, p. 15.

[62] Ibid., p. 16.

culminating in the codification of the tradition as written texts, the consolidation of the textual tradition underwent various stages of redaction. While redaction undoubtedly fixed the orality, oral text continued to be in circulation, creating a corresponding mnemonic process that often complemented and not contradicted the written tradition.[63] This exercise was influenced by parallel developments in exegesis, counter traditions, and socio-economic and political changes.

Religious communities from the tenth century onwards developed a distinct consciousness that attempted to absorb the diverse identities related to caste, occupation, and region, and in turn was influenced by them. The significant ruling dynasties such as the Pallavas, Cōḷas, and Pāṉṭiyas (and later on, the Vijayanagar Empire in the fourteenth century) interacted with various religious groups in order to validate their respective power networks through ritual authority.The religious communities in turn attempted to attract patronage from the royalty and the local chieftains in order to expand social influence and control over the temples, their resources, and administration. The individual religious communities evolved a pragmatic integrative paradigm and religious ideologies were articulated in the respective textual traditions by the ideologues of the community, usually the *brāhmaṇas*.[64] While on one hand, exegesis through written interpretations and commentaries became the elitist channel for transmission, on the other hand, rituals, festivals, and regular community singing of hymns in the temples became the main expression of popular faith and understanding of scripture. The systematic development and consolidation of the pilgrimage network further created a sacred geography for the community to interact and identify with, thereby strengthening group consciousness and affiliations. Always important in community life, the temple became even more significant in its role as a node binding diverse social groups in common practices of participatory devotion.

63. Dutta (2004), *Community Identities and Sectarian Affiliations*, pp. 44–5; Dutta (2007), \ 35 (9–10), pp. 22–3; R. Chamapakalakshmi (2012), *Religion, Tradition and Ideology*, pp. 105–6.

64. In the case of the Śaivas and the Vīraśaivas, the ideologues were from the non-brāhmaṇa *Vēḷāḷa* community and other powerful agricultural castes. A comparative analysis of the social attitudes of various religious traditions during this period is beyond the scope of this chapter.

In this context, Śaivism was successful primarily due to its careful presentation of an integrative paradigm that amalgamated Tamil *bhakti*, brāhmaṇical forms, and autochthonous cults. The evolution of the *Śaiva Āgamas* which laid down new forms of worship became the theological basis for converting and assimilating the local cult centres into Śaiva shrines. Sacred geography as delineated by the Nāyanārs became the blueprint for expansion of these sites into temple centres. Since the Nāyanārs in their hymns located maximum Śaiva sites in the Kāvērī region, this area consequently became the focus of religious and political development. Consequently, the local priests were initiated into Śaivism and constituted a new class of temple priests called *Śiva brāhmaṇas* who were ritually assigned a lower rank than *Smārta* (Vaḍama) *brāhmaṇas*. This created a hierarchy within the structure of the *brāhmaṇa varṇa*. With the aniconic *liṅga*, the Śaiva temples became institutions of integration and incorporated diverse cults that represented the religious traditions of various social groups.[65] The creation of a Śaiva pantheon with the incorporation of Murukaṉ and Durgā, representing a divine family, and the assimilative characteristic of the *liṅga* worship had wide appeal and broadened the social basis of Śaivism. It was adopted as the royal cult by the Cōḷa dynasty from the mid-tenth to the twelfth century, under Rājarāja I (c. 985–045 CE), Rājendra I, and Kulōttunga II (*c.* 1133–50 CE), which further enabled the consolidation of the Śaiva community. The compilation of Śaiva hymns and the composition of hagiographies were integral to the royal project, and contributed significantly to the evolution of the Śaiva scripture, *Tirumaṟai*. Its compiler, Nambi Āṇḍar Nambi, and Cēkkiḻar, composer of the Śaiva hagiography, *Periya Purāṇam*, were associated with the courts of Rājarāja I and Kulōttunga II respectively.[66] The royal patronage to Śaiva temples expanded the domain of liturgy and, consequently, the hymns of the four Nāyanārs, Appar, Cuntarar, Campantar, and Māṇikkavāccakar, were introduced in the temples as a part of the ritual singing. The apotheosis of these four

[65] See R. Champakalakshmi (1996a), 'From Devotion and Dissent to Dominance: The *Bhakti* of the Tamil Āḻvārs and Nāyanārs', in Champakalakshmi and Gopal (eds), *Tradition, Dissent and Ideology: Essays in Honour of Romila Thapar*, pp. 145–7; also see Peterson (1991), *Poems to Śiva: The Hymns of the Tamil Saints*, pp. 3–95.

[66] Champakalakshmi (1996b), 'From Devotion and Dissent to Dominance: The *Bhakti* of the Tamil Āḻvārs and Nāyanārs', p. 161.

Nāyanārs took place in the temples around the tenth century under the royal initiatives, mainly of Rājarāja I and Kulōttunga II.[67]

Another major philosophical system that evolved around the ninth century, influencing and reorienting the medieval Śaiva and Vaiṣṇava community exegesis, was Advaita or non-dualism, formulated by Śaṅkarācārya. Based on Vedānta/Upaniṣadic ideas, this system represented a consistent, intellectual, brāhmaṇical response to heterodox religious traditions.[68] In contrast to the popular aspect of Śiva and Viṣṇu as reflected in the hymns of the Nāyanārs and Āḻvārs, Śaṅkara's philosophy of Advaita representing *nirguṇa* Brahman (the concept of the divine as formless/without attributes) clearly addressed the intellectuals.[69]

The heavy royal patronage of Śaivism overshadowed the regional progress and presence of Vaiṣṇavism. Compared to the Śaiva temples, the construction of the Vaiṣṇava temples was on a minor scale. Other than the ninth-century Āḻvār, Tirumaṅgai, none of the Āḻvārs were apotheosized in the Cōḷa temples. Unlike the Śaivas, the Vaiṣṇavas were not a well-developed and organized community with a comprehensive textual and scriptural tradition. Vaiṣṇava attempts made in this direction in the late ninth and early tenth centuries resulted in the composition of the *Bhāgavata Purāna*, a work in which the exposition of Āḻvār *bhakti* was undertaken in Sanskrit for the first time. This 'Sanskritization of the Kṛṣṇa tradition' adopted the popular style of the *Purāṇa* narratives which drew heavily upon regional myths and fused the brāhmaṇical traditions with the folk cults.[70] However, the heavily classicized text coupled with its advaitic position—an effort to reconcile the *bhakti* mode with brāhmaṇical conventions—failed to make an impact on either the local population, the Śrīvaiṣṇava philosophical system itself, or the Cōḷa patrons.

Nevertheless, until the middle of the tenth century both Vaiṣṇavism and Śaivism received royal patronage under Parāntaka I (AD 907–55). Viṣṇu temples such as the Raṅganāthasvāmī temple at Śrīraṅgam were structurally elaborated upon, and donations for the celebration of one

67 Ibid., p. 147.

68 Pande (1998 [1994]), *Life and Thought of Śaṅkarācārya.*

69 Champakalakshmi (1996b), 'From Devotion and Dissent to Dominance: The *Bhakti* of the Tamil Āḻvārs and Nāyanārs', pp. 153–4.

70 Hardy (1983), *Viraha-Bhakti*, pp. 483–552; Champakalakshmi (1996b), 'From Devotion and Dissent to Dominance: The *Bhakti* of the Tamil Āḻvārs and Nāyanārs', pp. 140–1.

of the important Śrīvaiṣṇava festival, the *Paṅguṇi Uttiram*, were made.[71] State support was further evident from the presence of various local Kṛṣṇa and Rāma temples, a good example of the latter being the famous Rāma temple in Madurāntakacaturvedīmaṅgalam that was established during the reign of Parāntaka I.[72] As we shall see in the next chapter, this particular *brahmadeya* was strategically located on the route between Kāñcīpuram and Śrīraṅgam, and the *guruparamparās* link these two sites with important events in Rāmānuja's life. During this phase a conscious attempt was made to introduce ritual singing in the temples, and the 1,000-verse *Tiruvāymoḻi* of Nammāḻvār, a work steeped in mysticism and *bhakti*, was collected and put to music. In all probability a lack of resources prevented the Vaiṣṇavas from similarly augmenting the entire hymnal corpus. Hence, a comprehensive and systematic channel for the popular dissemination of Vaiṣṇava ideas of *bhakti* did not develop in the same manner as that of the Śaivas. Poor networks of interaction and a weak institutional structure precluded the development of a community with a strong and cohesive identity, ideology, and location, ensuring that the 'Śrīvaiṣṇavas' remained a discrete, scattered group in south India. Although temple inscriptions do explicitly refer to 'Śrīvaiṣṇavas', this was an honorary prefix of Vaiṣṇava *brāhmaṇas* and did not imply a community.

The significance of these Vaiṣṇava hymns was primarily due to the ideas and symbols that they expressed, which later formed the basis for Śrīvaiṣṇava theology and exegesis. The hymns in general and those of Nammāḻvār in particular were characterized by their stress on the concept of *prapatti* (emancipation through unconditional surrender to God). The hymns reiterated that *prapatti* could be attained by anyone, irrespective of the caste status of the individual devotee. These compositions were not only a protest against the exclusive and discriminatory nature of the *brāhmaṇa* socio-religious sphere, but also suggested an alternative that enabled the community of the Vaiṣṇava *bhaktas*, unified through practices of ritual worship, to transcend caste and its oppressive affiliations. The hymns underscored community bonds by emphasizing the merit of collective recitation in the temples. This is best exemplified in Nammāḻvār's *Tiruvāymoḻi*.

[71] Archaeological Survey of India, *South Indian Inscriptions*, Vol. XXIV, No. 7.

[72] Professor Champakalakshmi shared this information with me in the course of discussions on the Cōḷa patronage of Śrīvaiṣṇavism.

The Vaiṣṇava community consciousness was further highlighted and consolidated through the notion of pilgrimage. Through descriptions of the sites considered sacred by local cults, the hymns charted out a sacred geography for the community. This marked the beginning of the concept of pilgrimage, where each site was visited and sung into prominence. In his hymn *Periya Tirumaṭal*, the Āḻvār saint Tirumaṅgai mapped more than 90 such places. Further, the hymns downplayed the traditional status of Sanskrit, historically the language of religious expression, and instead emphasized the sacredness of Tamil, the language of the ordinary Vaiṣṇava devotee. The hymns also enhanced Tamil by claiming that it encapsulated the essence of the otherwise inaccessible liturgical schema of the *Vedas*. Thus, through Vaiṣṇava efforts a prominent regional language was exalted in its own right, as well as equated with Sanskrit, the language of scriptures. It should be noted that the ideas of a sacred geography, community singing, and Tamil as a sacred language were also articulated in the Saiva hymns composed around the same time.

All the ideas expressed in the hymns relate to the background of the Āḻvārs, who were mostly from marginalized castes. For instance, Nammāḻvār was a Vēḷāḷa, Tirumaṅgai was a non-*brāhmaṇa kalva* chief, and Āṇṭāḷ was a woman. Even some *brāhmaṇa* Āḻvārs, like Periyāḻvār, were from groups lower in the brāhmaṇical hierarchy. The transformation of local cult centres into Vaiṣṇava sacred sites was accompanied by the acculturation and assimilation of the cultic priests, who derived their status from the Āgamic forms of worship considered inferior to the Vedic forms; hence, a low ritual rank was assigned to them within the *brāhmaṇa varṇa*.[73] The *Caturvedin*s (Vedic *brāhmaṇa*s), the Smārtas and Vaḍamas (those who performed Vedic sacrifices)

[73] The discourse against caste and a catholic attitude of a community that included devotees from diverse background has led many scholars to conclude that the *bhakti* of the Āḻvārs was a radical protest against the conservative social norms. Undoubtedly, the elements of protest did assert themselves, but they should not be over-emphasized. In fact, the religion of the hymnists influenced by the contemporary socio-political environment evolved a conservative attitude that became synonymous with the dominant ideology of the subsequent period (the ninth to the twelfth century). See Champakalakshmi (1996b), 'From Devotion and Dissent to Dominance: The *Bhakti* of the Tamil Āḻvārs and Nāyanārs', pp. 135–63.

were superior to the temple priests, the social category to which the *brāhmaṇa* hymnists like Periyāḻvār, Toṇṭaraṭippoṭi, and Madhurakavi belonged. These complex socio-religious issues of caste, salvation, and pilgrimage would inevitably feature as a sub-textual assertion in the hagiographical narratives.

The tenth century witnessed an attempt to provide a theological–ritualistic justification for elaborating upon temple worship, intended to attract greater numbers of devotees and thus create a Śrīvaiṣṇava collective. Such a rationalization was provided in the works of Yāmuna, the *ācārya* immediately preceding Rāmānuja. Yāmuna's *Āgamapramāṇya*, written in Sanskrit, advocated a major ideological shift from an exclusive, metaphysical approach as represented in the *Vaikhānsa Āgama* to a more popular, ritualistic, and incorporative approach as represented in the *Pāñcarātra Āgama*. However, this shift which asserted the validity of the *Pāñcarātra* was a notional one initially and later became the ideological basis for the textual elaboration of liturgical practices in the post-Rāmānuja period, when the concept of community took on a wider resonance. Yāmuna's *Stotraratna*, which articulated the intellectual aspects of *bhakti-yoga*, also was an important text that was commented upon during this period.

By the eleventh and twelfth centuries, the Śrīvaiṣṇavas began to reorient their community base and structure more directly against the thrust of social and political changes. The Śrīvaiṣṇava efforts to create a definite sphere for community participation by introducing ritual singing and elaborate forms of worship strengthened their institutional networks, especially in the Raṅganāthasvāmī temples at Śrīraṅgam and Uttaramērūr during the reign of Rājendra I (c. 1012–44 CE).[74] Two inscriptions from Uttaramērūr of this period document the distribution of the food offered to the deity among the Śrīvaiṣṇavas reciting the *Tiruppādiyam* (a hymn) during worship, and also note the creation of an endowment of land for the maintenance of the three individuals assigned to regularly recite the *Tiruvāymoḻi* in the temple. Similarly, inscriptions dated to c.1085 CE make references to the recitation of the *Tiruvāymoḻi* of Nammāḻvār, the *Tirupaḷḷi-yeḻucci* of Toṇṭaraṭippoṭi

[74] Venkatachari (1978) *The Maṇipravāḷa Literature of the Śrīvaiṣṇava Ācāryas*. Venkatachari cites from, Sastri (1923), *The Colas*, Vol. II, pp. 479–80. These inscriptions are reported in the *Annual Reports on Indian Epigraphy* (1892) Nos 61 and 62; Sastri (1923), No. 176.

and donations made for the feeding of the Śrīvaiṣṇavas.[75] An inscription dated c.1088 CE notes that the hymns of Kulaśekhara Āḻvār were recited for three nights before the deity during the course of a festival in the Raṅganāthasvāmī temple at Śrīraṅgam.[76] Interestingly, the term 'Āḻvār' to define the twelve early Vaiṣṇava religious leaders began to be used only from the eleventh century onwards.

No inscriptions refer to Rāmānuja, though he lived in this era. Nevertheless, he had emerged as a significant philosopher and made a crucial intellectual contribution to the larger Vedantic discourse. This contribution, comprising his commentaries on the Vedas, *Brahmasūtra*, *Upaniṣads*, and *Bhagavadgītā* would subsequently acquire a central place in the Śrīvaiṣṇava textual tradition. The practice of interpreting canonical Sanskrit texts was a part of the larger Vedāntic tradition to which both the Advaita of Śaṅkarācārya and Viśiṣṭādvaita of Rāmānuja belonged. The latter's commentaries, introducing seminal ideas, emerged as an important philosophy during the eleventh–twelfth centuries in the Tamil region and infused the ancient texts with fresh meaning, enhancing their relevance.[77] As mentioned before, in his *Gītābhāṣya*, Rāmānuja acknowledged Yāmuna's works. This is a further corroboration of the practice of Sanskrit commentaries on the *Prasthāna Treyī* [*Upaniṣads*, *Brahmasūtra*, and *Bhagavadgītā*] transmitted through a lineage of *ācārya*s who acknowledged each other and presumably would have borrowed also from each other's works. Yāmuna acknowledged the preceptor Nāthamuni whose own works have not survived. He also recognized Nammāḻvār and, by extension, the *Tiruvāymoḻi*. Through these textual traces one can see the origin and trajectory of the concept of a *sampradāya* or a tradition as one thought, one movement, and, most significantly, one organization. The development of a *sampradāya*, however nascent at that time, marked the transition between the Vaiṣṇavism of the pre-Rāmānuja phase on the one hand and the Rāmānuja and post-Rāmānuja phase on the other. The functioning of the *sampradāya* generated two important genres of

[75] Archaeological Survey of India, *South Indian Inscriptions*, Vol. XXIV, Nos, 57, 58, 60.

[76] Ibid., Vol. XXIV, No. 63.

[77] Stietencron (2001), 'Charisma and Canon: The Dynamics of Legtimization and Innovation in Indian Religion', in Dalmia, Vasudha et al. (eds), pp. 14–38.

religious literature: the *bhāṣyas* (commentaries) and the *guruparamparās* (hagiographies), both lynchpins of the Śrīvaiṣṇava textual tradition.

From the thirteenth century onwards, the economic, social, and ritual activities around the temples increased. The paraphernalia around the deity became more complex and the numerous endowments received meant that an account and a record had to be maintained. This resulted in various groups competing with each other over the control and management of the endowments. In this context, the Śrīvaiṣṇavas whose *rakṣai* or protection is invoked emerged significantly as an organized group and this is epigraphically evident from their overarching control in the temple organizations.[78] Several Śrīvaiṣṇavas became the *Śrikāryam* (temple officials), replacing the *sabhās* (*brāhmaṇa* assemblies).[79] The temples now had shrines dedicated to the Āḻvārs. The temple of Āṇṭāḷ at Śrīvilliputtūr (Tirunelveli district) acquired local importance and she was considered the patron goddess of that region. For these reasons, this temple was patronized by the Pāṇṭiyas, the ruling dynasty of that area.[80]

Expansion of the temple rituals and office of the temple functionaries created a space for non-brāhmaṇical classes. This was significant and a special mention must be made of the *kaikkoḷas* (a powerful weaver community), whose presence in the temples was institutionalized through allotment of numerous duties to them and their participation in the rituals, donations, and administration increased.[81] *Kaikkoḷa Mudalis* were important temple officials. Epigraphic evidence emphasizes the

[78] Champakalakshmi (2012), p. 237.

[79] Archaeological Survey of India, *South Indian Inscriptions*, Vol. XXIV. See Pāṇṭiya, Hoysala, and Vijayanagara inscriptions for references to the participation and association of the Śrīvaiṣṇavas with the Raṅganāthasvāmī temple at Śrīraṅgam.

[80] Ludden (1989), *Peasant History in South India*, pp. 31–2.

[81] The inscriptions of the Raṅganāthasvāmī temple at Śrīraṅgam and Venkaṭeśvarasvāmī temple at Tirupati refer several times to the *kaikkoḷas* and their administrative duties. *Kōil Oḻugu*, the chronicle of the temple at Śrīraṅgam, also devotes considerable attention to the *kaikkoḷas* and Rāmānuja's role in assimilating them into temple services. See Archaeological Survey of India, *South Indian Inscriptions*, Vol. XXIV; and Tirumalai-Tirupati Devasthanam Epigraphical Series, Vols I–VI, 1933–34, S. Subrahmanya Sastri (trans./ed.) and 1935–38 Viraraghavacharya (trans./ed.). Also see *The Kōil Oḻugu: The Chronicle of the Śrīraṅgam Temple with Historical Notes* (1961), Rao (trans./ed.).

claims of the *kaikkoḷa*s for a higher ritual status. The Śrīvaiṣṇava hagiographic tradition credits Rāmānuja with the introduction of the non-brāhmaṇical classes into the temple's institutional sphere, but there is no epigraphic evidence to support this reformist claim. Nevertheless, the changing context and the simultaneous evolution of a vibrant intellectual discourse formed the basis for future development of the Śrīvaiṣṇava community. It has been pointed out that, 'under the leadership of early *ācārya*s, and in response to the presence of powerful non-brāhmaṇa local interests, *brāhmaṇa* authorities may have succeeded in realizing in practice, the ideal of inclusivism by allowing and enhancing the participation of "*śūdra*s" in administration and ritual life of the temple'.[82]

Therefore, the ethos of medieval *bhakti* was no longer characterized by devotional spontaneity as was in the case of the Āḻvārs. Sense of *bhakti* meant a studied systematization of the community structure that involved consolidating the hymnal past into a fixed scripture, bringing in the intellectual ideas in circulation, and creating a structure of a community with a broad social base, comprising a cross section of devotees. The institutional context for this *bhakti* was the temple and the *maṭha*s. In addition, *bhakti* involved the veneration of the Āḻvārs and the *ācārya*s who were now canonized into a cult of saints, the textual context of which were the hagiographies. The growing religious consciousness further consolidated the textual tradition and the institutions of the temples and the *maṭha*s. The *maṭha*s with their distinctive monastic lineages especially in the Vijayanagar and post-Vijayanagar period emerged as the centre of intellectual activities, redaction, and propagation of the textual tradition, including the hagiographies. The composition of the *Muāyirappaṭi* in the Parkāla *maṭha* was a result of these developments. Thus, the *maṭha*s emerged as the custodians of the Śrīvaiṣṇava tradition due to their important contribution in the organization of the canon, its preservation, and its transmission, associating it with the wider ethos of the community.

Similar developments can be seen in Śaivism, Vīra Śaivism, and Advaitism. In the Advaita philosophy, popular devotion and its modes of worship in temples were marginalized, and the establishing of Smārta *maṭha*s and the foregrounding of Sanskrit scriptures became essential for the dissemination of Advaita as a belief system as well as for its

[82] Chamapakalakshmi (2012), *Religion, Tradition and Ideology*, p. 239.

institutional developments. In contrast, the Śaiva *maṭhas* became the centre of the formation of the Śaiva Siddhānta philosophy with a large *vēḷāḷa* non-*brāhmaṇa* support that gradually overtook the leadership of the *maṭhas*. Thus the *maṭhas* became the institutional focus of these religious traditions and their respective community identities.[83]

THE TEXTUAL TRADITION AND THE ŚRĪVAIṢṆAVA COMMUNITY

By the end of twelfth century, three independent traditions circulated amongst the Śrīvaiṣṇavas: the Tamil tradition, comprising the hymns of the Āḻvārs; the liturgical tradition of the *Pañcarātra Āgama* that provided an ideological basis for the image worship and institutional framework of the temple; and the Sanskritic tradition of the Vedānta and Rāmānuja's commentaries on its canonical texts. These received traditions were collected, compiled, edited, and reworked upon with a careful selection of those ideas and beliefs that would reinforce community orientation and enable a cohesive sense of identity. These existent ideas, including *bhakti, prapatti*, temple worship, pilgrimage, and community affiliation, now became the fundamentals of exegesis in the Śrīvaiṣṇava textual canon. This canon was constituted by the hymns of the Āḻvārs codified into a corpus, the *Nālāyira Divya Prabandham*; the theology and philosophy transmitted through the mechanism of *sampradāya*; the commentaries or the *vyākhyāna*s or the *bhāṣya*s; the hagiographies or the *guruparamparā*s; and the liturgy or the *Āgamas*. The *sthalapurāṇa*s, a genre of pilgrimage texts that evolved after the fifteenth century, are a part of the textual tradition, but are not necessarily considered canonical.

This systematization of the textual tradition, which reflected a community consciousness and sense of belonging, acquired the status and authority of scripture and was finally encoded as a canon within Śrīvaiṣṇava religious culture. Further, its canonical status provided 'meaning and direction to the community as a whole and to each individual member by representing both the ultimate truth and means of attaining it'.[84] Implicit in this understanding of the canon was fixity and permanence, that is, nothing to be added or taken away.[85]

[83] Ibid., pp. 112–14; pp. 286–318.

[84] Stietencron (2001), 'Charisma and Canon', p. 14.

[85] Ibid., p. 15.

Despite a clearly fixed form, the contents of the canon could be interpreted and reinterpreted in the Śrīvaiṣṇava commentaries that were also a part of this tradition. In building up and establishing a tradition, the major concern of the ideologues of the community was the redaction of the texts into a cohesive stable structure. This redaction was indispensable for successful articulation and transmission of the Śrīvaiṣṇava philosophy and also aimed, as remarked by Eric Hobsbawm, to 'structure at least some parts of social life … as unchanging and invariant within the changing context'.[86]

The commentaries and the *guruparamparā*s had a specific function as an integral part of the Śrīvaiṣṇava canon.[87] The vast body of commentarial literature which concentrated on interpreting and commenting on the preexisting texts, especially the hymns of the Āḻvārs, itself became the subject of further commentaries and interpretations. Written on the principles of Viśiṣṭādvaita, these commentaries mainly focused on Nammāḻvār's *Tiruvāymoḻi* as a theological subject and this came to be known as the *Bhagavadviṣaya paramparā* in the commentarial tradition.[88] Śrīvaiṣṇava *vyākhyāna*s fixed the vast *Prabandham* corpus into a canon by including the occasional variants current at that time, thus resolving all the narrative ambiguities associated with oral transmission.

At every stage there was continuous scope for additions and elaborations. For instance, the *ācārya*s of the thirteenth and the fourteenth centuries—Vedāntadeśika on the one hand and Piḷḷai Lokācārya followed by Maṇavāḷamāmuṉi on the other—were copious producers of philosophical as well as commentarial exegesis, formulating important theological concepts over which numerous debates took place.[89] The ultimate significance of the commentarial tradition lies in the dynamics of these polemical debates which became an essential part of spiritual exegesis and the focus of the community. Even the ideas of Rāmānuja

86 Hobsbawm (1983), 'Introduction: Inventing Traditions', in Hobsbawm and Ranger (eds), *The Invention of Tradition*, p. 2.

87 For details on the Śrīvaiṣṇava textual tradition, see Dutta (2007), pp. 22–42.

88 Hardy (1983), 'Mādhvêndra Puri: A Link between Bengal Vaiṣṇavism and South Indian Bhakti', *Journal of Royal Asiatic Society*, pp. 245–8.

89 For details on the split of the Śrīvaiṣṇava community into the Vaṭakaḷai and Teṉkaḷai, see Mumme (1988), *The Theology of Maṇavāḷamāmuṉi: Toward an Understanding of the Teṉkalai-Vaṭakalai Dispute in the Post-Rāmānuja Śrī Vaiṣṇavism.*

and his works could be interrogated via scholarly debates. The commentaries were also intended to clarify certain key concepts relating to *prapatti, bhakti,* the role of Śrī as mediatrix, and so on.[90]

In the process of explication of textual ambiguities, conflicting arguments emerged, creating their own discord, between proponents and opponents within the community. It has been asserted that 'most of the commentaries are no longer familiar with the conventions of the Cankam poetry, a deficiency which has given rise to great many pseudo problems and which ultimately is responsible for the abstruse allegorical interpretations which became fashionable from the thirteenth century onward'.[91] It is these 'allegorical interpretations' that generated debates and the notional differences that crystallized into schools of thought that were the precursors of the formal schism with two distinct groups of adherents, the Vaṭakaḷais and the Teṉkaḷais. Similarly, the *guruparamparās* also exhibited the process of canon formation. These multi-layered and multi-textured hagiographical narratives infused Śrīvaiṣṇava tradition with a sense of history and cultural continuity, bequeathing ancient ideas and beliefs and conventions which gave legitimacy and credibility to the community and its religious practice. The commentarial tradition, especially the *Bhagavadviṣaya paramparā,* is recorded in the hagiographies in the life story of Rāmānuja, in which he is depicted as commissioning the writing of a commentary on the *Tiruvāymoḻi* to one of his close disciples who was also his cousin, Tirukkurkai Pirāṉ Piḷḷāṉ (twelfth century). This was the first commentary written in Maṇipravāḷa and known as the *Āṟāyirappaṭi* :

> On a certain occasion, seeing *Yatiśa* (Rāmānuja) contemplating the drift of a certain *Prabandha,* that son of Pūrṇa (Piḷḷāṉ) stated what *Yatiśa* was contemplating upon.
>
> Struck with wonder at the young man giving out what he himself arrived at on contemplation, believing that the young man knew it because of his descent from Nāthamuni, *Yatiśa* embraced him as his son in intellectual descent.

[90] See Carman (1981), *The Theology of Rāmānuja: An Essay in Interreligious Understanding*; Lipner (1986), *The Face of Truth: A Study of Meaning and Metaphysics in the Vedāntic Theology of Rāmānuja.*

[91] Hardy (1983), 'Mādhvêndra Puri: A Link between Bengal Vaiṣṇavism and South Indian Bhakti', *Journal of Royal Asiatic Society*, p. 244.

> Kurukeśavārya (Piḷḷāṉ) having become known both as the son of Rāmānuja *Yatiśa* and his sandal (pāḍuka), made the commentary on the last work of Śatārī (Nammāḻvār's *Tiruvāymoḻi*)
>
> Giving Piḷḷāṉ the name of Kurukeśvara, accepting the 6000 commentary of his, the establisher of the *bhāṣya* (Rāmānuja) fulfilled the third wish of Yāmunārya[92]

Interestingly, this commentary and subsequent ones were based on the doctrinal premises of Viśiṣṭādvaita and not on Āḻvār devotion, which imposed 'on the poems conceptual categories alien to their original spirit'.[93] However, some scholars hold that Piḷḷāṉ understood 'many of Nammāḻvār's verses in the light of Rāmānuja's theology, but conversely, Piḷḷāṉ's understandings of Rāmānuja's philosophy of the Vedānta' were 'affected by the sentiments in the Tamil hymns'.[94] The significance of this particular commentary lay in its bringing together Tamil and Sanskrit Vaiṣṇava theology and discussing issues that were neither present in Nammāḻvār's hymns or Rāmānuja's exegesis.[95] On the other hand, the *guruparamparās* devised their own strategies of reflecting upon the *Nālāyira Divya Prabandham* and the process of its canonization. The narrative project of incorporating the process of compilation and redaction of the *Prabandhams* within the hagiographical structure was closely linked to the history of the community as articulated by these hagiographies. This is discussed in the final section of this chapter.

Associated with the redaction of the *Prabandhams* was the composition of the *Rāmānuja Nūṟṟandādi*, a *stotra* (praise poem) of 108 verses dedicated to Rāmānuja composed around the twelfth or the thirteenth century and added to the corpus of the *Prabandham*, whose systematization and standardization of the number of hymns to be incorporated were gradually getting fixed.[96] Like other hymns sung collectively in

[92] Krishnaswami Aiyangar, *The Yatirājavaibhavam of Āndhrapūrṇa (Life of Rāmānuja)*, *ślokas* 81–4.

[93] Hardy (1983), 'Mādhvĕndra Puri: A Link between Bengal Vaiṣṇavism and South Indian Bhakti', *Journal of Royal Asiatic Society*, p. 245; Hardy (2001), 'The Formation of Śrīvaiṣṇavism', in Dalmia et al (eds), pp. 41–61.

[94] Carman and Narayanan (1989), *The Tamil Veda: Pillan's Interpretation of the Tiruvyamoli*, p. xi.

[95] Ibid., p. xiii.

[96] Hardy (1983), 'Mādhvêndra Puri: A Link between Bengal Vaiṣṇavism and South Indian Bhakti', *Journal of Royal Asiatic Society*, p. 250; Ramanujam (1973), *History of Vaishnavism in South India up to Ramanuja*, pp. 9–10. According to

temples as part of regular ritual worship, *Rāmānuja Nūṟṟandādi* was also meant to be sung or recited, thus reminding the devotee that along with Āḻvārs, Rāmānuja was also a part of a *paramparā* (community lineage), and was in philosophical continuity with the Āḻvārs. In actual fact, there was a gap of almost 200 years between the last Āḻvār (tenth century) and Rāmānuja (eleventh century).

Such accepted and textually reinforced continuity had important ramifications for community consciousness, as Rāmānuja was presented as both embodiment and vehicle of the hymnal ideas, which in actual fact did not have any direct influence on his writings. Integrating the *Rāmānuja Nūṟṟandādi* with the *Nālāyira Divya Prabandham* was also a clear attempt to link the Āḻvār mode of *bhakti* with the Viśiṣṭadvāita *bhakti* of Rāmānuja and unify the ideological and social groupings affiliated with each.

The co-existence and complex overlap of the Tamil and Sanskrit textual traditions had profound social and philosophical effects. Commentators and hagiographers either wrote only in one or other language or in a highly Sanskritized Tamil; and both *vyākhyānas* and *guruparamparās* were influenced by Āḻvār ideas as well as Rāmānuja's metaphysical theories. The *Rāmānuja Nūṟṟandādi*, composed and written in Tamil, was influenced by Rāmānuja's commentaries and his exegesis of Viśiṣṭādvaita. This *stotra* repeatedly emphasized that the correct interpretation of the Vedas was to be associated exclusively with Rāmānuja:

> When the faultless Veda became faulted and the whole world was ruled by Kali alone, there came the benevolent *muni* Rāmānuja[97] ... by the knowledge imparted by Rāmānuja, the contradictions of the Upanishads have been resolved, the lives of the polemics have ended, the Vedic seers have become elevated, the world has received much good, the twin *Karmas* of faulty lives have been destroyed.[98]

In the textual tradition this *stotra* has acquired a canonical status of a *prappana gāyatrī* (even if he cannot recite the *Prabandham*, a Śrīvaiṣṇava

---

him, 'While Vedānta Deśika would reckon the 4,000 including the *Rāmānuja Nūṟṟandādi* within the collection, Teṅkalai school not withstanding their high regard for the work, would reckon the 4,000 excluding it from the collection.'

97 *Rāmānuja Nūṟṟandādi* ('Ode to Rāmānuja of Tiruvaraṅgattamudanār'), trans. from Tamil by Srirama Bharati (2000), p. 743, verse 16.

98 Ibid., p. 752, verse 65.

is required to recite the *Rāmānuja Nūṟṟandādi* daily).[99] In fact, the importance of Rāmānuja as the most important *ācārya* of the community was completely established with several *stotras* dedicated to him, including *Yatirāja Saptati* and *Yatirāja Vimśati* by Vedāntadeśika and Maṇavāḷamāmuṉi respectively in Sanskrit, the language of most of the *stotras*.

The ideological framework of Śrīvaiṣṇava canon formation was the *Ubhaya Vedānta*, or the dual Vedānta (Sanskrit and Tamil). In general, the hymns of the Āḻvārs were considered as the Tamil Vedas and Nammāḻvār's *Tiruvāymoḻi* is especially referred to as the Tamil or 'Draviḍa' Veda. According to the Śrīvaiṣṇava tradition, these hymns and *Tiruvāymoḻi* in particular were not an imitation of the Sanskrit Veda.[100] Rather, they were revealed through the twelve Āḻvārs, of whom Nammāḻvār, as we will later see, is considered to have played a crucial role. The commentaries went to elaborate lengths to identify theological and structural similarities between the two Vedas, and the hagiographies provided the 'historical context' for this purpose.[101] The significance of the *Ubhaya Vedānta* was in its fundamental emphasis on a regional language, in this case Tamil, being equivalent to Sanskrit as a valid and authoritative scriptural language; thus by implication the Tamil *Prabandhams* were at par with the Sanskrit Vedas. However, the philosophy of the *Ubhaya Vedānta* had complex ramifications. The commentaries and hagiographies both register debates and undercurrents in the devotional narratives, arguing over the status of Tamil and Dravida Vedas in relation to Sanskrit and the Sanskrit Veda. The textual tradition sharply reflected the anxieties within the different groups of the Śrīvaiṣṇavas, and these polemics and tensions ultimately became the basis of the community splitting into the Vaṭakaḷai and the Teṉkaḷai.

[99] *Rāmānuja Nūṟṟandādi* is considered analogous to the *gāyatrī mantra*, which is supposed to be chanted by devout Hindus every day. Hence, *Rāmānuja Nūṟṟandādi* is the *gāyatrī mantra* for *prapannas*, that is, those seeking *prapatti* (complete surrender to God).

[100] Carman and Narayanan (1989), *The Tamil Veda*, p. 4.

[101] For an account of Śrīvaiṣṇava commentaries on the Tamil Veda and the avowed parallel of this corpus with the Sanskrit Veda, see Carman and Narayanan (1989), *The Tamil Veda*, pp. 3–12; also see Venkatachari (1978), Manipravala Literature, pp. 40–3.

HAGIOGRAPHIES AS HISTORY: CONSCIOUSNESS, MEMORY, AND TRADITION

The context of transmission of the *Nālāyira Divya Prabandham* from the Āḻvārs to *ācāryas* presented a story of the recovery of a lost tradition. This narrative of recovery implied that the hagiographers travel back to the past, link that past to the then-present context, and finally highlight the elements of continuity and change, thus creating a historical experience for the Śrīvaiṣṇava devotees that would be remembered over generations. Recounting how its hymns were collected and compiled, the *Divyasūricaritam* tells us that the Śrīvaiṣṇava preceptor Nāthamuni undertook a journey to various temples in south India, where the individual Tamil hymns of the Āḻvārs were sung. His intention was to collect by then the widely scattered 4,000 hymns of the Āḻvārs:

> Once, some holy men from Kurukāpurī (Āḻvār Tirunagari in Tirunelvelli district in Tamil Nadu) arrived at Vīranārāyaṇapuram, where Nāthamuni lived and sang 'Ārāvamudu' ten verses of Śrī Parāṅkuśa's (Nammāḻvār) hymn. Nāthamuni heard them and was very happy. He immediately left for Kurukāpurī, (the hometown of Nammāḻvār) with the purpose of listening to the rest. After paying respect to the god in the temple there, he came across a tamarind tree in whose trunk Parāṅkuśa *muni*, who had never slept was residing. Nāthamuni was disappointed as Saṭhagōpa (Nammāḻvār) rapt in yogic meditation did not meet him. Thereafter, in order to meet Saṭhagōpa, Nāthamuni recited twelve thousand times the ten stanzas of the hymns of Madhurakavi (who was the disciple of Nammāḻvār). Finally, Saṭhagōpaswāmī along with Madhurakavi appeared before Nāthamuni and transmitted the *Dvaya mantra* and Nammāḻvār's four works, with their respective meanings. Having received from Śrī Saṭhagōpa the meaning of the four *Vedas* contained in the Dravida *Divya Prabandha*, Nāthamuni meditated there and continued to reside in that place. However, the ever merciful Lord Kṛṣṇa at Vīranārāyaṇapuram appeared in his dream and asked him to come back and meditate upon these *Prabandhams* here. On his arrival at Vīranārāyaṇapuram, Nāthamuni with the help of his disciples set these thousand *Draviḍa* hymns to divine music in the temple at the behest of the god.[102]

[102] *Divyasūricaritam*, Ch. 16, *ślokas* 13–21.

This may be considered as the first attempt at creating a canon, albeit oral, within the hagiographical tradition. Such a recounting attempted to create an environment for community consciousness through a liturgical practice, the collective singing of the hymns in the temple. While providing a physical and a ritual space for the recitation of the hymns, the temple also generated and consolidated a participatory milieu for the oral transmission of spiritual culture, involving reciters as well as listeners, that is, the entire community of devotees, irrespective of their caste status. Further, the biography of Nāthamuni tells us about the construction of the oral tradition:

> The Cōḷa king had trained a lady to sing the Vedas. In order to test her, the king invited another lady singer to compete with her. He also invited several experts in music, including Nāthamuni. Nāthamuni thought to himself that since everybody does not know about the Tamil hymns, this will be a good opportunity to tell everybody about it. Thus, with the purpose of apprising about the hymns, Nāthamuni along with his disciples went to the Cōḷa court. The king requested Nāthamuni to judge the two women. Nāthamuni after listening to them gave his opinion. According to him, one lady's songs could be understood by everybody and another lady's songs could be understood by the god and those like him (meaning the *brāhmaṇas*). Then he explained the difference between the two through complex musical exercise that was accompanied by different kinds of tunes, rhythms and intonations. The king was happy and rewarded Nāthamuni. Thereafter, Nāthamuni taught the Draviḍa Veda with music and his text, the *Nyāyatattva*, to his disciples.[103]

Presumably the lady whose song was comprehensible to everybody was singing in Tamil, and Nāthamuni's explanations to everybody with musical notes were probably the Tamil hymns of the Āḻvārs or, as the account of recovery tells us, the *Tiruvāymoḻi* of Nammāḻvār. The account also describes a cardinal feature—the tradition of unbroken knowledge transmission through the *guru-śisya paramparā*.

The above account in the *Divyasūricaritam* recounts Nāthamuni recovering the hymns of Nammāḻvār only. The *Āṟāyirappaṭi* and *Muāyirappaṭi* tell us that Nāthamuni recovered, collected, and redacted the entire corpus of four thousand hymns, but gradually in stages. The *Āṟāyirappaṭi* narrates:

[103] Ibid., Ch. 16, *ślokas* 22–30.

One day some Śrīvaiṣṇavas from Mela nāḍu came to the temple and sang a verse from the *Tiruvāymoḻi* beginning with *Aravamuḍe* before the deity Maṉṉanār. Listening to this, Nāthamuni was greatly pleased. In the hymn, it was mentioned these songs were 10 within this 1000. Then Nāthamuni asked them, 'Do you know this *prabandha* completely?' They replied, 'We only know the 10 songs.' Nāthamuni asked, 'Do you have the *Śrīkośa* in your country? Are there people who learn and sing this?' They replied, 'We know this much and it is not in any other place.' He gave them the *tīrthaprasad* and they left. Nāthamuni realized that this *prabandha* must be in the Tirukurugūr area—the birthplace of Śaṭhāri.[104] Thereafter, he went to Āḻvār Tirunagari, reached the temple and worshipped Nammāḻvār and the god there and prostrated before Paraṅkuśadāsa, the disciple of Madhurakavi. He asked Paraṅkuśadāsa, 'Are there people who can recite the *Tiruvāymoḻi* and are there *Śrīkośas*?' To which Paraṅkuśadāsa replied, 'Both *Tiruvāymoḻi* and other *Divyaprabandhas* have been sung here, but for a long time they have become *pramuśita* (lost). But my *ācārya*, Madhurakavi taught me the *prabhandha, Kaṇṇinuṇciṟuttāmbu* and told me that if this *prabandha* is sung 12,000 times to the Āḻvār (Nammāḻvār), meditating on his feet, with the mind focused totally on him, the Āḻvār will be pleased.' Nāthamuni prostrated before Parāṅkuśadāsa and asked him in all humility to teach the *prabandha*. Parāṅkuśadāsa was pleased and recited for him the *Prabandham*. Thereafter, Nāthamuni went to the tamarind tree and to the Āḻvār recited *Kaṇṇinuṇciṟuttāmbu* 12,000 times. Nammāḻvār was pleased and asked, 'Why do you concentrate on me and recite?' To which Nāthamuni requested him to teach the *Tiruvāymoḻi* and other *Prabandhams*. Just as Kṛṣṇa gave Arjuna the *diyadṛṣṭi* (divine vision), Nammāḻvār gave Nāthamuni the *divyajñāna-cakṣu* (vision of divine knowledge) and gave the *rahasyatreya* (three secrets), *Tiruvāymoḻi*, the 3000 *Prabandhams* along with their meanings and *aṣṭāṅgayogarahasyas*. Nāthamuni was grateful.[105]

Is the *Āṟāyirappaṭi* trying to tell us through this lengthy narrative that these hymns, especially Nammāḻvār's hymns, were already known in the

[104] According to the *Muāyirappaṭi* (pp. 50–1), the Śrīvaiṣṇavas informed that they were from Tirunagari and were on pilgrimage to various *divyadesas*. On reaching Tirukuḍandai, they heard these hymns from the people who were worshipping the Āḻvārs in the temple there and learnt these hymns from them. The text further tells us that the Viṣṇu and his consort Lakṣmī enjoined Nammāḻvār to impart the hymnal knowledge to Nāthamuni.

[105] *Āṟāyirappaṭi*, pp. 117–19.

Tamil region, and Nāthamuni was aware of them but had not heard them, despite being a Vaiṣṇava? Interestingly, this narrative also provides the context for the transmission of tradition in which Nammāḻvār revealed the divine knowledge through the Tamil *Prabandhams*—both being a secret, as is evident by the repeated use of the adjective *rahasya*. The narratives also tell us that Nammāḻvār gave the meanings of the *Prabandhams*—probably indicating the commencement of the commentarial tradition. The *Muāyirappaṭi* betrays a Sanskritic bias in stating that in addition, Nammāḻvār also gave the *Tirumantra* (divine knowledge) and the *Vyāsasūtra* (a commentary on the Vedas), which explained the *Tirumantra* and the meanings of the *Vyāsasūtra*, along with the 4,000 *Prabandhams* and other secret meanings.[106]

In many ways, this narrative is reminiscent of the brāhmaṇical transmission of knowledge (like in the case of the Vedas) that is always secretive, prerogative of the select few, then revealed and commented upon. These accounts clearly represent an effort by the Sanskritic intellectual tradition of the Viśiṣṭādvaita to forge a link with the popular Tamil hymnal tradition, which understandably was lost to them and had to be recovered. Thus, the hagiographies were constructing a '*paramparā* (an uninterrupted sequence of *gurus* back to primordial times) that the 'Śrīvaiṣṇavism' or the 'Viśiṣṭādvaita' of the *Ācāryas* considered itself to be the direct descendant of the Āḻvār movement'.[107]

The following account emphasizes the dissemination of the knowledge to everybody and its popularization through ritual singing:

> Lord Maṉṉanār of Vīranārāyaṇapuram appeared in Nāthamuni's dream and commanded him to recite the *Prabandhams* at least once. Next day, Nāthamuni went to the temple, worshipped the Āḻvār and told him about the dream. The Āḻvār through the priest commanded Nāthamuni to go to Vīranārāyaṇapuram and let all the Śrīvaiṣṇavas who have the quality of looking at everybody equally, recite these hymns, so that everybody knows about it. Nāthamuni went to several sacred sites and came back to Vīranayanapuram and worshipped the deity Maṉṉanār and submitted to him the news that the Āḻvār had graced him by giving the *Divya Prabnadhams*. The deity there lamented that despite all his efforts through incarnations, things had gone wrong and because of the Āḻvār's *Prabandhams* they

[106] *Muāyirappaṭi*, pp. 50–1.

[107] Hardy (1983), *Viraha-Bhakti*, p. 243.

> would now be corrected. Hence god felt that such *Prabandhams* should not be lying as *pramuśita* (lost/idle). The Lord asked Nāthamuni to set them to music, so that everybody listens to them and learns them. Nāthamuni called his nephews and with their help set them to music. Just as Vyāsa propagated the Vedas, Nāthamuni also propagated the *Divya Prabnadhams* through beautiful tunes.[108]

Thus setting to tune, reciting and making the hymns accessible to everybody is the core of the narrative. The refrain that these hymns were *pramuśita* (lost/idle) shows that till then they were not put to music systematically. In the life story of Nāthamuni, the concept of music and the language, Tamil, is central to the transmission of the tradition and clearly shows that despite a scripture that has been written, orality persisted, was equally sacrosanct and perhaps more efficacious in creating a memory of the hymns never to be forgotten. The *Muāyirappaṭi* stated that Nāthamuni, who was a great *yogī*, felt that it was better to realize Kṛṣṇa through sweet music rather through *yoga*. Music and recitation created a remembrance involving everybody. Associated with recovery and remembrance was also the notion of something that was lost (*pramuśita*) or forgotten and this was repeatedly emphasized to strengthen the memorialization, which would prevent the loss for all times to come. Since the narratives also tell us that the singing of these hymns in temples had been discontinued, the memory of these hymns was institutionalized through a festival in the temple called *adyāyanōtasava* by none other than Rāmānuja himself. However, the *Muāyirappaṭi*, through the motifs of loss, recovery, and memory, recounts that it was Nāthamuni who, after receiving and reciting the hymns, instituted this festival.

> The elders present there were pleased and told Nāthamuni, 'Because of your efforts we got the special meaning of the *Tiruvāymoḻi*.' They narrated a story:
>
> Previously, Tirumaṅgaiāḻvār after worshipping Periya Perumāḷ (god) at Tiruvaraṅgam (Śrīraṅgam) installed Nammāḻvār there. During Mārgaḻi, starting from *śukla-ekādaśī*, *Tiruvāymoḻi* was to be sung along with the recitation of the Vedas and this was to be called *Tiruadyāyanōtsava*, to be conducted every year. Tirumaṅgai conducted at the behest of Periya Perumāḷ. Due to the passage of time, the Āḻvār did not come and the *Divya Prabandhams* were lost (*lupta*). This we have heard from our elders.

108 *Āṟāyirappaṭi* pp. 119–20.

> So Nāthamuni prostrated before the elders and said, 'God has remedied one shortcoming through me and now he will grant other wishes too.' He went to the temple and according to Tirumaṅgai's ordinance, went to Tirunagari, got the Āḻvār in a procession and for first 10 days, starting from *prathama*, 2000 verses that were *upaṅgas* were recited and *Tiruvāymoḻi* was recited for 10 days, starting from *ekādaśī* and rest of 1000 for one day-thus for 21 days *Adyāyanōtsava* was conducted. Thereafter, Nāthamuni went to Kuḍandai and worshipped the lord, installed Nammāḻvār and in the month of Mārgaḻi in the first 21 days conducted the *Adyāyanōtasava* ... thus firmly established the *Prabandhams*. Thus Nāthamuni went to Vīranārāyaṇapuram and with the help of his two nephews at the behest of Maṉṉanār, set the *Prabandhams* to music and thus propagated the *Tiruvāymoḻi*.[109]

The recovery, consolidation, and systematic articulation of the hymns through a social/collective practice—the festival—that continues into contemporary times was utilized to embed a specific historical memory as the primary vehicle for carrying forward the Śrīvaiṣṇava scriptural canon.[110] Such a mnemonic consciousness was crucial for the perpetuation of a tradition and history of the community.

The strategies and mechanisms of historical memories that would transmit and disseminate the Śrīvaiṣṇava tradition were inscribed in the very structure of the texts. Accounts of Rāmānuja commissioning Piḷḷāṉ to write a commentary on the *Tiruvāymoḻi* are another instance of hagiographic attempts to textually encode the process of memorialization. So are accounts of the marriage of Āṇṭāḷ (daughter of the important figure Periyar Āḻvār) to Raṅganāthasvāmī (the form of Viṣṇu at Śrīraṅgam), described in Chapter 12 of the *Divyasūricaritam*. Just before Āṇṭāḷ's marriage is to take place, her father declares to her that by merely listening to the glorious descriptions of the 108 sacred Śrīvaiṣṇava centres, an individual could attain *mokṣa* and accrue same kind of benefit and merit that was acquired by visiting them. This valorizing of the power of utterance suggests that in Śrīvaiṣṇava religious culture orality (liturgy, etc.) was given precedence over the physical ritual of pilgrimage; the underlying implication was that the carrying forward of the tradition through oral

[109] *Muāyirappaṭi*, pp. 51–3.

[110] Younger (1982), 'Singing the Tamiḻ Hymnbook in the Tradition of Rāmānuja: The "Adyayanōtsava" Festival in Srīraṅkam', pp. 272–93.

means was far more efficacious. The theme of the wedding of Āṇṭāḷ to Raṅganātha provided an occasion for asserting the community collective.[111] The wedding enabled the hagiographers to present a gathering of divine invitees, who were none other than various forms of Viṣṇu, in all 108 Śrīvaiṣṇava shrines. The text brings in the hymnal mode through adding Nammāḻvār, a non-brāhmaṇa Vēḷāḷa Āḻvār, and his *brāhmaṇa* disciple, Madhurakavi, to the gathering of exalted guests. The establishment of a network of interaction amongst these sacred centres of pilgrimage in Chapters 13 and 14 of the *Divyasūricaritam* and subsequently in other hagiographies further enhanced community consciousness.

Similar motifs of the community/collective recur through the texts, reiterating the notion of an ideal community and the transmission of sacred tradition. This interaction between the oral and the written narrative modes and the systematic assimilation of the former into the latter is evidence that the 'tradition had been appropriated by the literate *brāhmaṇa* who had also seen the potential value of controlling oral information on the past and recording it in a literary form relevant to emergent contemporary requirements'.[112] In fact, orality became a powerful mnemonic device.

Since the primary aim of the *guruparamparās* was to memorialize the lives of the Śrīvaiṣṇava religious leaders, the hagiographers freely embellished the biographies with the intention of projecting their subjects as exemplars. These texts are thus frequently considered unhistorical by modern scholars, and authors of the hagiographies have been accused of prioritizing mythology over historical objectivity. Such an opinion has emerged from the modern perceptions of myth and history as dichotomous and contradictory categories, despite a general acknowledgement that in Indian culture history and myths have always exhibited a symbiotic relationship. However, while clearly mythologizing the life stories of Śrīvaiṣṇava preceptors, the *guruparamparās* did manifest a historical consciousness. Embedded in the biographical narratives were elements of Śrīvaiṣṇava chronology, the history of institutions, especially the temples, the growth of the community over a period of time, and transmission of this knowledge through the channel of cultural

[111] *Divyasūricaritam*, Chs 12, 13, pp. 202–69.

[112] Thapar (1992), 'Society and Historical Consciousness: The Itihāsa-Purāṇa Tradition' in *Interpreting Early India*, p. 137–73.

memory.[113] The 'externalized history' in these hagiographies depicted the highest standards of spirituality in the form of Āḻvārs and *ācārya*s whose exemplary lives represented specific values and ethics identified as distinctively Śrīvaiṣṇava.[114]

Recounting the history of the community for the Śrīvaiṣṇava devotees, the *guruparamparā*s composed from the twelfth and thirteenth centuries onwards began with an account of the lives of the Āḻvārs. It was imperative to place these saints and their compositions as the fundamental entry point in the narrative project, since the Āḻvār hymns already in oral circulation contained significant themes for the future development of a cohesive Śrīvaiṣṇava ideology. The life stories of the Āḻvārs were followed by biographical accounts of the *ācārya*s, Nāthamuni (ninth century), Yāmuna (tenth–eleventh century), and Rāmānuja (eleventh–twelfth century), and their role in reinforcing community consciousness through a philosophical trajectory. Texts such as the *Divyasūricaritam* firmly situate the subject within a wider Vaiṣṇava framework and recount the lives of the Āḻvārs in a fixed sequence that came to be recognized as the standard Śrīvaiṣṇava chronology. Beginning with the Mudal Āḻvārs (Poygai, Bhudatt, and Pēy), the texts then proceed to narrate the lives of Tirumaḻisai, Nammāḻvār, Madhurakavi, Kulaśekhara, Toṇṭaraṭippoṭi, Tiruppāṇ, Tirumaṅgai, Periyāḻvār, and Āṇṭāḷ. Historically, Tirumaṅgai is the last of the Āḻvārs. We find that the *Āṟāyirappaṭi* and *Muāyirappaṭi* also, within their respective Tamil and Sanskritic frameworks, document a different order of the Āḻvārs.

However, the biographies of some of these saints overlapped in the text. The Mudal Āḻvārs were shown to be contemporaries, and interaction between them was the thematic basis of one of the earliest accounts. According to the narratives, in the course of their wanderings these three Āḻvārs arrived at Tirukkōvaḷūr one night, one after the other, in the same sequence as they are presented in the *guruparamparā*s (viz. Poygai,

[113] See Thapar (1992), 'Society and Historical Consciousness: The Itihāsa-Purāṇa Tradition', in Thapar, *Interpreting Early India*, pp. 137–73; also see Rao, Shulman, and Subrahmanyam (2001), *Textures of Time: Writing History in South India, 1600–1800*, pp. 1–23.

[114] As noted by Thapar (1992) 'Society and Historical Consciousness', p. 138, 'The record may be one in which historical consciousness is embedded: myth, epic and genealogy; or alternatively it may refer to more externalized forms: chronicles of families, institutions and regions, biographies of persons in authority'.

Bhudatt, and Pēy). They took shelter in a choultry near the Viṣṇu temple at Tirukkōvaḷūr. There was very little space, and each Āḻvār became independently conscious of a stranger having squeezed in beside them; they realized subsequently that it was the Lord Himself. Through their spirituality, they had a *darśana* or vision of Lord Viṣṇu, after which each inspired Āḻvār spontaneously composed 100 devotional verses each in Tamil, known as *Mudal Tiruvantādi, Irantāmtiruvantādi*, and *Muṉṟam Tiruvantādi*.

This narrative is an example of the hagiographic attempt to attribute contemporaneity to certain saints' lives, a textual element that was not historically valid. This strategy was applied sometimes to the Āḻvārs as a group, sometimes to both Āḻvārs and *ācāryas*, and sometimes to the *ācāryas* only; it generated a sense of 'communitas'. The hagiographic mythologization of the Āḻvār and *ācāryas* also functioned to reinforce the image of their being conduits for the sacred. For example, Nammāḻvār was considered to be the link between the divine and the temporal—it is said that at the behest of Viṣṇu, his minister, Viśvakasena, initiated the Āḻvār through the performance of rituals like the *pañcasamskāra* and *mantropadeśa* and handed down particular doctrinal customs and injunctions.[115]

These influential embedded and externalized histories of Śrīvaiṣṇava preceptors also provided a context for how religious institutions and functionaries negotiated various interests both within and outside the community. In this connection, the narratives present accounts emanating from within the community regarding opposition to Rāmānuja. Hostility from the *brāhmaṇa* priests within the Śrīvaiṣṇava community at the Rāṅganāthasvāmī temple at Śrīraṅgam and being saved by the intervention of none other than lord Viṣṇu or by his own initiatives had implications for conflicting interests and power struggle within the Śrīvaiṣṇava community. Since the hagiographers themselves were directly or indirectly associated with Rāmānuja and his successors who were now powerful within the

[115] These Śrīvaiṣṇava rites, central to religious initiation (*dīkṣai*), comprise five features: (a) *tapas*, branding of the shoulders with conch and discus, iconic attributes of Viṣṇu; (b) *puntaram*, wearing of the *nāmam* or the sect-mark symbolizing the feet of the Lord; (c) The utterance of divine name to the initiator *Nārayāṇadāsa*; (d) *mantīrattrayam*, the imparting of certain sacred utterances; (e) the handing over of a *śāligrāma*, a black ammonite stone considered auspicious, or similar objects of daily worship.

temples, the *guruparamparās* may be seen as a means of constructing a specific past that would validate the claims of one particular group—in this case, affiliated to Rāmānuja—either aspiring for power or having already acquired it. In the latter case, the hagiographies function as a mechanism for legitimizing this social and ideological authority. Externally, sectarian discourse against other religious groups—Śaivas, Advaitins, Jainas, and Buddhists—manifesting in the hagiographies reflected Śrīvaiṣṇava anxieties in relation to the social base, patronage, and community formations. For instance, the story of Tirumaṅgaiāḻvār stealing of the golden idol of Buddha to finance the construction of the boundary wall of the temple at Śrīraṅgam is a well-known account of fierce piety that justified theft and violence against another religious tradition.

These texts also registered the changing attitudes towards power. Various tellings within the same text gradually proceeded from the themes of right to access to the temple, as in the case of the untouchable Tiruppāṇāḻvār (who was denied entry to the temple because of his *pāṇār* status), to the assertion of *bhakti* or *prapatti* as the true devotional path, to control over the temple administration, to royal patronage, expansion of the Śrīvaiṣṇava social base and community networks. The latter themes were highlighted and made to converge in the biographical delineation of Rāmānuja.

Thus, the hagiographies served the crucial function of confirming the socio-religious and political contexts in which Śrīvaiṣṇava tradition and identity were constructed and reinforced. Some of the narratives also established Śrīvaiṣṇavism as a subversive ideology within the political framework. This is illustrated by the story of Tirumaṅgaiāḻvār, who served as chieftain of a Cōḷa ruler but came into conflict with the king when he started diverting state resources towards the service of the Vaiṣṇava *bhaktas* (a virtuous act, according to Śrīvaiṣṇavism). Finally, Tirumaṅgai lost his chieftaincy and took to robbery in order to continue his act of serving the devotees. The examples of Ālavandar and Kulaśekhara Āḻvār (a Cera King), who renounced their kingdoms for the faith, reflect an ideological aversion to power and material benefits. However, this textual description of the incompatibility between political authority and religious ideology is in fact a total reversal of the complementary relationship that existed between the Āḻvārs and the royalty. The Āḻvār hymns presented a strong legitimizing rationale for the hierarchies of kingship and court, and formed the ideological basis for Vaiṣṇava temple iconography, particularly in the late Pallava and early Cōḷa periods (eighth to tenth centuries AD).[116] As mentioned earlier in this chapter, the conscious efforts of the Cōḷas in the eleventh century to consolidate the Śaiva basis of their ideology resulted in a conspicuous absence of patronage to Vaiṣṇavism. Therefore, the delineation of a hostile state not only explained the neglect or marginalization of Śrīvaiṣṇavism as compared to Śaivism in this period, it also instilled the feeling of superiority and pride in the community. Thematic renderings of such aggression can be found in the life story of Rāmānuja who faced persecution at the hands of the Cōḷa ruler and had to flee (thereafter, that sovereign paid a heavy price, ultimately losing his life).

Undoubtedly, the Śrīvaiṣṇava hagiographers were conscious of both their scriptural and social functions. They collected and selected the life stories of the Āḻvārs and *ācāryas* from the narratives already in oral circulation. The hagiographical narratives were distributed in two categories: the 'Āḻvārs' (those steeped in devotion and spontaneous in their expressions) and '*ācāryas*' (those engaged in metaphysical discourse and involved in the organization and life of the community). While modern biographers refer to both 'Āḻvārs' and '*ācāryas*' under the inclusive term 'saints', in actual fact each category had specific associations with the formation of the Śrīvaiṣṇava scriptural canon and its place in devotional practice and community life. In the case of Rāmānuja, for instance, the narratives gradually move towards delineating him as an *ācārya* and construct a specific cultural memory to reinforce this as a dominant characteristic.

Thus, it may be said that Śrīvaiṣṇava hagiography as a narrative project developed at a time when there was a cultural transition from an interiorized engagement with ideology and metaphysics to a more inclusive, externalized representation. From twelfth to fifteenth centuries, hagiographies emerged as a dominant mode of historical telling as well as a means to inscribe the Śrīvaiṣṇava scriptural canon for the benefit of a community that considered these texts sacrosanct. Hagiographic delineations of the spiritual genealogy/sequence of preceptors, the Āḻvārs and the *ācāryas*, were so influential that these accounts continue to be used today as fundamental sources for secular modern biographies of the Śrīvaiṣṇava 'saints'.

[116] Champakalakshmi (1996a), 'From Devotion and Dissent to Dominance: The *Bhakti* of the Tamil Āḻvārs and Nāyanārs', pp. 142–55.

CHAPTER THREE

Texts, Contexts, and the Śrīvaiṣṇava Community

> Then in the Pīṅgala year auspicious for the world, on *śuklapañcamī* of the Caitra month on Thursday having the constellation Ārdra, and in the Siṁhalagna, there appeared (was born) in the wife of Keśavasomayajīn a receptacle of luster, which represented a portion of Ādiśeṣa, for vindicating the tenets of the Vedānta system and for expelling (destroying) the deluded systems of thought, both external and internal (to the Vedānta).
>
> Then Śrīsailapūrṇa came to Bhūtapuri and saw his wonderful nephew. He gave him, as a protective measure the mark of discus and conch and also the name Rāmānuja.
>
> *Yatirāja Vaibhavam*, *śloka*s 6–7[1]

The Śrīvaiṣṇava *guruparamparā*s describe the birth of Rāmānuja as an *avatāra* or incarnation of Ādiśeṣa, the thousand-hooded snake on which Viṣṇu sleeps. According to the texts, such an incarnation was imperative so that he could restore order and dispel all the 'deluded systems

[1] V. Varadachariar (ed.) (1978), *Yatirāja Vaibhavam of Āndhrapūrṇa* (*Vaṭuka Nambi*).

of thought' that were distorting Vedānta on earth; hence Ādiśeṣa, the god's loyal servant, took the form of Rāmānuja and manifested amongst the Lord's Bhāgavata devotees. The hagiographies, namely *Yatirāja Vaibhavam*, *Divyasūricaritam*, *Āṟāyirappaṭi*, and *Muāyirappaṭi* present this intimate connection with divinity early on, emphasizing that the narrative was about the life of an extraordinary individual who had no parallels.[2] According to the *Divyasūricaritam*, 'In Toṇḍaimaṇḍala, there is a *mahāgrahāra* called Pudūr. In this place, there lived *brāhmaṇas* steeped in *bhakti* at the lotus feet of the Lord and followed the path of Vedānta.'[3]

The hagiographies confirm that Rāmānuja was born in a well-known *brāhmaṇa* family in the *brāhamaṇa* settlement of Śrīperumbudūr in Toṇḍaināḍu.[4] The narratives in the *Divyasūricaritam* describe at great length the intellectual expertise of the Śrīperumbudūr *brāhmaṇas*, who followed the Vedānta tradition.[5] Further, we are told that Rāmānuja was born into the *āsūri kula*, supposedly an elite and erudite *brāhmaṇa* lineage. His father Āsūri Keśavācārya was an expert in performing *yajñas*.

The *smārta* lineage of Rāmānuja is highlighted in the *Yatirāja Vaibhavam*, *Āṟāyirappaṭi*, and *Muāyirappaṭi* by the association of his father, Āsūri Keśavācārya, a *dīkṣitar* with Periyanambi (Sanskrit: Śrīśailapūrṇa), a Śrīvaiṣṇava of Tirupati whose preceptor was Yāmuna. Compared to *Divyasūricaritam*, these texts provided more details about Rāmānuja's birth and kin.[6] We are told that Periyanambi lived at Tirupati and tended the flower garden there as a form of service to the Lord. Having learnt the Vedānta from Yāmuna and expected to carry forward this tradition, he met two young men who were well versed in Vedas and Vedāngas. These two men were Kamalanayana (Sanskrit: Puṅdarīkākṣa) from Madhuramaṅgala and Keśavāsomayājī from Bhūtapūri, both places being close to each other and situated near Kāñcīpuram. Impressed by their knowledge, Periyanambi proposed a match for his two sisters, Bhūmīdevī and Śrīdevī. The elder sister Bhūmidevī married Keśavāsomayājī and the younger sister Śrīdevi married Kamalanayana. Both men were branded thereafter with the Vaiṣṇava marks of conch and discus. A son was born to Keśavāsomayājī and Bhūmidevī, whom Periyanambi blessed with the marks of conch and

2 *Divyasūricaritam*, Chapter 17, *ślokas* 5–8.

3 Ibid., *śloka*1.

4 Ibid., *śloka* 3–10.

5 Ibid., *śloka* 1.

6 *Āṟāyirappaṭi*, p. 140.

disc and named him Rāmānuja. *Āṟāyirappaṭi* and *Muāyirappaṭi* also give similar details. In addition, they tell us that Periyanambi felt that the baby had the luster of Rāma's younger brother, Lakṣmaṇa, and hence named him Iḷaiāḻvār (young āḻvār), the Tamil name for Lakṣmaṇa.[7] The texts used this occasion to inform about the birth of Rāmānuja's cousin Govinda Bhaṭṭar to Kamalanayana and Śrīdevī. Initiated also by Periyanambi, the hagiographies highlighted this kinship as a precursor to the narratives on Govinda Bhaṭṭar's significant role in Rāmānuja's life story.[8] Interestingly, *Divyasūricaritam* gives us information about Rāmānuja's sister. The reference is in context of his renunciation and the text tells us that he renounced all his friends and family, except his sister's son, Vādhula Dāśarathi.[9]

However, all the hagiographies are unanimous about astral details of Rāmānuja's birth. The precise documentation of the time of birth and the planetary configurations at that moment indicated that the hagiographers wanted to fix the birth of Rāmānuja as an event that was to be an auspicious part of the Śrīvaiṣṇava religious calendar, ensuring its embedment in Śrīvaiṣṇava cultural memory. Further, early in the *Divyasūricaritam* we encounter one of the most important Śrīvaiṣṇava theological concepts: the relationship of transcendence and immanence, as manifested through the divine *arcavatāra*s (incarnations of Viṣṇu through which the Lord descends on the earth in order to be close to his devotees): Since God wished to reside amongst his dearest devotees, Ādiśeṣa was made to take birth as Rāmānuja.[10]

The reference to 'Toṇḍaimaṇḍala' earlier in this chapter demonstrates the Śrīvaiṣṇava hagiographers' intent to use the description of Rāmānuja's birth to simultaneously introduce other themes central to the project of structuring his biography: the social milieu of the *brāhmaṇa*s, the *agrahāra* or *brahmadeya* (the *brāhmaṇa* settlement); the geography of the Tamil region (Toṇḍaināḍu); Vedānta metaphysics; a Vaiṣṇava mythic framework (the *avatāra* concept); Vaiṣṇava religious practice, as shown in the branding of Rāmānuja with a conch and discus, both sacred marks of Viṣṇu; and finally the spread of Vaiṣṇavism. Clearly, the hagiographers were familiar with such an environment and were themselves a part of it. Written between twelfth and fifteenth centuries, much after Rāmānuja,

[7] *Āṟāyirappaṭi*, pp. 140–41; *Muāyirappaṭi*, pp. 73–4.

[8] *Āṟāyirappaṭi*, p. 141; *Muāyirappaṭi*, p. 75.

[9] *Divyasūricaritam*, Chapter 17, *śloka* 71.

[10] *Divyasūricaritam*, Chapter 17, *śloka*s 7–8.

the texts exhibited a detailed knowledge of the past with regard to the historical context in general and that associated with the Śrīvaiṣṇava community in particular. In addition, the hagiographers often reflected upon the past from their current perspectives. Thus, the narrative logic of the hagiographies in relation to the delineation of Rāmānuja can be properly understood only if the various layers of historical times reproduced in the texts and in which the texts themselves were situated are analysed.

This chapter will discuss the historical context within which the narratives were situated. The first section, while discussing institutions of *brahmadeyas*, temples, and *maṭhas* and the context that influenced them, will analyse the ways in which the hagiographies presented their narratives to highlight the Śrīvaiṣṇava negotiation with these institutions. The second section will discuss the changing social base between the twelfth and fifteenth century. This section foregrounds the narrative structures that will be discussed in the next two chapters with regard to the delineation of Rāmānuja as an *ācārya* and a dissenter. The third section will discuss the historical context of Kāñcīpuram, Tirupati, Śrīraṅgam, and Mēlkōṭe as significant political and economic centres that also became the centres of Śrīvaiṣṇava activities. Through the hagiographical agency of Rāmānuja, a network of interaction developed between these regions with Śrīraṅgam at the centre. This complex provided a focus to the religious consciousness of the Śrīvaiṣṇavas. The discussion will focus on Śrīraṅgam as an institutional centre.

BRAHMADEYAS, TEMPLES, *MAṬHAS*, AND NETWORKS OF CONTROL

The *guruparamparā* texts focused a major part of their narratives on the *brahmadeyas* and temples, two key institutions whose importance stemmed from their respective ability to integrate diverse social groups and consolidate state structures. Controlled by the *brāhmaṇas* of different religious communities, the *brahmadeyas* and temples were repositories of different ideological paradigms that ritually organized composite socio-political systems based on hierarchy and power.

> At the apex of this society stood the royal family, as the authors and patrons of the temple, who were invariably associated with the main structures like the shrines (*vimānas*) and gateways (*gōpūras*). Royalty was followed by the ritually pure *brāhmaṇa* priests performing, worship, an administrative elite, dominant agrarian and mercantile groups involved in temple

> administration and the hierarchy ended up, with the lower categories of agricultural worker, craftsmen and menials in the temple service.[11]

Entrenched at the top of this stratification were powerful political groups and the *brāhmaṇa* community themselves. Since the latter were prime negotiators of and instrumental in the consolidation of state systems, they were heavily patronized, and a particularly significant form of patronage was tax-free land grants in some of the most fertile areas of the Tamil region. The hagiographies did not miss the crucial significance of the *brahmadeyas* and temples as centres of power and status and the association of the *brāhmaṇas* with them; thus, Śrīperumbudūr as Rāmānuja's birthplace and Madurāntakacaturvedīmaṅgalam as the site of landmark Śrīvaiṣṇava events (such as Rāmānuja's initiation into the Śrīvaiṣṇava community) acquired further importance for the hagiographers by virtue of being *brāhmaṇa* settlements.

From the sixth century onwards, the expansion and integration of various peasant settlements in the river valleys and the transformation of the tribal population into settled peasant communities provided a base for the emergence of new state systems. Beginning with the Pallavas of Kāñcīpuram in the north, the Pāṇṭiyas of Madurai in the south, and the Ceras in the southwest, by the ninth century these political processes culminated with the Cōḷas in the Kāvēri valley. The consolidation of these states depended on the integration of various local and supra-local institutions, mainly the *nāḍus*, *brahmadeyas*, and temples.[12]

[11] R. Champakalakshmi (1995), 'State and Economy: South India, Circa A.D. 400–1300', in Romila Thapar (ed.), *Recent Perspectives of Early Indian History*, p. 309.

[12] For a general discussion on these institutions, see Gurukkal (1993), 'Towards the Voice of Dissent: Trajectory of Ideological Transformation in Early South India', pp. 2–22; Gurukkal, 'The Beginnings of the Historic Period: The Tamil South', in Romila Thapar (ed.) (1995), *Recent Perspectives of Early Indian History*, pp. 246–74; Champakalaksmi (1996b), *Trade, Ideology and Urbanization: South India 300 BC to AD 1300*, pp. 230–330; Champakalaksmi (1989b), 'The Study of Settlement Patterns in the Cōḷa Period: Some Perspectives', *Man and Environment*, 14 (1): pp. 91–101; Champakalaksmi (1995), 'State and Economy: South India. Circa A.D. 400–1300', in Thapar (ed.) (1995), pp. 275–317; Karashima (1984), *South India History and Society: Studies from Inscriptions, A.D. 850–1800*; Stein (1980), *Peasant State and Society in Medieval South India*; Veluthat (1993a), 'Religious Symbols in Political Legitimation: The Case of Early Medieval South India', pp. 23–33; and Veluthat (1993b), *Political Structure of Early Medieval South India.*

As a 'peasant micro-region' and a regional eco-type, the *nāḍu* was already existent and, from the seventh century onwards, had increased substantially in number, representing a process of agrarian expansion based on irrigation projects sponsored by the Pāṉṭiyas and Pallavas in the wet and dry areas. Often such an expansion took place at the expense of the erstwhile tribal population, who eventually were settled as peasants. The Palar-Cheyyar valley in the north and Vaigai-Tāmbraparaṇi in the south, locales of the Āḻvārs, exhibited such agrarian developments. These river valleys also witnessed a proliferation of *brahmadeyas* and temples sponsored by royal dynasties that recognized the potential of these two institutions for restructuring and integrating the economy and society. This function of *brahmadeyas* and temples stemmed from canonized Vedic-Purāṇic-Śāstraic discourse that provided the social rationale for integrating diverse peasant and tribal groups through the institution of caste. Since *brahmadeyas* were the repositories of better irrigation technology and farming methods, the land granted to them became a state-controlled mechanism for the extension of agriculture into unsettled areas and extraction of surplus from various peasant groups.

For instance, the temples controlled by the *brāhmaṇas* and situated in the *brahmadeyas* and the *veḷḷān-vagai* (non-brāhmaṇa villages) provided a space for ritual integration of new entrants within the *varṇa-jāti* paradigm. The tribal divinities were mythologized within the Āgamic mould and incorporated within the *Itihāsa-Purāṇa* tradition, enabling the configuration of a universalistic pantheon. The hierarchical structure of the *varṇāśramadharma* was relevant in these villages, where the distribution and circulation of resources took place within the authority structure of landed rights. Besides peasants, various categories of chiefs, artisans, and craftsmen were incorporated through ritual ranking within the temples. Thus, commanding an allegiance of various local groups, this institution generated economic activities of diverse nature that eventually became the basis of urbanization.

Efficiently linking peasants, local chiefs, and other groups to the royalty, both *brahmadeya* and temple were also utilized as institutional channels for transmission and dissemination of the royal ideology. The epic-Purāṇic myths through classicized notions of sovereignty influenced the ideals of kingship, projecting the king as the ideal *kṣatriya*. The *brāhmaṇas* provided a genealogy consisting of various mythical lineages, impressive ceremonial titles and often a *brahma-kṣatra* (*brāhmaṇa-kṣatriya*) status.[13] Further, this royal ideology represented a 'cosmological world-view' through asserting the divine origins of the ruler and his close identification with Purāṇic personalities.[14] Through his incarnations (especially the Trivikrama *avatāra*), Viṣṇu symbolized the universal king, projecting an 'incorporative kingship' that 'shared sovereignty between the king and the local chieftain'.[15] In this connection, Sanskrit became the official language as its classical, scriptural, and liturgical status lent 'dignity and resonance to an upstart king'.[16]

These ideological frameworks became crucial for reordering of polity in the sixth- and seventh-century contexts of hectic regional warfare, shifting boundaries, and political fluctuations. Naturally, then the location of the royal centres coincided with the sites of major temples and *brahmadeyas*. In particular, Kāñcīpuram and Madurai (the respective capitals of the Pallavas and Pāṇṭiyas) with their large and influential temple complexes embodied these integrative processes.[17] The connotations of *kōyil* acquired a new dimension through the modes of royal patronage: earlier a reference to the palace, it now came to include the temple as well. The sites became interchangeable, with both representing the temporal and the sacred spheres that mandated unquestioning obedience to a two-fold authority, king and God.

With the consolidation of the Cōḷas in the tenth century, the centre of political activities shifted from Tōṇḍaināḍu (with Kāñcīpuram as the capital) to Cōḷanāḍu with the capital at Tañjavūr. The Pāṇṭiyas

[13] Dirks (1976), 'Political Authority and Structural Changes in Early South Indian History', *Indian Economic and Social History Review*, (13) 2: 125–57; Veluthat (1993a), 'Religious Symbols in Political Legitimation', pp. 27–8; and Champakalakshmi (1995), 'State and Economy: South India, Circa A.D. 400–1300', in Romila Thapar (ed.), *Recent Perspectives of Early Indian History*, pp. 306–7.

[14] Champakalakshmi (1996a), 'From Devotion and Dissent to Dominance: The *Bhakti* of the Tamil Āḻvārs and Nāyanārs', in Champakalakshmi and Gopal (eds), *Tradition, Dissent and Ideology: Essays in Honour of Romila Thapar*, p. 156.

[15] Veluthat (1993a), pp. 23–33.

[16] Ramanujan (1993), *Hymns for the Drowning: Poems for Visnu by Nammalvar*, p. 106.

[17] For a detailed study of the urban complex of Kāñcīpuram, see, Champakalakshmi (1996b), *Trade, Ideology and Urbanization: South India, 300 BC to AD 1300*. New Delhi: Oxford University Press, pp. 371–424.

continued to rule from Madurai and provided a formidable opposition to the Cōḷas. Continuing with the Pallava system of utilizing the *nāḍus*, *brahmadeyas* and temples for political integration, both the Cōḷas and the Pāṇṭiyas further enhanced their institutional potential and created new configurations, the *vaḷanāḍu* and *nagaram*.

The process of agrarian expansion that created the crucial resource base to the Cōḷas and Pāṇṭiyas shaped the wet zone areas of the Tamil subregions, particularly in the Kāvēri and Tāmraparaṇi valleys. The villages of these territories became the centre of the king's authority and financial claim, as well as that of his chiefs.[18] By the thirteenth century, 550 *nāḍus* had come into existence, indicating a large number of agricultural settlements, mostly in the Kāvēri valley of Cōḷamaṇḍalam.[19] The proliferation of *brahmadeyas* and temples located in the *nāḍus* of these river valleys were also instrumental in extending agriculture. These two institutions implemented the royal irrigation projects, thus acquiring the crucial right to organize and manage production and water resources, often through with the *Vēḷāḷa* community, powerful non-brāhmaṇa landowners in the *nāḍus*, who also participated in temple administration along with the *brāhmaṇas*.[20] Created through royal initiative, the *brahmadeyas* and temples were often strategically situated in areas dominated by non-brāhmaṇa villages to ensure the loyalty of other castes that provided essential manpower for the vast irrigation projects.

One direct consequence of the ninth-century agrarian expansion was the escalation of commercial activities that led to the growth of market centres, *nagarams*, and a network between them that linked towns and villages to the *mānagaram*, a larger town that was usually a royal centre and a port. Commerce led to the development of new trade routes and

[18] See footnote 51 for references on this theme.

[19] Champakalakshmi (1995), 'State and Economy', p. 286.

[20] The tenth-century conversion of the *brahmadeyas* into *taṉ-kūṟus* or *taniyūrs* by the Cōḷas led to the emergence of independent revenue units (separated from the *nāḍus*) that had significant economic and political ramifications. *Taniyūrs* acquired several villages (*piḍāgais* and *purams*) and craft centres. A new type of *nāḍu* called the *perimalai nāḍu* evolved around *taniyūrs*, comprising *Vēḷāḷas* and cultivators. For details on *taniyūrs*, see Stein (1980), *Peasant State and Society*, pp. 141–72; Champakalakshmi (1995), 'State and Economy', pp. 286–305; Champakalakshmi (1997), *Re-Appraisal of a Brāhmaṇical Institution: The Brahmadeya and Its Ramifications in Early Medieval South India*, unpublished paper.

urban centres that linked remote and newly conquered regions with the core settled areas and the coast.[21] The spread of guild activities and trading associations, namely the Ayyāyoḷe 5000, Tamil Tiśai Āyirattu Aiññūṟṟuvar, foreign merchant organization, and Añjuvaṇṇam stimulated the expansion of the mercantile community with its diverse groups of merchants, artisans, craftsmen, and itinerant traders. One such community that became prominent in the ninth century was the Nagarattār, the powerful mercantile community whose members applied the *ceṭṭi* suffix to their names. Often the mercantile communities invested in agriculture and gifted to the temples, further strengthening their integration and interdependence with religious institutions. The *kaikkōḷa*s, a powerful weaver community with significant links to the temples acquired further importance through religious groups attempting to assimilate them in order to project a liberal outlook.[22] By the ninth century, clusters of *brahmadeya*s and temples had developed into urban centres that connected the village resource base to the royal, priestly, and social elites, successfully situating a range of populations, faiths, and affiliations within the same material complex.[23]

Thus, the *nāḍu*s, *brahmadeya*s, temples, and *nagaram*s with their respective assemblies (*ūr*, *sabhā*, and *nagaram*s) controlled the local distribution process and facilitated the collection of revenue from different areas, particularly the peripheral territories, acting 'as interdependent agents of the Cōḷa state synthesis' and bringing the villages 'close together in a system of unified political organization and economic change …'[24] Due to their overarching ideological and social framework of the *varṇa-jāti* paradigm (discussed earlier in this chapter), the *brahmadeya*s and temples became increasingly crucial as a means for the legitimizing of the political authority asserted by the local kings and the chiefs, and thereby rationalizing 'royal power with minimum use of

21 Champakalakshmi (1995), 'State and Economy', pp. 279–99.

22 Ramaswamy (2006, 2nd edn), *Textiles and Weavers in Medieval South India*, 35–62.

23 The multi-temple complexes of Kāñcīpuram and Tañjāvūr emerged as important politico-urban centres. The economic reach of the temple at Tañjāvūr extended over the whole of Cōḷa kingdom as well as the northern part of Sri Lanka. See Champakalakshmi (1996b), *Trade, Ideology and Urbanization*, Chapters 6, 7, 8.

24 Champakalakshmi (1995), 'State and Economy', p. 290.

force by the state'.[25] Linking the villages, various peasant communities and the local chiefs to the political network of the Cōḷas and Pāṇṭiyas, these institutional structures made common governance possible over vast regions.[26] By the end of the twelfth century, the clusters of agrarian settlements both in the wet and dry zones were constituted by various agricultural and artisanal castes. *Brāhmaṇas* and *Vēḷāḷas* emerged as dominant, followed by the *Paḷḷars, Paṟaiyas, Vāṇiyars*, and several others, hierarchically arranged within the caste structure but closely bound through interdependent economic relationships.[27] Most regional peasant groups armed themselves and built alliances with local tribes in efforts at self-protection and to counter the usurpation of resources that characterized a climate of ongoing economic uncertainty and military oppression. In several areas the *Kaikkōḷas* formed their own armed bands and identified as 'merchant-warriors'.[28]

[25] Kulke (1982), 'Fragmentation and Segmentation versus Integration? Reflections on the Concepts of Indian Feudalism and the Segmentary State in Indian History', *Studies in History*, 4 (2): 237–63.

[26] The nature of the Cōḷa state has been a subject of historiographical debate. Burton Stein's theory of the segmentary state has been subjected to criticism. According to Stein, *nāḍu* was the smallest segment, an ethnic unit with an autonomous, unchanging character. The Cōḷa state was a weak state with its control restricted to the core region, Cōḷanāḍu. The rest of the kingdom was governed through *brahmadeyas* and temples. The Cōḷas exercised ritual sovereignty, without any centralized system of taxation and an organized army. War booty was the source of income and Cōḷa military strength depended on the caste and guild armies. However, this view does not take into consideration the internal dynamics of the Cōḷa polity, society, and economy. See Burton Stein (1980), *Peasant State and Society in Medieval South India*. Delhi: OUP. For critiques, see Champakalakshmi (1981), 'Peasant State and Society in Medieval South India: A Review Article, *Indian Economic and Social History Review*, 18 (3/4): 411–26; Ramaswamy (1982), 'Peasant State and Society in Medieval South India: A Review Article', *Studies in History*, 4 (2): 307–19.

[27] For instance, in the Pāṇṭiya kingdom, the hilly regions with their tribal population were linked to the core area dominated by the *Vēḷāḷa* peasant groups on the basis of economic exchange. The hilly regions provided forest products in exchange of agricultural products from the peasant regions. See Ludden (1989), *Peasant History in South India*, pp. 15–41.

[28] Mines (1984), *The Warrior Merchants: Textiles, Trade and Territory in South India*.

Embedded in this diverse socio-political fabric, the temples formed the most crucial as well as stable links between royalty and society, and between the various social strata. The 'superordinate' character of the temple was evident in its complex role in the strengthening of territorial sovereignty at the local level, through temple-mediated negotiations and transactions that culminated in a network of alliances between the royalty and the various locality chiefs. Such alliances were significant in a contemporary situation marked by warfare, unsteady boundaries, and shifting frontiers. Shared institutional power structure manifested in the devotional practice of gift-giving to the temple deities, a custom that enabled the strategic redistribution of resources and political power. The kings' gifts to the temples were socially re-circulated on a large scale in the form of ritual goods, for instance daily *prasādam* (food offerings), that stimulated a range of economic transactions. The local chiefs also made gifts to the king or donated to the temples in the name of the king, in turn receiving titles and honours that enabled them to become the members of the royal alliance network. Occasionally, these chiefs made grants to temples outside their own domain, thus building their individual power networks and replicating the royal redistributive system. Though the notion of religious merit was an important aspect of ritual gift-giving, the kings and the chiefs principally used it as a mechanism for the negotiating mutual support in the political sphere. However, by 1300 AD the Cōḷa rulers had reorganized the *nāḍus* into large and cohesive *vaḷanāḍus* (artificial revenue and political units), thus bringing multiple chieftaincies directly under Cōḷa authority.

Apart from political presence, the temple was also an ideological mechanism for the medieval south Indian states, binding the belief systems of various social groups. The Āḻvār hymns had already created a context for dialogue between the universalized Purāṇic religion and the region's autochthonous cults, through which the latter were assimilated into the brāhmaṇical paradigm that dominated the temple. This incorporation was a result of the political dynasties' realization that *bhakti* was the 'best religion ... to hold ... society and its state together'.[29] The liturgical emphasis on the hymnal metaphors of power and strength as personified in the various forms of Śiva and Viṣṇu

[29] Kosambi (1962), *Myth and Reality*, p. 32; quoted in Kulke (1993b), *Kings and Cults: State Formation and Legitimation in India and Southeast Asia*, p. 11.

and popularized by the saints' compositions served to reinforce the prevalent political ideology that was based on the epic-Purāṇic pattern. Consequently, the hymns became the source of inspiration for the construction of several canonical temples with elaborate iconography that had an embedded political subtext, the various cosmic/heroic representations of Purāṇic deities analogous to a monarch and his absolute power. The deities acquired royal characteristics and the hectic temple activities, daily as well as annual, for instance festivals—all had the characteristics of the royal paraphernalia. For the first time, the region's political geography coincided with its sacred geography and the Kāvēri region, the core of Cōḷanāḍu, experienced hectic temple construction. Śrīraṅgam developed into a major political node as well as a sacred centre of Vaiṣṇavism.

In this context of political integration and legitimation, as well as social, agrarian, and commercial development, the religious communities attempted to create a niche for themselves, consolidate their social base, and multiply their networks of religious influence. In the absence of any challenge from the heterodox sects, these communities focused on the expansion through competing for patronage by the royalty and the local chieftains. The *ācāryas* (i.e., ideologues and theologians) now formally assumed the role of proponents of *bhakti*, earlier fulfilled by the Āḻvārs, and through influence in the temples and *maṭhas* imposed a concrete institutional frame upon the Āgamic-Purāṇic devotional paradigm. It was in this context that Yāmuna's *Āgamapramāṇya* and Rāmānuja's commentaries on Vedānta themes and texts, subsequently termed Viśiṣṭādvaita, assumed importance for the Śrīvaiṣṇavas.

By the end of the eleventh century, the region's religious groups, particularly the Śrīvaiṣṇavas, reoriented their community base and structure against the context of social and political changes. The gradual marginalization of the *brahmadeyas*, due to the exhaustion of their institutional capacity for socio-political integration, and consequently, the rising importance of the temples and *maṭha* had institutional ramifications for these communities. Twelfth- and thirteenth-century Pāṇṭiyas and the Cōḷa records cite several instances of the *brahmadeyas* converted into *veḷḷān-vagai* villages and donated as *devadānam* to the temples. Either the *brāhmaṇas* migrated from the Tamil country to the northern regions or converged increasingly towards the temples, further highlighting the latter's significance. This coincided with continuing decline of the Cōḷa administration and the re-emergence of the local chiefs. In addition, migration from the Karnataka region accelerated after the Hoysala occupation of the Kāvēri delta. The altered regional power structure led to an expansion of agriculture, and subsequent increase in land transactions, and increased private and temple holdings, particularly in the non-brāhmaṇa villages. This created a hierarchy in terms of landed rights with the *Vēḷāḷa*s gaining prominence as the dominant group, an appropriation of social privilege that led to increased tensions within the agrarian community. The growth of urban centres and the intensification of commerce contributed to the rising importance of the *nagaram*s as sites for the transactions of merchants and craftsmen, especially the weaver community of *Kaikkōḷa*s. This economic surge altered prevalent hierarchies, with various non-brāhmaṇa groups, including artisans, aggressively aspiring to higher (i.e., twice-born) caste status that would ensure their permanent inclusion within the *brāhmaṇa*-dominated ritual space of Śrīvaiṣṇava temples.

This strategic bid for social mobility culminated in a regional 'societal crisis' in the twelfth century, with the conflicts between artisans and agriculturists, influential artisan sub-castes such as the *Kaikkōḷa*s and Sāliyas, hill and forest people and the different merchant groups.[30] The existing social structure, in the absence of a regional variant of *kṣatriya*s and *vaiśya*s, crystallized the non-brāhmaṇa communities comprising various occupational, caste, and ethnic groups into a dual vertical division of the *Valangai* (Right-hand castes) and *Iḍangai* (Left-hand castes). However, the *Vēḷāḷa*s remained outside this division, like the *brāhmaṇa*s.[31] The temples were quick to forge new links in this altered social environment. The popular religion of the Śaivas and Vaiṣṇavas responded to the new configuration by accommodating the diverse ethnic groups and new group formation within a unified and ideologically sanctioned community paradigm. Thus, the twelfth century was a crucial period for the reconstruction of Śrīvaiṣṇava social frameworks, with religious groups vigorously competing to acquire masses of *bhakta*s through an expanded theological orientation that included non-brāhmaṇical elements.

30 See Champakalakshmi (1995), 'State and Economy', p. 296.

31 Ibid., pp. 295–97; Champakalakshmi (2012), pp. 239–44; Appadurai (1974), 'Right- and Left-Hand Castes in South India', pp. 216–59; and Ramaswamy (2006[1985]), pp. 58–9.

Thus, the Śrīvaiṣṇava textual tradition evolved and was gradually codified into a scriptural canon in a more expansive social milieu, reflected in the *guruparamparā* presentation of the Āḻvārs and the *ācāryas* as universalized narratives that would have broad community appeal.[32] This has been discussed in the previous chapter. However, it needs to be reiterated that the diverse social background of the Āḻvārs, ranging from Nammāḻvār (a *Vēḷāḷa*) and Āṇṭāḷ (a woman) to Tiruppāṉ (an untouchable) and Kulaśekhara (a chieftain), are offered along with narratives on Rāmānuja that, despite being presented within the Sanskritic framework of Vedānta, depict him as a dissenter who opposed the socio-cultural hierarchies that privileged the *brāhmaṇas*. The *Divyasūricaritam* illustrated Rāmānuja's inclusive ideology and democratic approach in several ways: he was supposed to have had a *śūdra* teacher, Tirukacci Nambi (Kāñcīpūrṇa); he severed marital ties with his wife because she misbehaved with his teachers on the grounds of their being his social inferiors; he ensured that the temple was accessible to *śūdras* and that non-brāhmaṇas were part of the temple administration, etc. These and other instances of Rāmānuja's actions depict a spiritual leader with catholic personality suggesting that liberal Śrīvaiṣṇava *brāhmaṇas* were appropriate leaders of the community. The social transformation documented in the hagiographies has endured over the centuries, and the Śrīvaiṣṇava community today is constituted by diverse social groups, ranging from Aiyangar *brāhmaṇas* to Piḷḷais, Mudaliyars, *Vēḷāḷas*, Kaḷḷars, and Iṭaiyars.[33] The description of the funeral of Rāmānuja in the hagiographies gives an idea of the composition of the Śrīvaiṣṇava community from twelfth to fourteenth centuries.[34] In addition to registering these crucial social changes, the *guruparamparās* also documented shifts in the dominant politico-economic context. The early years of Rāmānuja were situated within Kāñcīpuram, an important urban and religious centre. The narrative focus on Śrīraṅgam in the Kāvēri region and the community networks in the Tāmbraparaṇi river valley indicate the hagiographic intent to foreground some of the most politically and economically important regions of South India in the agriculturally rich riverine areas. Accounts dwell at length on the perennial contest for maximum control of temple

[32] Hardy (2001), in Dalmia, et al., p. 52.

[33] Ibid.

[34] See Chapter II, p. 59.

resources, especially of the Raṅganāthasvāmī temple at Śrīraṅgam, and on strategic negotiations with the Cōḷa and Pāṉṭiyas rulers. Similarly, Ramanuja's travel to Tirupati and his conflict with the Śaivas over the control of the temple was an attempt on the part of the hagiographers to provide a legitimizing context to the community to strengthen its control over this region whose prominence grew between the thirteenth and fifteenth centuries

> Having accepted with due obeisance Hayagriva, daily worshipping the family god Varada, he came again to Venkaṭādrī, having overcome all hostile systems of religion.
>
> 'Śrī Śrīnivāsa with his weapons, disc and conch, which had been given over to his devotee (Toṇḍaiaiman Rājā) is Śiva and no other', argued the Śaivas; Yatiśvara (Rāmānuja) prescribed them a test. Having agreed, they then placed within the sanctum the disc and the conch and the trident; and locked up the door. In the morning all of them opened the door together and examined.
>
> The Śaivas seeing Śrī Śrīnivāsa wear the conch and disc, having broken the trident were driven by Yatiśvara, Śrī Śailapūrṇa felt highly pleased.[35]

Inevitably, the Śrīvaiṣṇava efforts to develop strong textual, institutional, and devotional traditions were seen as a threat by the Śaivas, who were experiencing a similar social churning; their scripture and liturgy also reflect the emergence of new groups. The canonical *Tirumuṟai* and the Śaiva hagiographies *Tiruttoṇṭar Tiruvantāti* and *Periya Purāṇam* fix the number of saints at sixty-three and identify them as belonging to a wide caste spectrum, from *brāhmaṇa* to *paraiya*. However, other than Appar, Campantar, Cuntarar, and Māṇikkavāccakar whose devotional works comprise the core of Śaiva scripture, the rest of the Nāyanārs are of doubtful historicity. As with Śrīvaiṣṇava *guruparamparā*s, Śaiva hagiographic focus on the low-caste background of the Nāyanārs was a deliberate projection of a popular movement. Interestingly, the hagiographers as well as the compilers of the scriptural canon were themselves usually upper-caste—prominent instances being Nambi Āṇḍār Nambi (a *brāhmaṇa*) and Cēkkiḻar (a *Vēḷāḷa* from the ruling family).[36]

35 Krishnaswami Aiyangar (1909 [1985]), *The Yatirājavaibhavam of Āndhrapūrṇa, ślokas* 89–92; Also see, *Āṟāyirappaṭi*, p. 228; *Muāyirappaṭi*, pp. 107–08.

36 Champakalakshmi (1996a), 'From Devotion and Dissent to Dominance: The *Bhakti* of the Tamil Āḻvārs and Nāyanārs', pp. 135–63.

The systematic incorporation of other popular Śaiva traditions within a single framework gradually evolved into a Śaiva Siddhāṅta movement in the fourteenth century. The twelfth-century inclusion of the Tamil Siddha tradition through the prominent presence of the Siddha saint Tirumular, who emphasized Śiva and Murukan worship, reflected an attempt in this direction.[37] This inclusion of 'anti-brāhmaṇical and unorthodox elements into the traditional Śaiva order' and the creation of Tirumular's canonical work *Tirumantiram* inspired the Śaiva Siddhānta movement of the fourteenth century that was based on the Agamic tradition.[38] Significantly, the *Tevāram* acquired a sacred status within Śaiva Siddhānta, despite there not being a single commentary on this work. The movement's integrative characteristic reinforced the social roles of the non-brāhmaṇas, especially the artisan and the weaver groups who had become economically powerful in the twelfth century and were demanding greater ritual and administrative participation in the temples. The Śaiva pantheon, liturgy, and rituals came to include popular folk elements, and despite a secure place in the Śaiva religious framework, the non-brāhmaṇa devotees sustained their allegiance to the local deities.

The founding of Śaiva religious institutions, especially the *maṭhas* led by the Mudaliyār Santāna (mostly from twelfth- and thirteenth-century *Vēḷāḷa* lineages), further widened the catchment area of Śaiva *bhakti*. Moreover, Smārta and Śrīvaiṣṇava organizational structures replicated those of the Śaiva monastic institutions.[39] Although brāhmaṇical in orientation, the Smārta *maṭhas* emerged as major power centres for resource control for the royalty, especially in the Vijayanagar period, when they became the legitimizers for the upcoming kingship.[40]

After the twelfth century the Śrīvaiṣṇavas also developed a religious infrastructure of *maṭhas* that framed the independent tradition of Śrīvaiṣṇava ācāryic identity. With the decline of the *brahmadeyas* and marginalization of the *brāhmaṇas* after the twelfth century, the *maṭhas*, as influential custodians of the religious canon, gained control over the temples and temple lands. Located mostly in trading and weaving

[37] Ibid., pp. 148, 159–60.
[38] Ibid.
[39] Ibid., pp. 153–63.
[40] Ibid., p. 162.

centres, they attracted royal and mercantile patronage and were able to invest and participate in long-distance trade while enhancing their resource base.

Before the period of Rāmānuja, that is, in the eleventh century A.D. references at Tirupati, Śrīraṅgam, and Tirukkōvalūr to the *maṭha* seem to refer to a physical space within the temple where the Śrīvaiṣṇavas were fed or lived. Donations were made for this purpose and the *maṭha* was named after the donor, like the Kaḍavarāyā *maṭha* and the Madurāntaka *maṭha* at Śrīraṅgam, the Pallavarāyan *maṭha* at Tirupati, and Cittirameḻi *maṭha* at Tirukkōvalūr. These *maṭhas* did not have a head. During Rāmānuja's period, epigraphical reference to the *maṭha* is absent. It is only from the fourteenth century A.D. onwards that the epigraphical references to *maṭhas* point towards an institutional organization with a hierarchy of religious functionaries, including non-brāhmaṇa with a *jīyar* as the head having a large number of disciples. For instance, the Periya Jīyyaṅgār *maṭha* at Tirupati had *ekākī* Śrīvaiṣṇavas (those without threads) and *kaikkoḷas* as the servants of the *maṭha*. Therefore, one can conclude that initially *maṭha* was loosely structured and hence was a mere physical space within the precincts of the temple. In the Vijayanagar period, this physical space was transformed into a concrete institutional organization with a well-structured lineage. Amidst such intense religious development and socio-cultural transformation, sectarian rivalries amongst the *maṭha* centres became more frequent, especially in relation to acquiring the patronage of diverse economically and socially powerful groups. This was further reflected in the fourteenth and fifteenth centuries, with the migration of new social groups and the founding of the Vijayanagar Empire.

The hagiographies realized the crucial role of the *maṭhas* and incorporated them as narrative motif to highlight the importance and power of the Śrīvaiṣṇavas *ācārya*. The *Āṟāyirappaṭi* and *Muāyirappaṭi*, especially focus on the *maṭha* as the centre of the ācāryic activities. All the Śrīvaiṣṇavas *ācāryas* including the non-brāhmaṇa Tirukacci Nambi, one of the *gurus* of Rāmānuja, was the head of a *maṭha*. According to these narratives, Rāmānuja was also the head of a *maṭha* at Śrīraṅgam and by virtue of this, controlled the temple administration. The power of the head of the *maṭha* is evident by the initiatory rites that resemble the coronation of a ruler. Known as *paṭṭābhiśekam*, which literally means 'coronation' to the episcopal throne, it involved a series of rituals in which the community participate as the spectator. Thus, the *maṭha* head emerged as a powerful personality in the Vijayanagar period with an impressive hierarchical organization as well as networks of interaction and control.

THE CHANGING ŚRĪVAIṢṆAVA SOCIAL BASE FROM THE TWELFTH TO THE FIFTEENTH CENTURIES

The socio-religious trajectories of the twelfth century continued into the thirteenth, with the gradual decline of Cōḷa power and the emergence of numerous regional dynasties intensifying the uncertain political situation. The Kākatīyas of Wārangal in the interior Telugu country, the Hoysalas of Dvārsamudra in the Karnataka region, and the Pāṉṭiyas of Madurai in the Tamil country were the most formidable powers to reckon with. Amidst shifting political boundaries and fluctuating alliances, the core riverine areas of Kāvēri, Peṉṉār, Tāmbraparaṇi, and Kṛṣṇa-Godāvarī, containing numerous agricultural settlements and important trading centres, became the focus for competitive resource appropriation during this period. The control over these areas was crucial for both the Hoysala and Kākatīya kingdoms, located in the rocky areas of low rainfall and scarce natural resources, and hence unable to generate agrarian surplus and trade.[41] The Kākatīyas subsequently took over the area from Telaṅgāna to the rich agricultural land and ports of the Kṛṣṇa-Godāvarī delta and while Hoysalas occupied the western coastal area from the Konkan to Goa and Mālabār. The Hoysalas also shifted their capital from Dvārasamudra to Kaṇṇanūr near the Kāvēri delta in the Tamil region, where the Pāṉṭiyas were already making inroads. The tension between these two powers manifested in their competitive patronage extended to the Vaiṣṇava temple of Raṅganāthasvāmī and the Śaiva temple of Jambukeśvaram, situated on either side of the Kāvēri at Śrīraṅgam.[42]

The invasions by armies of the Delhi Sultanate under Alauddin Khalji and Muhammad bin Tughlaq in the fourteenth century disturbed the political configurations in south India, especially of the Hoysalas,

[41] Stein (1989), *Vijayanagara*, pp. 13–27; Talbot (2001), *Precolonial India in Practice: Society, Region, and Identity in Medieval Andhra*, pp. 38–86.

[42] *Kōil Oḷugu*. Rao (ed. and trans.) (1961), pp. 35–68.

Kākatīyas, and Pāṉṭiyas, and culminated in the establishment of the Sultanate at Madurai.[43] In this phase of turbulent political transition, the Vijayanagar Empire, founded in the fourteenth century with its capital at Hampi in Karnataka, emerged as a consolidated ruling power. This initiated a series of strategic alliances that integrated the peninsular region south of river Kṛṣṇa by bringing together the three cultural zones of Tamil Nāḍu, Andhra, and Karnataka. Finally, the defeat of the Madurai Sultan at the hands of Kumara Kampana of Vijayanagar pushed the regional frontier to the southernmost point of India. Various political groups, especially the Vijayanagar kings and the Telugu warriors who represented Vijayanagar in different regions of the peninsula, legitimized their power and sovereignty by projecting themselves as the saviours of mankind. They became culturally identified as the destroyers of the 'Tulukkas' (i.e., 'Turkish' invaders from the north), restorers of the dhārmic order and temple worship disrupted due to plunder by northern armies, and founders of the new stable political order.[44] The theme of invasions often deployed in the inscriptions and the numerous

[43] There were two sets of forays into south India by the rulers of the Delhi. The first set of invasions was from *c.* 1296 CE onwards, when Alauddin Khalji (*c.*1296–1314 CE) conducted successful expeditions against the Yādavas of Devagiri (Maharashtra), Kākatīyas of Wārangal (Andhra Pradesh), Hoysalas of Dvārasamudra (Karnataka), and the Pāṉṭiyas of Madurai (Tamil Nāḍu). Since their main motive was the acquisition of wealth, these states were not annexed but were reduced to a tributary status. Governance of the distant south from Delhi was considered politically imprudent. The second set of invasions took place during the reign of Muhammad bin Tughlaq (*c.*1324–51 CE). Motivated by the imperialist desires of expansion and control, these invasions proved to be counterproductive for the Sultan as Tughlaq governance in the south could not withstand the pressure of constant rebellions by local chiefs and officials. Ultimately, the Sultanate was routed and two important polities established their control, viz., the Vijayanagar kingdom with its capital at Hampi (Karnataka) and the Bahamani kingdom with its capital at Gulbarga.

[44] For a similar theme, see Chattopadhyaya (1998), *Representing the Other? Sanskrit Sources and the Muslims (Eighth to Fourteenth Century)*; Thapar (1971), 'The Image of the Barbarian in Early India', *Comparative Studies in Society and History*, 13 (4): pp. 408–36; Thapar (1992a), *Interpreting Early India*, pp. 60–88; and Talbot (1995), 'Inscribing the Other, Inscribing the Self: Hindu-Muslim Identities in Precolonial India', *Comparative Studies in Society and History*, 37 (4): pp. 692–722.

political biographies of this period influenced modern historiography, for instance the thinking of scholars of the 1960s, who projected the founding of the Vijayanagar Empire as a Hindu response to Muslim incursions.[45] However, a different narrative emerges when the historical context is analyzed. In a situation of rapid political transition, the acceptance of this custodial image by various religious groups gave the political leaders an access to region's temples and monastic organizations, and the vast resources they commanded. Conversely, the religious communities controlling the temples received the protection and patronage required for their further consolidation.

From thirteenth century onwards, temple and polity were inextricably linked with each other and their interaction became the basis of a new social formation. The most important factor underlying these developments was the phenomenon of migration.[46] From the end of the twelfth century, Kannada and Telugu peasant groups migrated from areas of marginal resources to the wet riverine regions, 'receiving new traditions and religious symbols from the valley culture and leaving their own marks on the society of the rice-belt'.[47] Fluctuating political boundaries, ever-mounting military requirements of the regional kingdoms, especially of the Vijayanagar Empire, and the expansion of the agricultural frontier contributed to the increasing migration of the Telugu warrior class to the river valleys and peripheral areas of potential development. Referred to as the *nāyakas*, they impinged upon the pre-existing local power groups and their respective spheres of control and emerged as the major benefactors of the temples and *maṭhas*, thereby promoting religion, especially Śrīvaiṣṇavism at the local and supra-local levels. Migration also brought into prominence a new class of itinerant merchants and traders, several of whom gradually settled and emerged

[45] For example, Sastri (1958), *A History of South India: From Prehistoric Times to the Fall of Vijayanagar*, pp. 264–312.

[46] Ludden (1989), *Peasant History in South India*, pp. 15–100; Stein (1989), *Vijayanagara*, pp. 14–25; Breckenridge (1985), 'Social Storage and Extension of Agriculture in South India, 1350 to 1750', in Picola (ed.), *Vijayanagar—City and Empire: New Currents of Research*, pp. 41–68; Bayly (1992), *Saints Goddesses and Kings: Muslims and Christians in South Indian Society, 1700–1900*, pp. 12–65.

[47] Bayly (1992), *Saints Goddesses and Kings*, p. 23.

as powerful landowners. The inscriptional references to the *Kaikkōḷa*, *Vāniya*, *Śikku Vāniya*, *Vyāpārī*, *Mayilāṭṭi*, *Kaṉmaḷa*, and *Kōmaṭṭi* traders, and *Pattanūlkār* (silk weavers) from Saurāṣtra point to the development of a brisk trade and increased craft production which found a thriving market in Vijayanagar's dominions. Migrants settled in many stages. For instance, the *Pattanūlkār*s supposedly migrated from Saurāṣtra, briefly settled in the city of Vijayanagara, and then moved on to finally settle in the pilgrimage centers of Kāñcīpuram, Madurai, and Rāmeśvaram.[48] The emergent mercantile communities were the followers of different religious traditions—Śaiva, Vaiṣṇava, and Islam.[49] However, most of the migrant merchants and traders were Vaiṣṇavas. Their lavish sponsorship of Śrīvaiṣṇava temples helped to spread the faith, and the Vēṅkaṭēśvara temple at Tirupati and the Nārāyaṇasvāmī temple at Mēlkōṭe emerged as significant institutions due to the patronage of both the *nāyaka*s and the merchants. These two sacred centres received exhaustive treatment in the *guruparamparā* accounts with reference to Rāmānuja's initiatives and reforms.

Some migrants moved en masse, that is, as a community; others as individuals or with their families and clans.[50] Apart from the groups mentioned above, peasant communities and agricultural specialists such as Śāṉars (tank-diggers) constituted a migratory group that significantly modified the existent regional demographic. New irrigation technology and forms of production were introduced that 'established new domains for competition over territorial control',[51] even as migration integrated the dry upland areas and the river valleys of Kāvēri and Tāmraparaṇi. By the fifteenth century, agrarian expansion not only took place in the naturally wet areas but also in the dry zones through artificial irrigation technology, especially tank and well irrigation. Landowners and peasants alike, each in their domain of capital and labour respectively supported the implementation of the new technology, particularly in the black

[48] Breckenridge (1985), 'Social Storage and Extension of Agriculture in South India, 1350 to 1750', p. 44.

[49] Bayly (1992), *Saints, Goddesses and Kings*, pp. 42–55.

[50] Ludden (1989), *Peasant History in South India*, p. 51; Breckenridge (1985), 'Social Storage and Extension of Agriculture in South India, 1350 to 1750', p. 45.

[51] David Ludden, *Peasant History in South India*, p. 46.

soil region. However, in these dry upland zones the agriculturists came into conflict with the social group of hunters and pastoralists, and the encounter often led to the latter being assimilated into the agricultural community. These changes enabled the emergence of a warrior peasant class, both economically and politically powerful, and primarily non-*brāhmaṇa* and Telugu in composition. The settlement of the migratory Telugu or the Vaḍuga groups in the central Deccan and the Tamil wet regions often displaced the older Tamil peasants and landholders, especially *brāhmaṇas* already settled there, and created a new class of landed magnates and new groups of artisans and merchants. Further, some of the locally entrenched *Vēḷāḷa* landed communities emerged as big landowners with titles such as *nāḍudaiyan* or *nadalvan*. Local and migrant landed communities customarily paid regular tribute to the Telugu commanders of the Vijayanagar army, and allied themselves with the local chieftains. In this context, the *Reḍḍi*s, *Vēḷāḷa*s, *Gavunḍa*s, and *Manrāḍi*s further enhanced their position as the dominant strata of peasantry, and acquired armed power. Further, new networks of relations were forged between the dry upland zones and the wetland agricultural community. Thus, the whole of peninsular India witnessed a concerted warrior-peasant effort that culminated in a new regional order upheld through the coercive power of the new warrior kings.[52]

Each agricultural zone (dry, mixed, and wet) had a distinct social and material milieu. Kinship networks organized into specific caste groups were important for striking alliances and creating exchange networks in relation to control of agricultural production.[53] The *nāṭṭavar*s of the Cōḷa period, mainly *Vēḷāḷa*s bound by kinship ties, transformed themselves in the Vijayanagar period due to migrant flux and changes in the landholding system. The medieval configurations of the *nāḍu*s vanished, replaced by a set of sub-regions defined as the rural hinterlands of towns along major transport and communication routes.

By the fourteenth century, new changes in military technology were introduced through the *nāyaka*s as a military class. The older political and military elites based in the wet zones relied on these *nāyaka*s for protection. From late fourteenth century onwards, the *nāyaka*s became more influential, as they were 'protectors, patrons, and arbiters, whose

[52] Ibid., pp. 43–4.

[53] Ibid., p. 65.

power rested first on military might, and more essential in the long run on their resourcefulness in their transactions with the existing dominant elites in temples and local assemblies'.[54] The restructuring of the state administration further increased the power of the *nāyaka*s who by then had developed a strong local base and found ways to successfully bind together into a community the agriculturalists of the wet rice-belt and migrants who had not yet fully settled in the territory. They also encouraged commercial activities and often employed merchants and money-lenders in administration.[55] By the seventeenth century, independent *nāyaka* states emerged in Tiruchchirapalli, Madurai, and Tañjāvūr.

Amidst such ongoing politico-economic and social flux, religion proved to be a major stabilizing influence, and the religious domain was not just dominated by the religion of the *Vēḷāḷa*s and *brāhmaṇa*s. Against this backdrop of migration of various social groups and the growing power of the martial communities in both wet and dry areas, the worship of warrior goddesses became popular. This period registered a dramatic increase in the Amman shrines, which had become new cult centres for the *nāyaka*s and the *poligār*s.[56] These cult centres were associated with the particular lineage god who had a local appeal and also with big brāhmaṇical temples. This integration was effected through the concept of divine marriage that linked the two lineages (brāhmaṇical and non-brāhmaṇical), enabling a kinship network which the woman, in this case, the goddess, was both the 'lynchpin' of the connection between lineages, and the substrate of the new relationship. According to marriage norms within Dravidian kinship frameworks, the reciprocal exchange of gifts and resources took place for several generations.[57] Hence, a large

[54] Ibid., p. 45.

[55] For a detailed description of *nāyaka*s, see Karashima (1994), *Towards a New Formation: South Indian Society under Vijayanagar Rule*; and Karashima (2002), *A Concordance of Nāyakas: The Vijayanagar Inscriptions in South India*.

[56] Stein (1978), 'Temples in Tamil Country, 1300–1750 A.D.', in Stein (ed.), *South Indian Temples: An Analytical Consideration*, pp. 11–45; and Bayly (1992), *Saints, Goddesses and Kings*, pp. 27–30; Dutta (2003), 'The Politics of Religious Identity: A Muslim Goddess in the Śrīvaiṣṇava Community of South India', pp. 157–84.

[57] Hudson (1978), 'Siva, Minaksi, Visnu: Reflections on a Popular Myth in Madurai', in Stein (ed.), *South Indian Temples: An Analytical Reconsideration*, pp. 106–18; Trautmann (1981), *Dravidian Kinship*, pp. 91–315; Bayly (1992),

pantheon was created, comprising local/folk warrior gods and goddesses and the brāhmaṇical/classical deities of Śiva and Viṣṇu.[58] This schema embodied the devotional trajectory of a vast cross-section of society earlier linked primarily in a hierarchical manner through temple rituals. Further, non-brāhmaṇical *Vēḷāḷa* village priest also now participated along with *brāhmaṇa* priests in the ritual activities of the large temples that were thus closely linked with the village deities through a priestly network. The religious domain became more complex as some of the migratory groups carried their own gods and goddesses from outside the Tamil region into the new territories, and 'constructed a new temple, thereby creating a cross-section of worshippers beyond the locality and developing a network of inter-regional devotion and pilgrimage'.[59]

Such a scenario provided religious communities with many opportunities to consolidate their social base. The major agenda for the religious community was the integration of the diversities within the overarching community paradigm. In this context, the textual tradition whose evolution and structure has been discussed in the last chapter evolved a philosophy cutting across caste lines. The construction and consolidation of Śrīvaiṣṇava identity should be examined within the context of hagiographic myths and legends and temple ritual practices that attempted to maintain a delicate balance between the different groups of believers. Political and economic aspects of identity converged in the temples, which had become a central mechanism for developing agricultural policies and inter-community networks with the help of powerful temple-based sectarian leaders. The numerous endowments made by diverse social groups generated resources that were managed and invested by the temples in tank irrigation, through which territories of limited agricultural potential were transformed into zones of high-yielding mixed agriculture, the base of a flourishing trade in food and cash crops. Various temple centres linked the wet agricultural zones with the dry upland areas, and these links enabled Mēlkōṭe, Tirupati, Śrīraṅgam, Tañjāvūr, and so on, to emerge as major

---

Saints, Goddesses and Kings, pp. 39–40; Uberoi (ed.) (1993), *Family, Kinship and Marriage in India*, pp. 13–75; Kapadia (1995), *Siva and Her Sisters: Gender, Caste, and Class in Rural South India*, pp. 2–67.

[58] Susan Bayly (1992), *Saints, Goddesses and Kings*, pp. 31–3.

[59] Ibid., p. 39.

nodes of Śrīvaiṣṇavism where sectarian leaders were able to systematically exert their strength.

It is worth examining the relationship between the temples' primary benefactors (the Vijayanagar rulers and chiefs) and the sectarian leaders enmeshed in temple politics. On one hand, both needed and took support from each other; on the other hand, sectarian rulers used the temple as a base for building power, and were also in a position to make endowments. Arjun Appadurai identifies an asymmetrical relationship between the rulers and the sectarian groups:[60] while the rulers conferred honour as well as resources in the form of gifts upon the latter, the latter in turn only rendered honour to the rulers. Despite such an asymmetrical relation, the state still patronized the temples for two reasons. First, the state was not interested in directly investing the crucial domain of irrigation, for this brought the additional responsibility of providing labour and managing finances, activities that sectarian leaders, with their social influence, could perform more capably. Two, gifting to the temple and its functionaries was an act of merit that was inevitably recorded and eulogized in the inscriptions. However, the underlying motive was to gain the greatest possible access to the temple and be a part of the ceremonial framework that included other social groups over which the *rāya*s and chiefs wanted to assert control. The temple and its functionaries were instrumental in legitimizing their benefactors' political authority, and festivals and pilgrimages became were important occasions for the enactment of this ritual association. The donees were regularly honoured with a part of the donated foodstuffs, which were then sold and the proceeds reinvested in irrigation-based activities.

In this context, the notion of a lineage emanating from the Āḻvārs, Rāmānuja, and even Rāmānuja's close disciples became significant. The hagiographies through their narratives in addition to delineating Rāmānuja as the most important *ācārya* also delineated the disciples of Rāmānuja as prominent *ācārya*s on the basis of their avowed proximity to him. Therefore, associating or attaching to one of the ancestries of these Āḻvārs and *ācārya*s on the part of the Śrīvaiṣṇava religious leaders provided a reference point to project themselves as legitimate religious authority and lay claim over the temple resources and hon-

60 Appadurai (1981), *Worship and Conflict under Colonial Rule*, pp. 63–104.

ours. For instance, the Uttama Nambis and Kanḍāḍais claiming to be descendants of Periyāḻvār and Mudaliāṉḍāṉ (one of the earliest and closest disciples of Rāmānuja) respectively emerged prominently in the Raṅganāthasvāmī temple at Śrīraṅgam during the Vijayanagr period. A brief discussion on the Kanḍāḍais will be taken up in Chapter 5 in the context of their non-brāhmaṇa disciples and their administrative position in the temple. With reference to the family of Uttama Nambis, the fifteenth-century epigraphs provide several instances of their prominence as *sthānika*s (managers) of the temple, conducting festivals, installing images, receiving several honours and land grants, supervising repairs and constructions and donating horses, gold, and other valuables lavishly to the temples.[61] The details in one of the inscriptions show the bargaining power of the Uttama Nambi *vis-à-vis* the Vijayanagar ruler. The inscription recorded that the Uttama Nambi who was then the *Sthānika* of the temple at Śrīraṅgam made a representation to the king for restoration of some concessions customarily granted to the *Sthānika* on a particular occasion. It was further reported that a royal order was passed to that effect and in addition, the king granted to Uttama Nambi a village, some tax-free land in another village, temple honours and enjoined the officials to execute all orders given by Uttama Nambi with regard to the temple, indicating the acknowledgement of absolute power to be enjoyed by the latter in the temple administration.[62] In another one such instance, Uttama Nambi along with the *maṭha* head, Śrīraṅganārāyaṇa Jīyar, made a representation to the king for a gift of land in four villages. This epigraph highlighted the nexus between the Vijayanagar ruler, religious leaders, and *maṭhadhipati*. It tells us that Uttama Nambi had instituted a service in the temple in honour of Vijayanagar ruler Devarāya Mahārāya I. In return, Uttama Nambi and his brother Chakrarāya were made the agents of the temple, exempted from the payment of the taxes on the land granted in the four villages, received remunerations in cash and kind and a share in the contributions to the temple from these villages.[63] The importance of Uttama Nambi is further accentuated in the epigraphs as a signatory to

[61] *South Indian Inscriptions*, Vol. XXIV, Nos 306, 307, 313, 319, 323–5, 329, 331.

[62] Ibid., No. 309. No dates given.

[63] Ibid., No. 310. No dates given.

land transactions along with Śrīraṅganārāyaṇa Jīyar and some powerful chiefs.[64]

Therefore, the power of the sectarian leaders grew with the generation of resources on such a massive scale and control over it. The sectarian leaders imitated the royal paraphernalia and behaved like minor kings themselves. Despite these ongoing fractures, oppositions, and appropriations, temple, king, and religious leaders were symbiotically linked in apparent service to deity and community. Śrīvaiṣṇava *bhakti* as formulated by Rāmānuja provided a distinctive symbolic umbrella, providing political benefactors the necessary wide orbit of collective influence and, as frequently reiterated in the hagiographies, offering an integrative paradigm of community.[65]

RELIGIOUS COMPLEX AND ŚRĪRAṄGAM: THE CENTRE OF THE ŚRĪVAIṢṆAVA COMMUNITY

Within the *guruparamparā* texts, the Raṅganāthasvāmī temple at Śrīraṅgam emerged as the most important sacred centre for the Śrīvaiṣṇavas in general, and for the activities of Rāmānuja as the community's supreme *ācārya* in particular. Historically, both the temple and the town were based on religious ideologies and identities, and politically legitimated structures of power and dominance. All these factors generated processes from within that enabled Śrīraṅgam to grow as a centre of trade as well as a sacred centre, with a focus on urbanization. From the period of Kulōttunga Cōḷa I till Hoysala rule was established in the Tamil region, that is, from the eleventh to the fourteenth centuries, Śrīraṅgam and its temple catalyzed the growth of a large prosperous hinterland which created a complex economy and raised the Śrīvaiṣṇava community to a position of religious and economic significance in the region. Between the eleventh and the twelfth centuries, the temple functioned as a prominent negotiator in land transactions in which large parcels were bought, sold, and leased out for paddy cultivation. This was also the time when *brahmadeya*s were on decline.

[64] Ibid., No. 328, *c.*1432 CE.

[65] Breckenridge (1985), 'Social Storage and Extension of Agriculture in South India, 1350 to 1750', pp. 55–6.

The migration of new groups into the Kāvēri region, and the consolidation of the already settled sections of the population there had an effect on Śrīraṅgam. Commanding the allegiance of various local groups, the institution of Raṅganātha temple generated diverse economic activities that eventually became the basis of systematic urbanization. Within this context, the land transactions made by the temple at Śrīraṅgam play a crucial role in developing a hinterland that had the capacity of generating a surplus. Most of the villages being gifted, bought, and sold were in the Cōḷamaṇḍalam area, the hinterland including the Tiruchchirapalli, Maṉṉārguḍi, Lālguḍi, Kumbhakōṉam, and Tañjāvūr regions—all wet fertile areas draining into the Kāvēri. Occasionally, the temple directly leased land to tenant agriculturists, *kanmis* for a fixed period in return for a stipulated amount of paddy.[66] The ongoing involvement of the pastoral community through gifts of cows and agricultural products indicated that the hinterland may have included the agro-pastoral zone along with the wet areas of cultivation. Both the temple and town of Śrīraṅgam expanded their resource base, and there is epigraphic evidence of the wealth they generated. One inscription, for instance, refers to the temple giving loans to the *sabhā*s of *brahmadeya*s in decline, like Candralekhaicaturvedīmaṅgalam, whose leaders attempted to pay back their debt by selling their own land.

The Pāṉṭiya occupation of the deltaic region in the fourteenth century caused an expansion of the fertile hinterland, as part of its territory was being gifted from areas of Pāṉṭiyanāḍu, especially from the wet regions of the Tāmbraparaṇi river valley. Pāṉṭiyan records at Śrīraṅgam document the creation of new *brahmadeya*s carved out of the older ones like the Vikramacōḷacaturvedīmaṅgalam. This was clearly an attempt to restructure and reorder village settlement patterns and establish political control. Like the Cōḷa *brahmadeya*s, the new Pāṉṭiya entities commemorated different rulers, for instance, Kaliyugarāmancaturvedīmangalam, Koḍaṇḍarāmacaturvedīmaṅgalam, and Ravivarmacaturvedīmaṅgalam, named for Jaṭāvarman Sundara Pāṉṭiya. House-sites, pathways, and land grants were given to the *brāhmaṇa*s inhabiting these *brahmadeya*s, and Pāṉṭiyan records clearly stipulate that should an occasion arise for the donees to sell the land assigned to them, transactions should be confined to their own community or to the Bhāgavatas.

66 *South Indian Inscriptions*, vol. XXIV, no. 36.

Such a rearrangement of the hinterland, where new *brahmadeyas* were created from the villages of the older ones, and the development of Śrīraṅgam reflect the changing socio-economic context. By the twelfth and the thirteenth centuries, new political and agricultural groups, especially from the dry upland areas of Deccan, migrated towards the fertile deltaic region forcing a need for new avenues of agrarian expansion. Consequently, focus shifted to the area around Śrīraṅgam which, apart from a favourable ecology, had the prior distinction of being an important Śrīvaiṣṇava centre. This fundamental reconfiguration of the hinterland began in the late eleventh century and gathered momentum in the thirteenth and the fourteenth centuries with the conquest of Śrīraṅgam by the Pāṉṭiyas. The new dynasty immediately sought to alter and broaden the administrative arrangement within the temple as well as its social base by involving more groups, including a large number of non-brāhmaṇas, in contrast to the previous system in which temple affairs were entirely in the hands of one group of functionaries. This politically strategic reorganization was also an economic necessity, for both town and temple were entirely dependent on the administration's systematic and steady extraction of agricultural surplus from the hinterland. A large number of land grants were made by various political groups who also instituted temple services in their names. Dynastic genealogies, for instance, of the Telugu Cōḷas, and accounts of battle victories, for instance, of the Sundara Pāṉṭiya over the Hoysala king Somēśvara, were inscribed on the temple walls. Inscriptional evidences refer to various mercantile groups making land grants to the temple. The *Kudiraiceṭṭis*, a horse-dealer community from Malaimaṇḍalam, were the major donors, and some temple inscriptions record gifts of gold by '*Paradesi-savāsi* merchants', probably a group of itinerant traders. The *kaikkōḷas*, a weaver community, as mentioned before, appear to have been temple servitors. By the fourteenth century Śrīraṅgam was a significant node of regional power, and the temple of Raṅganātha had evolved as an institution for new mechanisms of political legitimation and a conduit for political as well as socio-religious expediency.

Śrīvaiṣṇava religious ideology, as mirrored in its textual tradition that developed during this period, represented a major cultural confluence, with the integration of the Tamil hymns of the Āḻvārs, the Viśiṣṭādvaitic philosophy of Rāmānuja, and adoption of the *Pañcarātra* system of worship that brought together the Tamil and Sanskrit traditions. With regard to this new liturgical cohesion, the hagiographic delineations of Rāmānuja confirm his importance as a spiritual and community leader in Śrīraṅgam, where he protested against social hierarchy and introduced other modes of reform, such as the sharing of ritual space by non-brāhmaṇa devotees. From the end of the twelfth century onwards, Śrīraṅgam was the backdrop of all Śrīvaiṣṇava religious activities, theological as well as liturgical, and the evolution of the charismatic figure of Rāmānuja coincided with the emergence of new groups in search of new ways to consolidate and legitimize their political and social presence. Moreover, a favourable ecology made Śrīraṅgam and its surrounding areas ideal for the development for agrarian resources. Patronage by the political elite and prosperous merchant groups, gifts of land as sites for temple ceremonies such as recitation of the hymns, especially the *Tiruvāymoḷi*, and for celebration of festivals and ritual activities enhanced the social role and function of the temple, and from the thirteenth century onwards, the Śrīvaiṣṇava *brāhmaṇa*s became increasingly entrenched in the temple administration. All these developments (economic, political, and ideological) gave Śrīraṅgam the character of a religious town that was a major pilgrimage centre for the Śrīvaiṣṇava community. Inscriptions record pilgrims from Kāśmīradeśa (north India) and Malaināḍu, and also document the town/temple visits of important sectarian leaders. In textual terms, the Āḻvār hymns had accorded primacy to Śrīraṅgam, and the hagiographies, while mapping 108 *divyadesa* particularly highlighted the sacredness of Śrīraṅgam as a pilgrimage site and extolled its association with Rāmānuja. In fact, the entire pilgrimage narrative is punctuated with references to Rāmānuja's organizational and intellectual activities at Śrīraṅgam. The ideological framework of *ubhaya vedānta*, along with various social, economic, and political processes, accommodated a diverse population of *bhakta*s, although in a hierarchical manner. This was evident in the layout of the settlement, where the religious and political elites were—and still are—based in proximity to the sanctum, with quarters within the inner four temple walls; lower-caste groups such as artisans, craftsmen, and temple servants live further away, within the three outer walls.

Two socio-political trends emerged in association with Śrīraṅgam in the fourteenth century, and remained prevalent, particularly after the establishment of the Vijayanagar Empire. First, as discussed earlier in this chapter, a crucial and expedient relationship developed between sectarian leaders and new political groups. Second, there was a crystallization and assertion of caste identities, an instance being the self-identification of merchants as '*Traivarṇika*', that is, of *vaiśya* caste; another instance is the increased presence of Śāttada Śrīvaiṣṇavas, a group of non-brāhmaṇas who worked in the temple as well as at the *Rāmānujakutams* (feeding houses where pilgrims collected). Both trends are reflected in the hagiographers' continual emphasis on the low-caste status of the Āḻvārs, the irrelevance of caste for salvation, and the social reforms instituted by Rāmānuja.

Like Śrīraṅgam, there were other temple centres which were of importance to the Śrīvaiṣṇavas and hagiographical association of Rāmānuja with these sites further enhanced their importance. These were the temple centres at Mēlkōṭe, Tirupati, and Kāñcīpuram. Situated in the Mandya district of Karnataka, Mēlkōṭe emerges in the hagiographical sources as an area developed by Rāmānuja while in exile as he was escaping the persecution of the Cōḷa ruler. Further, the narratives tell us that Rāmānuja went to Karnataka through Toṇṇūru and Sāligrāma and finally established the Nārāyaṇasvāmī temple at Mēlkōṭe.[67] We are also told that Rāmānuja's sojourn brought this part of Karnataka, which was initially populated by the Jainas within the ambit of Śrīvaiṣṇavism.[68] By the fourteenth century, the legends of Rāmānuja's visit to Mēlkōṭe were well known and this association enhanced the temple's importance in the local as well as supra-local Śrīvaiṣṇavas organizational network. For instance:

> On the northern bank of Sahyajā (Kāvēri), on the Nārāyaṇagiri which is much higher than all the places, dwells god Nārāyaṇa himself. The command of Yatirāja (Rāmānuja) which is borne on the head by the virtuous, which is the crusher of evil doctrines, is not easy to grasped [sic] by the dull.[69]

Like in other temple centres, Rāmānuja was the source of legitimacy and credibility for the temple organization, rituals, and festivals

[67] *Epigraphia Carnatica. Vol. VIII (Mysore Archaeological Series)*. 1889–1955; Gopal (1983), *Sri Ramanuja in Karnataka*, pp. 3–39.

[68] The epigrahical evidences of the fourteenth century already reflect the contribution of Rāmānuja towards Mēlkōṭe in their introductory part (i.e., the *praśasti*). Most of them commence with the formulaic, 'Obeisance to illustrious Rāmānuja' (*subham astu śrī Rāmānujāya namah*).

[69] No. 32 in Gopal (1983), *Sri Ramanuja in Karnataka*, p. 128.

of Mēlkōṭe. For example, the temple functionaries that is,—the group of fifty-two as well as the *maṭha* itself traced their lineage through their respective association with Rāmānuja. These fifty-two referred as *tirukulattār* in the hagiographies were supposed to be non-brāhmaṇas, who were given access to the temple and its administration by none other than Rāmānuja himself. Most of the inscriptions refer to the fifty-two as the 'establishers of the philosophy of Rāmānuja, first disciples of the establishers of the Vedic religion, terror to conjurers, confounder of the maintenance of doctrine of illusion, establisher of the six *darśanas* Rāmānujācārya, worshippers of the divine feet of god Tirunārāyaṇa of Yādavagiri'.[70] The epigraphical evidence shows that by the time Vijayanagar Empire was established in the fourteenth century, they had already emerged as a significant group in the Nārāyaṇasvāmī temple.

Similarly, the temple centres at Kāñcīpuram and Tirupati developed into strong local bases for the sectarian leaders and their institutional organizations and drew numerous followers from all over South India. Our discussion till now has already underscored the significance of these two places in the hagiographical narratives on the Śrīvaiṣṇava in general and Rāmānuja in particular. These two centres along with Śrīraṅgam, from the twelfth and the thirteenth centuries onwards emerged as the source of the network of control that spread and crossed the Tamil as well as the southern border and subsequently by the fourteenth and the fifteenth centuries, provided a strong institutional base to the Śrīvaiṣṇava religious leaders. For instance, important Śrīvaiṣṇava families like the Tātācāryas, Kanḍāḍais, and Uttamanambis and the *maṭhas* developed their power base in these two centres. From fourteenth century onwards, the development of the Veṅkateśvara temple at Tirumala-Tirupati as a major centre of pilgrimage and Śrīvaiṣṇava activities was due to the royal patronage of the Vijayanagar Empire. The epigraphical reference mentions numerous *jīyars* and *Vaidika brāhmaṇas*—all of whom at different points of time exercised some kind of control over the temple organization. Many of them came from regions outside Tirupati. For example, the Kanḍāḍais came from Śrīraṅgam. Even the *maṭhas* at Naṅguneri, Tirukkuruṅguḍi, and Āḻvār Tirunagari appear to be donors at Tirumala-Tirupati. This highlights the institutional significance of the temple for the Śrīvaiṣṇava community identity, as these *maṭhas* of the

70 *Epigraphia Carnatica*, vol. VIII, no. 134, 140, and so on.

southernmost regions did not seem to figure in the other two temple centres (viz., Kāñcīpuram and Śrīraṅgam). The Periya Jīyar *maṭha* and the Cinna Jīyar *maṭha* based at Tirumala-Tirupati also drew followers from all over South India.

Thus, this chapter attempted to analyse the historical context of the hagiographies that also influenced the context within them. The hagiographies registered a reaction and their respective narratives were a comment on the historical context, which were either conforming to the context or subverting it or both, depending on the situation. However, amidst all these representations there was an agenda to evolve an ideal that would outlive the context. In addition to the exegetic ideal that was articulated in the textual tradition, these hagiographies were also articulating a spatial ideal in which areas like Śrīraṅgam, Kāñcīpuram, Tirupati, and Mēlkōṭe amongst others, were delineated as sacred. Often referred as Vaikuṇṭha (the heavenly abode of Viṣṇu), these areas had a historical trajectory of their own in which the religious context was also enmeshed. Some of these regions were already a part of the sacred geography of the Śrīvaiṣṇavas, but with the changing political geography and state interventions in the institutional development of *brahmadeyas*, temples, and *maṭhas*, these areas became crucial for the resource base of the Śrīvaiṣṇavas, a point that the hagiographies did not miss. The historical reality of the contesting claims was recorded in the narratives but with the purpose of representing the superiority of the tradition. Rāmānuja was always victorious, God intervened invariably on his behalf and redeemed the situation and finally everybody had to acquiesce to Rāmānuja's religious authority and, by that extension, to the Śrīvaiṣṇava ideal. Reminiscent of the motifs of the political conquest, these hagiographical narratives delineated Rāmānuja as the most important *ācārya* of the community—a theme that will be discussed in the next chapter.

CHAPTER FOUR

Rāmānuja as an Ācārya

Myself with Śrī is the highest reality. Difference (between the self and Myself) is the doctrine acceptable to Me. Self-surrender or *prapatti* is the infallible means (for *mokṣa*). Remembrance of Me during the last moments (of one's life) is not necessary. Release from bondage (is certain) at the end of life (to those who have taken to *prapatti*). Mahāpūrṇa is the respectable *ācārya*.

Yatirāja Vaibhavam, śloka 40

Yatirāja then composed the *Vedārthasaṅgraha*, and the *Vedāntasāra, Vedāntadīpa*, and the *Śrībhāṣya* for the *Vedāntasūtra* and a gloss on the *Gītā* and taught them to Vātsyeśa and others.

Yatirāja Vaibhavam, ślokas 70[1]

[1] Both the *ślokas* are cited from *Yatirāja Vaibhavam of Āndhrapūrṇa* (*Vaṭuka Nambi*), V. Varadachariar (ed.), 1978. In the case of the translated *ślokas* quoted in the main text, the particular edition will be cited in the references. Otherwise, the references of the specific *śloka* or *ślokas* cited in the footnotes pertain to both the editions.

This chapter describes various *guruparamparā* themes that contributed to inscribing Rāmānuja as an unsurpassed exegete and supreme *ācārya* of the Śrīvaiṣṇava community. The hagiographies are unanimous about the fundamental concepts of Śrīvaiṣṇava exegesis: (*a*) Viṣṇu with his consort embodies the ultimate truth; (*b*) *Jīva* (individual self) is separate from Brahman (Supreme Being); (*c*) those surrendering themselves completely to him, i.e., practising *prapatti*, will attain *mokṣa*, or be released from earthly bondage and the cycle of rebirth; and (*d*) the act of remembering God in the last moments of one's life is not necessary for one's salvation/emancipation.

In the hagiographies of Rāmānuja, the most important *ācārya* of the Śrīvaiṣṇava community, these ideas are explicated by none other than Lord Viṣṇu himself. The primary site for the transmission of the exegesis was the Varadarāja temple at Kāñcīpuram, where Rāmānuja spent his early years before becoming a renunciate and migrating to Śrīraṅgam. The hagiographies tell us that Rāmānuja wanted to become Tirukacci Nambi's disciple. Tirukacci Nambi was a non-*brāhmaṇa* Śrīvaiṣṇava devotee and served Lord Varadarāja by fanning him regularly at Kāñcīpuram. Referred to as *gajendra dāsa*, narratives associated Tirukacci Nambi as the disciple of Ālavandar or Yāmuna, who was during that time the *ācārya* at Raṅganāthasvāmī temple at Śrīraṅgam. This association also highlighted the Śrīvaiṣṇava network between Kāñcīpuram and Śrīraṅgam. Rāmānuja, we are told, one day went to Tirukacci Nambi's *maṭha* and requested him to convey to the Lord certain questions that bothered him. He further urged Tirukacci Nambi to communicate to him the Lord's reply. Tirukacci Nambi meditated upon the Lord, connected with Him, posed Rāmānuja's queries, and conveyed the Lord's reply (which has been cited at the beginning of this chapter) to Rāmānuja.[2]

Thus, the significance of these ideas was highlighted by locating them in the portion or the chapter dealing with the biography of Rāmānuja through a *guru* whose position of authority, despite being a non-*brāhmaṇa*, was represented on the basis of his direct communication with god. Through the life story of Rāmānuja, Śrīvaiṣṇava exegesis was transmitted and the revelation of each exegetical aspect was contextualized in

[2] *Divyasūricaritam*, Ch. 17, *śloka*s 48–54; *Āṟāyirappaṭi*, pp. 167–8; *Muāyirappaṭi*, p. 88.

a separate narrative—all of which converged to delineate Rāmānuja as the most significant *ācārya* of the community. This chapter's epigraphs summarize the crucial constituents of Śrīvaiṣṇava exegesis and its association with Rāmānuja and his doctrinal compositions themselves.[3]

The first section will discuss the larger hagiographical trends that specifically modelled Rāmānuja as an exemplar/ideal for the subsequent *ācārya*s of the Śrīvaiṣṇava community, reflecting the worldview and general expectations of an ordinary Śrīvaiṣṇava in relation to the qualities desirable in an *ācārya*. The second section describes the polemics and sectarianism in the hagiographies that demarcated an exclusive Śrīvaiṣṇava territory in the domain of metaphysics by projecting Rāmānuja to be an intellectually superior exegete. The third section demonstrates the narrative strategies through which the entire Śrīvaiṣṇava tradition came to be embodied in the representations of Rāmānuja. The fourth section will discuss the hagiographic accounts of Rāmānuja's activities in relation to the spread of the community networks and their ramifications for Śrīvaiṣṇava identity. Section five analyzes the textual devices through which particular *stotra*s that have always been a part of the everyday domestic as well as liturgical practices in the Śrīvaiṣṇava community memorialize Rāmānuja as an *ācārya*.

Thus, these narratives in the hagiographies composed between the twelfth and fifteenth centuries, while engaged in bringing together the discrete ideas and practices within a particular Viśiṣṭādvaita–Śrīvaiṣṇava frame, were also attempting to create a distinct tradition and an ideal community, providing a template for the subsequent generations.

RĀMĀNUJA AS AN *ĀCĀRYA*: IDEAS, IMAGE, AND THE ŚRĪVAIṢṆAVA COMMUNITY

Rāmānuja is known to be one of the most important thinkers in Indian philosophy. His seminal contribution is the theistic interpretation of Vedānta/Upaniṣadic ideas. These interpretations have placed Rāmānuja

[3] The *Divyasūricaritam* adds the *Gadyatraya* and *Nityānuṣṭhāna* or *Bhagvadāradhāna* (manual of daily worship) to Rāmānuja's compositions. See *Divyasūricaritam*, Ch. 18, *śloka*s 10. For the question of authenticity, i.e., whether some of these works were actually authored by Rāmānuja, see Carman (1981), *The Theology of Rāmānuja*, pp. 18–23.

amongst the intellectually important philosophers such as Śaṅkara, Madhava, and Vallabhācārya. The *Śribhāṣya*, Rāmānuja's commentary on the *Vedāntasūtras*, has been regarded as a decisive work that interpreted Vedānta within the ideological framework of Vaiṣṇava thought, countering the idea of oneness of Brahman (Supreme Being) and *jīva* (the individual soul) postulated by Śaṅkara's Advaita. This major reworking of a core metaphysical argument was undoubtedly the origin of the Śrīvaiṣṇava exaltation of Rāmānuja as a supreme *ācārya*. As stated in a popular modern biography of Rāmānuja:

> Sri Rāmānuja (1017–1137 A.D.) is chronologically second in the line of three celebrated scholar-saints of South India who made significant and lasting contributions to the revival of Hinduism. Sri Śankara who systematized the Advaita philosophy and Sri Madhva who advocated the Dvaita Philosophy appeared a little before and after Rāmānuja, respectively. All these three noble souls re-established and revitalized the Vedāntic thought after a thorough and systematic refutation of the non-Vedic systems like Jainism and Buddhism. They also successfully repulsed the pure conservative Vedic ritualism of the Mimamsakas and upheld the validity of the metaphysical speculations of the Upanishads.[4]

Though Rāmānuja's ideas are systematized under the philosophical term 'Viśiṣṭādvaita', he never used this term himself for his own philosophy. Neither does one find it in the *Divyasūricaritam, Yatirāja Vaibhavam, Āṟāyirappaṭi*, or *Muāyirappaṭi. Divyasūricaritam* narrates that Goṣṭhīpūrna declared, 'From today this *Haridarśana* will be named after you (Rāmānuja)', and the other three texts use the term, *Lakṣmaṇa darśanam, Emperumānār darśanam*, and *Rāmānuja siddhānta*, respectively, for Rāmānuja's theology.[5] It has been suggested that in the post-Rāmānuja period, the Śrīvaiṣṇava commentators such as Sudarśana Sūrī and Vedāntadeśika used the term 'Viśiṣṭādvaita' to describe Rāmānuja's ideas.[6] Interestingly, Madhva's *Sarvadarśanasaṃgraha*, a description of various philosophical systems probably written during the sixteenth

4 Narasimhachary (2007 [2004]), *Makers of Indian Literature: Sri Ramanuja*, p. 9.

5 *Divyasūricaritam*, Ch. 18, *śloka* 3; *Yatirāja Vaibhavam*, *śloka* 59; *Āṟāyirappaṭi*, p. 195; *Muāyirappaṭi*, p. 96.

6 Narasimhachary, (2007 [2004]), *Makers of Indian Literature*, p. 14.

century, also uses the term *Rāmānuja darśanam* ('the Rāmānuja system') for this particular metaphysical framework.[7]

Rāmānuja darśanam, later called 'Viśiṣṭādvaita', presented an alternative model for the perception of god in which the divine (in this case, Viṣṇu) had attributes—in other words, Brahman was *saguṇa*, not *nirguṇa* (without attributes) as posited in Advaita. Through this mode of 'qualified monism', Viśiṣṭādvaita countered the Advaita theory of undivided, immutable oneness as the nature of the Absolute. Unequivocally theistic, Viśiṣṭādvaita emphasized that though the individual soul was inherently one with Brahman, in ontological terms it was separate and had a conscious existence of its own. The qualities of the Absolute were characterized by both immanence (*paratva*) and transcendence (*saulabhya*), this simultaneity making him accessible to an ordinary devotee who could then establish a personal relation with him. Unlike Śaṅkara, Rāmānuja advocated the fulfilment of the social obligations by an individual. The relation between man, god, and matter was characterized as *śarīra-śārīrī bhāva*, where 'the universe forms the "body" of the Lord, in a metaphorical sense. Like any physical body possessed by a living being the body of the Lord also, viz., the Universe, is invariably supported by Him for His exclusive benefit or Excellence'.[8]

Written in Sanskrit, Rāmānuja's ideas took the form of commentaries. Hence, there emerged a new literary genre within the Śrīvaiṣṇava textual tradition in which the exposition of religious philosophy took the form of elaborate interpretations and discourse. The hagiographies claimed that Sarasvatī, the goddess of learning and the arts, was so impressed with his prolific commentarial skills that she bestowed upon him the honorific term *bhāṣyakāra* and gifted him with the image of Hayagriva (a form of Visnu).[9] As a coherent system of ideas, Rāmānuja's *darśana*, which soon acquired authority both within and outside the community and gave him an exalted status, placed Śrīvaiṣṇavism on an equal footing with other religious traditions, especially the Advaita-Vedānta tradition

[7] Madhava Acharya, *The Sarva-Darśana-Saṃgraha* (1961; trans. E.B. Cowell and A.E. Gough), pp. 64–86.

[8] Narasimhachary (2007 [2004]), *Makers of Indian Literature*, pp. 13–14. Also see Carman (1981), *The Theology of Rāmānuja*, pp. 65–124, and Julius Lipner (1986), *The Face of Truth: A Study of Meaning and Metaphysics in the Vedāntic Theology of Rāmānuja*, pp. 63–96.

[9] *Yatirāja-Vaibhavam, śloka* 88; *Āṟāyirappaṭi*, p. 226; *Muāyirappaṭi*, p. 106.

which had already developed a systematic theology by the twelfth century. In fact, the commentarial tradition in the post-Rāmānuja period, comprising the various textual metaphysical expositions, engaged with his ideas and structured their polemics on its basis. Consequently, different opinions emerged that often became the basis of the schism into the Vaṭakaḷai and Teṉkaḷai.[10]

Since the Śrīvaiṣṇava *brāhmaṇas* primarily constituted the hagiographers' target audience, it is to be expected that the focus of the hagiographies was the exhortation and vindication of the Vedic tradition. This was reinforced through the descriptions of his early life within the Vedic tradition. After Rāmānuja's ceremonial initiation into brahmanahood (rice-taking, boring of the earlobes, tonsure, and investiture with the sacred thread), the texts laud his prodigious intellect. Rāmānuja's precocity was evident when at an early age he mastered the Vedas and the Vedānta.[11] The hagiographers also exalted Rāmānuja through emphasizing his status of renunciate, considered the highest spiritual attainment and one that additionally was an essential qualification for the position of an exemplary Śrīvaiṣṇava *ācārya*. Repeated reference to Rāmānuja as *Yatirāja* ('Lord of Renunciates') and the title of the hagiography *Yatirāja Vaibhavam* demonstrates the importance of formal renunciation as both a spiritual virtue and ideal and, by extension, the exalted position of renunciates in the acaryic lineage.

The initiation of Rāmānuja into the world of *sanyāsi* or *yati* (equivalent to an ascetic) was described in a dramatic way. The narratives tell us that Rāmānuja was very upset with his wife after she humiliated the wives of his *gurus*, Mahāpūrṇa/Periya Nambi and Kāñcīpūrṇa/Tirukacci Nambi. Deeply distressed, he became a *sanyāsin*, left his family, donned saffron robes, took the *tridaṅḍin* (the three-pointed staff) and also retained the signifiers of brahmanhood—the sacred thread and the tuft of hair.[12] This was in sharp contrast to practices of *sanyāsa* at Advaita and Śaiva *maṭhas* in south India, whose members had to commit to lifelong

[10] For instance, Vedāntadeśika's *Śataduṣaṇī*. See Chari (2004 [1961]), *Advaita and Viśiṣṭadvaita*, pp. 1–18.

[11] *Divyasūricaritam*, Ch. 17, *ślokas* 1-9; *Yatirāja-Vaibhavam*, pp. 9–11; *Āṟāyirappaṭi*, pp. 140–1; *Muāyirappaṭi*, p. 73.

[12] *Divyasūricaritam*, Ch. 17, *ślokas* 69–71; *Yatirāja Vaibhavam*, *ślokas* 51; *Āṟāyirappaṭi*, pp. 173–4; *Muāyirappaṭi*, p. 91.

celibacy and renounce all physical markers of *varṇa* status and social affiliation. Therefore, the status of the renunciate was articulated not in contradiction to the status of a householder. Rather, it exhibited consistency with the brāhmaṇical ideals. From the texts it appears that the essential qualifications for becoming an *ācārya* and head of the *maṭha* were that the candidate should be a *brāhmaṇa* well versed in the Vedas and Vedānta, a householder, and preferably belonging to an important Śrīvaiṣṇava *brāhmaṇa* lineage. Further, Rāmānuja's commentaries on the *Vedāntasūtras*, *Bhagavad Gītā*, and the *Upaniṣads* from the perspective of Viśiṣṭādvaita still conformed to the larger Vedāntic tradition, thus providing the Śrīvaiṣṇava community with a metaphysical space to identify with and articulate within. Combining the perfections of a superior exegete and a *sanyāsin*, the figure of Rāmānuja easily lent itself to the hagiographic project of delineating a charismatic Śrīvaiṣṇava *ācārya* who was also an exalted leader of the community.[13]

However, it must be emphasized here that Rāmānuja's intellectual genius as a theorist and commentator did not make him exceptional. After all, these paradigmatic discursive projects had been already undertaken by other commentators, such as Śaṅkara and Bhāskara before him. His singularity was derived from his spiritual zeal and stress on practices of personal devotion for the path-breaking transformation of the Śrīvaiṣṇava devotional community that expanded to include non-*brāhmaṇa* devotees along with its exclusive groups of brāhmaṇical disciples. Contextualized within the Vedantic traditions, this unambiguous democratization of spiritual culture was indeed considered a radical development.

The hagiographic delineation of Rāmānuja as an *ācārya* was also associated with the centrality of tradition in the evolution of community consciousness. As has been stated previously, the hagiographic construction of

[13] In this section, concepts about the delineation of Rāmānuja as a charismatic *ācārya* are drawn principally from analyses by Vasudha Dalmia, Heinrich Stietencron, and Friedhelm Hardy. See Dalmia, 'Introduction' in Dalmia et al. (eds) (2001), *Charisma and Canon: Essays on the Religious History of the Indian Subcontinent*, pp. 5–13; Stietencron (2001), 'Charisma and Canon: The Dynamics of Legitimization and Innovation in Indian Religions', pp. 14–38, in Dalmia et al. (eds) (2001), and Hardy, The 'Formation of Śrīvaiṣṇavism', pp. 41–59 in Dalmia et al. (eds) (2001).

the past was influenced by contemporary concerns, a process which began in the twelfth century. Rāmānuja was placed at the centre of this process as a charismatic religious leader whose position of authority was verified by virtue of his ideas being a part of the Vedāntic tradition.[14] Thus, the textual tradition in general and the hagiographies in particular were engaged in the process of creating a canon, codifying pre-existing ideas along with interpretations and comments of the codifier and modified and added to the structure of that tradition. This canon of which the *guruparamparā*s were a part constructed their narratives to legitimize Rāmānuja's status and charisma and reinforce his spiritual and social authority. Under these circumstances, the reworking of the tradition and tracing of an integrated *sampradāya* of preceptors in reverse order from the historical to the mythological—Rāmānuja to Yāmuna to Nāthamuni to Nammāḻvār and finally to Viṣṇu—could have been a mechanism of establishing claims over the rich temple resources and patronage. This explains the self-conscious attempt by the commentators and the hagiographers to synthesize the Tamil and Sanskritic strands of the *bhakti* tradition.

Could it be that there were competing groups present within the Raṅganāthasvāmī temple and the Śrīvaiṣṇava *brāhmaṇa*s engaged in evolving the tradition were the dominant amongst them or were trying to assert their domination? Tensions within the community over the control of the temple at Śrīraṅgam were obvious. The hagiographies make an oblique reference to the intensity of the rivalry that led to an unsuccessful attempt to poison Rāmānuja (who was at that time the *Śrīkāryam* of the temple), and Garuḍavāhana Paṇḍita was associated with Rāmānuja's attempt to restore order after the latter discovered the conspiracy. According to the *Divyasūricaritam*, after Rāmānuja discovered that milk and *jāmun*—a toxic combination—had been offered to the God, he punished the culprit. Thereafter, he installed a Dhanvantrī shrine and attached an *ārogyaśāla* to it. Rāmānuja then formally placed Garuḍavāhana Paṇḍita in charge of the *ārogyaśāla* and assigned him the daily task of offering the God the medicinal concoction that was to be prepared by him.[15] While the text seems to suggest that the offence was against the deity, the target of the crime was obviously none other

[14] Stietencron (2001), in Dalmia et al. (eds), *Charisma and Canon*, pp. 14–16.

[15] *Divyasūricaritam*, Ch. 17, *śloka*s 86–7.

than Rāmānuja. This incident was exclusive to *Divyasūricaritam*, whose author, Garuḍavāhana Paṉḍita, as discussed in Chapter 1 recorded it to legitimize his status and therefore does not appear in the other hagiographies. However, *Yatirāja Vaibhavam*, *Āṟāyirappaṭi*, and *Muāyirappaṭi* record yet another incident of an attempt to poison Rāmānuja:

> Then at one time, knowing the food *bhikṣā* (which an ascetic should receive from others) was mixed with poison (*kadācidviṣyukyabhikṣām*), Yatirāja fasted for three days. On hearing this, two eminent preceptors (Goṣthīpūrṇa and Mahāpūrṇa) reached Śrīraṅgam quickly from Goṣthīpūra. Those two preceptors asked Yatirāja who welcomed and bowed to them to accept daily the food certified (purified) by Praṇatārtihara who with great concern took care of his body. He (Yatirāja) too did accordingly.[16]

This Praṇatārtihara was Kiḍāmbiāccān Piḷḷai, one of the closest disciples of Rāmānuja from Tirupati, who after this incident in the hagiographies is declared as the bodyguard of Rāmānuja:

> When Uḍaiyavar (Rāmānuja) went to the *ghāts* to bathe, there was a crowd jostling against each other and trying to get close to him. One of them appointed a *gṛhasta* (householder) to give food that was mixed with poison to Uḍaiyavar. The *gṛhasta* asked his wife to do so and she refused. She then removed the poison, offered the food and prostrated before Rāmānuja. Rāmānuja was puzzled after accepting the offering, threw it in the Kāvēri and started fasting. Tirukacci Nambi came to know about this and by afternoon reached the *ghāts* to meet Rāmānuja. Rāmānuja with all the disciples prostrated before him. Tirukacci Nambi did not ask Rāmānuja to get up. Kiḍāmbiāccān Piḷḷai who was standing nearby was agitated and told Tirukacci Nambi that in this hot sand, not asking Rāmānuja to get up was too severe a test. Tirukacci Nambi was impressed with this attitude and said that he was looking for someone like Kiḍāmbiāccān Piḷḷai who was solicitous to Rāmānuja and commanded that thereafter Kiḍāmbiāccān Piḷḷai would be the only one who cooked for Rāmānuja.[17]

This episode was a potential reference point on the basis of which the descendants of Kiḍāmbiāccān Piḷḷai could claim their rights in the temple honours and resources in the later period.

[16] *Yatirāja Vaibhavam of Āndhrapūrṇa* (*Vaṭuka Nambi*), V. Varadachariar (ed.) 1978, *śloka*s 68–9.

[17] *Āṟāyirappaṭi*, pp. 202–3; Also see *Muāyirappaṭi*, p. 102.

Post-fourteenth-century hagiographies record that Tiruvaraṅgatta Amudanār, composer of the *Rāmānuja Nūṟṟandādi*, belonged to the rival group and attempted to poison Rāmānuja as he was envious of Rāmānuja's increasing influence. His conspiracy was discovered, but Rāmānuja forgave him and initiated him into the community. Certain stanzas in this *stotra* exhibit a penitential tone, with the composer lamenting that he had sinned, was deceitful, had committed terrible deeds of sin, committed misdeeds in the past, and was now completely won over by Rāmānuja:

> O Rāmānuja, Benevolent as the dark cloud! Who in this wide world can understand the nature of your grace? I was the very hotbed of sin. On your own you came and accepted me. Today your noble qualities are sweet as ambrosia to my lowly self's soul.[18]

Such portrayals of Rāmānuja as compassionate, pragmatic, and astute, a leader who could resolve disputes and unify the community, were necessary for the legitimation of the Śrīvaiṣṇava *brāhmaṇas*' claims to positions of authority and control over temple resources. These delineations of Rāmānuja as a charismatic and benevolent figure also mediated the important task of introducing innovations in the temple. The character of Rāmānuja as inscribed by hagiographers in this period became the focus of religious identities and negotiations for the subsequent period, and this was evident from the kinds of claims to religious authority being made by various groups, especially with regard to their respective genealogies or *ācāryaparamparās*. The origin of the lineage in most of the cases was traced to Rāmānuja. In this manner, each group with its individual lineage claimed to represent the legitimate Śrīvaiṣṇava tradition.

Thus, the competing factions and their hagiographers made concentrated efforts to project Rāmānuja as their own extraordinary and powerful preceptor, project a model of the ideal *guru* and *ācārya* that was based on his qualities and proximity to god. Early renderings of this ideal, found in the *Divyasūricaritam*, *Yatirāja Vaibhavam*, *Āṟāyirappaṭi*, and *Muāyirappaṭi*, were elaborated upon in the later texts that show a steady accretion of laudatory narratives around the figure of Rāmānuja. The textual strategies consisted of first highlighting Rāmānuja's extraordinary qualities and exalting him as an *ācārya* par excellence. Once this

[18] *Rāmānuja Nūṟṟandādi*, verse 25. See also verses 23–4 and 27.

was established, the hagiographers strategically introduced narratives of sectarianism, described changes in liturgy and rituals, questioned existing ideas, and revived older ones. Finally, they depicted Rāmānuja resolving conflicts and tensions by asserting his charismatic authority. These narratives reflected the anxieties and interests of certain groups with whom the hagiographers were associated; through the image of Rāmānuja they were putting forth their own agendas and claims, often questioning the existing traditions within and outside the Śrīvaiṣṇava community. Thus, Rāmānuja and his charisma became a reference point for the legitimate introduction of new motifs and trajectories. In addition, the hagiographic endeavour succeeded in generating the archetype of a particular behavioural pattern through stories of Rāmānuja's exemplary actions, a model of ideal behaviour in any circumstance. The narratives represented Rāmānuja as unflinchingly upholding the cause of Śrīvaiṣṇavism against all odds, even if this commitment meant fighting powerful rulers. The self was always secondary. Ever humble, he remained polite even in the most adverse and aggressive circumstances, however strong the provocation might be. Hence, such an exemplary behaviour reinforced his already sacred status (he was considered an incarnation of Ādiśeṣa). This ideal behaviour also came to represent Śrīvaiṣṇava virtues in general.[19]

On one hand, the *guruparamparā*s exalted Rāmānuja as extraordinary and exclusive; and on the other hand, they inscribed him as a just and compassionate figure, equally accessible to everyone. Clearly, the hagiographers were addressing two sets of audiences, each holding Rāmānuja as an exemplar in its worldview. One set were the elite *brāhmaṇa ācārya*s for whom Rāmānuja was the embodiment of an ideal leader of the community, and the other set were the common Śrīvaiṣṇava devotees for whom Rāmānuja was an ideal *guru*, so much so that the 'god and *guru* in their relation to the devotee tend to be exchangeable and almost identical'.[20] Through their construction of a particular image of Rāmānuja as an inspiring *ācārya* as well as an enlightened *guru* the hagiographers were trying to create a specific religious consciousness through community ideals, to be emulated, assimilated, and practised in a specific Śrīvaiṣṇava lifestyle. These values delineating Rāmānuja as an exemplar

[19] Hawley (1987), *Saints and Virtues*, pp. xiii–xviii.

[20] Stietencron (2001), in Dalmia et al. (eds), *Charisma and Canon*, p. 24.

in many ways contributed to the notion of an ideal Śrīvaiṣṇava. The *guruparamparā* narratives clearly asserted that Rāmānuja was second to none and that his ideas were the ultimate truth; no other interpretation could influence them.

One significant way of institutionalizing Rāmānuja as the most important *ācārya* of the community was the installation of his image in temples. The tradition informs us that Rāmānuja himself did this in his own lifetime:

> That chief of ascetics who had a host of disciples who were governed by *śāstras* and codes of good conduct, and well known for their good behaviour, was proffered a request by some (among them). And (hence) Yatirāja embraced three idols (of his) and ordered that they should be installed at Śrīraṅgam, Śrīperumbudūr and Yadugiri (Mēlkōṭe), giving them (idols) to them. May he, who is protecting the entire world, protect me with his glances.[21]
>
> Then Rāmānuja *muni* after instructing people in his ideas, establishing the singing of the *Prabandhas* of Saraoyogi, Sathagopa Sūrī and other *divyasūrīs* at Śrīraṅgam and installing their images along with his own image, waited eagerly for the attainment of the *paramapada*.[22]

The installation of Rāmānuja's images during his lifetime and symbolically infusing life in them through his embracing of these idols was indeed a unique way of creating a remembrance that would evoke devotion and reverence, thus attempting to erase any doubts about the Śrīvaiṣṇava tradition's credibility. The *Muāyirappaṭi* highlighted the imperativeness of memorialization. It narrates that Piḷḷāṉ and Mudaliāṇḍāṉ requested Rāmānuja to give permission to install his own images; otherwise nobody would remember his *siddhānta*.[23] The *Āṟāyirappaṭi* even provides iconographic details, thus concretizing and fixing the memory.

> Kanḍāḍaiāṇḍāṉ (disciple) requests Rāmānuja to give an *arcavigraha* of himself at Śrīperumbudūr, the place of his birth. Rāmānuja agrees. Kanḍāḍaiāṇḍāṉ calls a sculptor and describes to him how Rāmānuja should be sculpted: 'He should have 12 *nāmams*, a *tridaṇḍa* (three pointed

[21] *Yatirāja Vaibhavam of Āndhrapūrṇa (Vaṭuka Nambi)*, V. Varadachariar (ed.) 1978, *śloka* 110.

[22] *Divyasūricaritam*, Ch. 18, *śloka* 97.

[23] *Muāyirappaṭi*, p. 131.

> staff), *kāśaya* (saffron robe), *śika* (tuft of hair), and thread, seated on a lotus, wearing a garland of *tulasi* and lotus beads, should have the *añjalimudra* (in a pose of folded hands praying to the gods), and radiance like a sun.' The sculptor made the images according to the instructions and placed it before Kaṇḍāḍaiāṉḍāṉ, who showed it to Rāmānuja. Rāmānuja looked at it and embraced it tightly and infused it with entire strength (*sarva śakti*) and wrote to Kaṇḍāḍaiāṉḍāṉ, in a letter that it should be installed during the *puśya māsa* (month) on the *guru puśya* day.[24]

Hagiographical description of this 'institutionalization of charisma' was intended to permanently embed Rāmānuja as the paramount *ācārya* and *guru* within the Śrīvaiṣṇava tradition.[25] By fixing the status, were the hagiographers attempting to foreclose any rival claim that was in circulation or could have arisen? A focus of individual and community identity, the image was so revered that it acquired a near-divine aura. The continuous interaction between the devotee and Rāmānuja-as-image unified the community; and this projection of Rāmānuja as supreme *ācārya* was effectively creating 'public religious spheres' through its function as a pivot of the Śrīvaiṣṇava devotional experience.[26]

SECTARIANISM, IDEAS, AND THE COMMUNITY

A feature common to most modern biographers of Rāmānuja is the comparison with Śaṅkara, whose Vedāntic interpretation of Advaita is always considered to be abstract and intellectual while Rāmānuja's Viśiṣṭādvaitic schema is considered to be more comprehensible to the average *bhakta*, implications being that it was less intellectual. Indeed, such perceptions have been so influential that even noted historians such as A.L. Basham commented that

> Rāmānuja was not as brilliant a metaphysician as Sankara, but Indian religion perhaps owes even more to him than to his predecessor. In the centuries immediately following his death, his ideas spread all over India, and were the starting point of most of the devotional sects of later times.[27]

[24] *Āṟāyirappaṭi*, pp. 302–3.

[25] Stietencron (2001), in Dalmia et al. (eds), *Charisma and Canon*, pp. 25–7.

[26] Ibid., p. 26.

[27] Basham (1994), *The Wonder That Was India*, p. 335.

One also needs to question the conceptual categories within modern Indian philosophy in the nineteenth and twentieth centuries, whereby Śaṅkara's Advaita came to be recognized as 'philosophy' and Rāmānuja's Viśiṣṭādvaita as 'theology'. Implicit in these categorizations was the idea that philosophy was objective and analytical, while theology was intuitive and oriented towards salvation of the self as the goal. Such an understanding was rooted in the influence of Western ideas on the Indian thinkers who, while studying classical Indian texts to analyse the self and the other, were also evolving strategies to defend the Indian tradition and uphold its dignity against Western thought and its claims of intellectual superiority and domination. However, such a discursive reformulation of the supposed two non-interactive domains of knowledge systems, viz., 'philosophy' represented by Śaṅkara's Advaita and 'theology' represented by Rāmānuja's Viśiṣṭādvaita, collapse in the pre-modern period. Rāmānuja's commentaries engaged with the ideas of Advaita and he himself appeared to be in constant dialogue with the Advaita philosophy of Śaṅkarācārya, whose subsequent followers were probably in touch with Rāmānuja. This is obvious as the traditions of that period tell us that Rāmānuja's family belonged to a Smārta lineage. The Smārta *brāhmaṇas* were the followers of the *smṛiti* tradition (the traditional 'remembered' texts like the *Manusmṛiti* and *Gṛihyasūtras*). According to their philosophy, the Brahman was 'the infinite reality of pure consciousness into which the soul is ultimately absorbed after the illusory experiences are transcended through *mokṣa* or release'.[28] Thus, they were followers of Śaṅkara's philosophy and recognized the five deities, namely, Viṣṇu, Śiva, Śakti, Ganeśa, and Śūrya (*pañcayātana),* but were not sectarian and could not be classified as Vaiṣṇava or Śaiva or Śākta.[29] It should be noted that Śaṅkara himself belonged to eighth-century Kerala and so could not possibly have met Rāmānuja.

[28] Jackson (1991), *Tyāgāraja: Life and Lyrics*, p. 31.

[29] The *smārtas* were known to synthesize the non-*brāhmaṇa* devotion with their traditional rituals and thus laid the foundation of the religiosity characterized by *bhakti*. They were known to have incorporated the non-*brāhmaṇa* beliefs in such a manner that they were acceptable to the orthodox *brāhmaṇas*. Therefore, they were credited for 'sanskritizing' *bhakti*. At the same time, they presented the traditional structure in such a manner that it was more accessible to the non-*brāhmaṇas*. For details, see Jackson (1991), *Tyāgāraja*, pp. 31–2 and 62–3, fn 7, 10, and 11.

It needs to be pointed out that this comparison in modern biographies between Śaṅkara and Rāmānuja and their ideas being 'more abstract' and 'more accessible', respectively, is not an understanding projected by the hagiographical narratives. The texts did not declare that Rāmānuja's ideas were any less metaphysical than the pure monism of Advaita. Through its association with the Vedic canon, Viśiṣṭādvaita too was shown to be structured within a highly Sanskritized framework not comprehensible to the average devotee. Hence it devolved upon later Śrīvaiṣṇava hagiographers and theologians to create an accessible Tamil tradition through the building of a canon and finally by merging the Tamil and Sanskritic traditions, with Rāmānuja as the embodiment of this unique synthesis.[30] The narratives in the four hagiographies, especially the *Āṟāyirappaṭi*, are replete with discussions on the relation of the self to the Brahman, the achieving of salvation, and other such crucial theological issues.

However, a careful reading would confirm that Rāmānuja's *bhakti* with its heavy Sanskritic bias was indeed more intellectual than popular. The 'popular' element of Viśiṣṭādvaita is its clear emphasis on all devotees, regardless of caste status, having equal access to divine grace through personalized devotional practices rather than through classical liturgy and priestly mediation. Several commentaries discussed this fundamental principle of non-discrimination in the light of the social and political situation dominated by various politically powerful non-brāhmaṇa communities such as the *Vēḷāḷas* and *Kaikkoḷas*. Like the hagiographies, these commentaries also sought to validate the 'popular' perspectives by identifying interpretations of the corpus of Tamil hymns in Rāmānuja's expositions. The later commentaries invariably attempted to show that Viśiṣṭādvaita with its conceptual fulcrum of *saguṇa* Brahman, the divine with attributes, was more comprehensible to an ordinary devotee than Advaita, which postulated the abstruse and complex notion of *nirguṇa* Brahman, the formless Absolute.

There are also some modern biographies that do not find much difference between the ideas and activities of Śaṅkara, Rāmānuja, and Madhvācārya, (a twelfth–thirteenth century religious leader from Karnataka known for

[30] See for instance Jagadeesan (1977), *History of Srivaishnavism in the Tamil Country (Post Ramanuja)*, pp. 175–83; also see K.K.A. Venkatachari (1978), *The Manipravala Literature of the Srivaisnava Acaryas*, pp. 16–21.

the Dvaita interpretations of the Vedānta) and their interpretations of the Vedānta. As noted by a modern biographer:

> Very often it is wrongly believed that these three saints represented three mutually contradictory and inconsistent systems of thought and that there is more of divergence than unity in their teachings. Nothing can be farther from the truth. Depending upon the times and situations of the human society, in which they lived, they were obliged to teach their fellow men what they thought was best in their interests. Doctrinal divergences and dialectical debates notwithstanding, all these three giants of spirituality tried to bring the entire nation, rather humanity, under one unique umbrella of Vedantism. … If we can indulge in a sort of metaphor, liberation is a beautiful mansion to reach which, Śaṅkara, Rāmānuja and Madhva built a flight of steps in different periods of time. Thus the life and works of these three saints were mutually complementary but not contradictory.[31]

Such a view clearly underscores the 'modern' perception of these medieval thinkers, which reads them from the perspective of an integrated Hinduism based on the Vedas and Vedānta. However, the three 'giants of spirituality' in their own times were clearly aware that they were articulating different, though linked, philosophies. This is seen, for instance, in the invocation/first *sūtra* of Rāmānuja's commentary *Śrībhāṇya*:

> May the gods on earth [i.e. Brāhmaṇas] drink daily the speech nectar of the son of Parāśara [Vyāsa], taken out of the midst of the milky ocean of the *Upaniṣads*; which is the reviving means of the souls with the vitality gone away owing to the powerful scorching up of fire of worldly existence; which is well preserved by Predecessor-teachers. [Which was] kept at a distance [i.e. not sufficiently intelligible] owing to the conflict of many ideas [of various schools of thought] but [now] brought within the reach [of all] in our words.[32]

Modern writings connecting and sometimes eliding the two influential thinkers often ignore the fact that the era between Śaṅkara and Rāmānuja witnessed the production of two more influential advaitic commentaries on Vedānta: one by Bhāskara and the other by

[31] Narasimhachary (2007 [2004]), *Makers of Indian Literature*, pp. 9–10.
[32] Ramanuja, *Brahmasutra*: 1: 2.

Yādavaprakāśa, a near-contemporary of Rāmānuja. Rāmānuja produced his *bhāṣya* subsequent to these works, and in the historical context is likely to have been in contact with Yādavaprakāśa. There must have been circulation of ideas and philosophical discussion that was a part of the intellectual climate to which Rāmānuja belonged.

This interaction is highlighted in the hagiographical narratives that describe the relationship between Yādavaprakāśa and Rāmānuja in antagonistic terms. After informing us about Rāmānuja undergoing the various lifecycle rituals customary for a *brāhmaṇa*, hagiographies describe his prodigious intellect that grasped difficult metaphysical ideas and mastered equally difficult texts such as the Vedas at a young age.[33] We are also told that after some time he got married, and that he subsequently migrated to Kāñcīpuram, an important religious and trading centre.

Here he became a disciple of the *guru* Yādavaprakāśa, a famous Advaitin and intellectual renowned for his interpretations of Vedānta. In the course of his learning, Rāmānuja often questioned his *guru*'s interpretation of the *Upaniṣads*.[34] Moreover, for his formulation of Viśiṣṭādvaita he chose the very *śrutis* his teacher was using as references for the established exposition of Advaita, and this brought him into direct opposition with Yādavaprakāśa. This tension between the teacher and the disciple represented the contradictions between the Viśiṣṭādvaita and Advaita systems of philosophy, where the latter was well established. The ideological tensions between teacher and disciple are reflected in the hagiographies that extol Rāmānuja's brilliance and erudition and reiterated that in the course of his learning Rāmānuja often questioned his *guru*'s Advaitic interpretation of the *Upaniṣads*, and countered the arguments by 'Sadvaita' interpretations.[35]

The narratives also highlight Yādavaprakāśa's failure and Rāmānuja's success in dealing with practical situations involving the expression of devotional powers, such as relieving the king's son from the affliction of

[33] *Divyasuricaritam*, Ch. 17, *ślokas* 9–10.

[34] For narratives regarding Rāmānuja and Yādavaprakāśa, see *Divyasūricaritam*, Ch. 17, *ślokas* 10–11, 16–34; *Yatirāja Vaibhavam, ślokas* 12–32; *Āṟāyirappaṭi*, pp. 142–52; *Muāyirappaṭi*, pp. 75–81.

[35] *Divyasuricaritam, śloka* 11. The term used is 'Sadvaita', associated with Viśiṣṭādvaita, implying 'with Dvaita'; it should not be confused with the Dvaita philosophy of Mādhvācārya.

a *brahmarākṣasa*. This particular story established Rāmānuja as extraordinary and the Viśiṣṭādvaita philosophy as superior and was the origin of the intellectual incompatibility between Rāmānuja and Yādavaprakāśa, who became envious of his disciple's success. One of the disagreements over the interpretations that culminated in the breaking-point was when Rāmānuja with all humility corrected his *guru* over an elucidation of a *śruti* text:

> One day, when Rāmānuja was massaging Yādavaprakāśa with oil, a *śiṣya* came to Yādavaprakāśa to clarify a particular doubt over a passage in the *Chāndayoga Upaniṣad*. This passage had a word *kapyāsam*, meaning of which was not clear. Taking the word to mean the posterior of a monkey, Yādavaprakāśa explained the passage as follows: The two eyes of the golden Puruṣa, that is the lord, are like two lotuses which are red like the posterior of a monkey. On hearing this interpretation, Rāmānuja was very upset and tears like flames of fire rolled down from his eyes onto the thigh of Yādavaprakāśa who asked Rāmānuja what his problem was. Rāmānuja expressed his grief over his teacher's 'unbecoming explanation' and said that he never expected this from a wise person like Yādavaprakāśa. Yādavaprakāśa replied, 'I am also very much grieved at your audacity. Can you interpret the passage in any better manner?' When Rāmānuja said he could, Yādavaprakāśa responded sarcastically, 'Fine, very good, I see, you wish to become better than Śankarācārya.' Then Rāmānuja provided an alternate explanation that *kapyāsam* means 'blossomed by sun' and the passage would then read as, 'The eyes of that Puruṣa within the golden solar orb are as lovely as the lotuses blossomed by the rays of the sun.'[36]

However, the *Divyasūricaritam* narrates this differently while retaining the main theme, that is, the superiority of Rāmānuja/Viśiṣṭādvaita over Yādavaprakāśa/Advaita.[37] The *Divyasūricaritam* does not cite the monkey–lotus analogy as the core of the dispute: interestingly, this appears much later in the text in a muted form, when Rāmānuja goes to visit the Śārada Pītha (whose location is not revealed). Here Rāmānuja met Sarasvatī, the goddess of learning who was already impressed with

36 As quoted in Swami Ramakrishnananda (1986), *Life of Sri Rāmānuja*, pp. 80–2.

37 See *Divyasūricaritam*, Ch. 17, *śloka*s 32–3, where it is recounted that Rāmānuja was upset with Yādavaprakāśa's incorrect interpretation of a sentence from the *śruti* text.

Rāmānuja and gave him the permission to use her books. Rāmānuja was surprised at Sarasvatī's generosity and could not help asking her the reason for such benevolence. Sarasvatī told him that she was impressed with his interpretation of *kapyāsam*, adding that while Śaṅkara compared this with the posterior of a monkey, Rāmānuja's comparing the term to a lotus flower was both correct and refined. Thereafter, Sarasvatī took Rāmānuja's composition *Vedārthasaṅgraha*, placed it in front of all wise men, and then placed it on her head as if dispelling all other interpretations which were nothing but distortions of the Vedānta.[38] Even Śaṅkara who predated Rāmānuja by almost three centuries was not spared. This account is present in the *Āṟāyirappaṭi* as well as in the *Muāyirappaṭi*; however, the latter does not mention the *kapyāsam* analogy in this context.[39] Though *Yatirāja Vaibhavam* mentions Sarasvatī's acknowledgement of Rāmānuja's superiority, the sectarian overtone deriding Śaṅkara is absent.[40] Interestingly, except *Divyasūricaritam*, the rest of the texts refer to Rāmānuja's *Śrībhāṣya* as the text that Sarasvatī out of reverence placed on her head.

All the hagiographies make Rāmānuja's interpretations of various *Upaniṣadic* verses the point of a radical departure from the Advaita. While these versions used it to reinforce the larger theme of direct rivalry between Rāmānuja and Yādavaprakāśa, they also inform us about Rāmānuja's fame and the veracity of his interpretations over the Advaita, one which even the goddess of learning acknowledged. These narrative strategies consolidated the figure of Rāmānuja as exceptional and powerful, conveying to the audience that his interpretations of Vedānta were final and could not be challenged further. In fact, the story of the *brahmarākṣasa* ridicules the Advaita followers through the figure of Yādavaprakāśa and upholds the Viśiṣṭādvaita followers through the figure of Rāmānuja:

> As soon as Yādavaprakāśa saw the son and the possession of *brahmarākṣasa* over him, he immediately started chanting the *mantras*. On hearing Yādavaprakāśa chanting the *mantras*, the *brahmarākṣasa* was besieged with rage and ridiculed Yādavaprakāśa and declared him completely ignorant. The *brahmarākṣasa* asserted that he knew about all the past births

38 Ibid., Ch. 18, *ślokas* 13–16.

39 *Āṟāyirappaṭi*, p. 226; *Muāyirappaṭi*, p. 106.

40 *Yatirāja Vaibhavam*, *śloka* 88.

of Yādavaprakāśa and himself. In the course of the argument that ensued, Yādavaprakāśa challenged the *rākṣasa* to reveal all about their respective past births. The *rākṣasa* informed that, 'In the past birth you were a chameleon (lizard) living near the banks of a pond in an *agrahāra*, named Madurāntaka. When some learned Vaiṣṇava men were on their way to participate in the festivals, they stopped here, rested and ate. Their leftover rice was consumed by you. As a result of the consumption of these sacred leftovers, you were redeemed and hence were born in a human form in this birth. I was a *brāhmaṇa* who along with other *brāhmaṇas* performed the *yajñas*. In one of the *yajñas*, I erred and with the result I was reborn as a *brahmarākṣasa*.'

Pointing towards Rāmānuja, the *rākṣasa* then said, 'This incarnation of Śeṣa (the snake on which Viṣṇu is resting), who has been sent on this earth to protect mankind, is someone I am scared of. If he asks me to leave the body of this boy, I will immediately obey. In fact, his sweet words will release me from this body and will give me *mokṣa* or salvation.' After saying this, the *brahmarākṣasa* fell at the feet of Rāmānuja. Thereafter, Yādavaprakāśa ordered Rāmānuja to command the *rākṣasa* to leave the body of the prince. Rāmānuja obeyed his *guru* and commanded politely the aggrieved *brahmarākṣasa* to leave the body, the sign being the breaking of a branch of the *pīpal* tree. The *rākṣasa* left the body of the prince and while going broke the branch of the *pīpal* tree. The king was happy and rewarded Rāmānuja lavishly. Thereafter, Rāmānuja gave all the endowments to his *guru*.[41]

Subsequently, the *guru* and disciple had further serious disagreements on scriptures and metaphysics. Yādavaprakāśa became so annoyed with Rāmānuja's interpretations that he asked Rāmānuja to leave his *āśrama*. Interestingly, the hagiographies inform us that the rivalry was so intense that the embittered Yādavaprakāśa conspired to take Rāmānuja's life. Rāmānuja was saved by the divine intervention of Viṣṇu and some fellow disciples such as his cousin Govindabhaṭṭa. In these versions Yādavaprakāśa, on the pretext of taking his disciples on a pilgrimage

[41] *Divyasūricaritam*, Ch. 17, *ślokas* 16–31. This story is also recounted in a similar manner in the other hagiographies, namely *Yatirāja Vaibhavam*, *ślokas*17–19, *Āṟāyirappaṭi*, pp. 150–2, and *Muāyirappaṭi*, p. 80. However, there are slight variations. For instance, in the *Āṟāyirappaṭi*, it is a princess who is possessed by the *brahmarākṣasa* who promises to leave the body only after Rāmānuja placed his 'lotus feet' on his head.

to the holy banks of the Ganga (according to some hagiographies, in Benares), planned to kill Rāmānuja, but his evil designs were revealed to Rāmānuja by Govindabhaṭṭa while the group was passing through a forest. In order to save his life Rāmānuja hid in the forest, while the other disciples proceeded onwards. However, Rāmānuja's feeling of helplessness did not last long. He soon encountered a hunter and his wife who offered to take Rāmānuja safely back to Kāñcīpuram. The hagiographies disclose that this pair was none other than Viṣṇu and his consort, Lakṣmī. Somewhere along the way Rāmānuja went to bring water from a well for the thirsty couple. He returned to find that they had disappeared, and that from where he was standing he could see the temple towers of Kāñcīpuram. He realized then that he had been saved by none other than Viṣṇu and Lakṣmī, in the guise of hunter and huntress.[42] Though the Yādavaprakāśa–Rāmānuja rivalry comprises a substantial part in the *Divyasūricaritam* (Chapter 17), the tenor is comparatively less sectarian. In fact, this text does not mention the conspiracy hatched by Yādavaprakāśa to kill Rāmānuja, Rāmānuja being saved by Govinda Bhaṭṭar, and finally by the Lord and his consort in the guise of hunter and huntress.

The ideological dissent against an established system of Advaita within a traditional *guru–śiṣya* method of disseminating knowledge was also associated with the organization of the community, conversion, especially of the Advaitins, and the consequent spread of Śrīvaiṣṇavism. The hagiographies are thus most graphic in their description of the Yādavaprakāśa–Rāmānuja rivalry. Could it be then that, with the emergence of the Vijayanagara Empire and the increasing political influence of the Advaita-oriented Śriṅgērī *maṭha* in the fourteenth and fifteenth centuries, the Śrīvaiṣṇava hagiographers' presentation of the *guru*–disciple rivalry was in fact symbolic of broader claims—that is, competition with regard to royal patronage and the acquisition of religio-political power? Since the conspiracy to kill Rāmānuja and the divine intervention are not recounted in the *Divyasūricaritam*, can one then assume that this was an earlier text, written around the twelfth–thirteenth century when the historical context was relatively less complex?

Therefore, the hagiographies were in their own way expressing the Viśiṣṭādvaita rivalry with the Advaita doctrine. In the *Divyasūricaritam*,

[42] *Yatirāja Vaibhavam, ślokas* 23–9; *Āṟāyirappaṭi*, pp. 143–6; *Muāyirappaṭi*, pp. 75–7.

Ārāyirappaṭi, and *Muāyirappaṭi* this rivalry is elaborated through a greater textual focus on the concrete performance of Rāmānuja's miracles, a proof of his ability to deal with practical matters that was to be useful later. In the *Yatirāja Vaibhavam*, the focus is more on the disagreement over the interpretations of the meanings of the *śruti*, with the discursive trajectory entirely tilted towards the metaphysics of Vedānta, the source of the *guru*–disciple conflict that resulted in Yādavaprakāśa's plot to murder Rāmānuja. Such variations were due to the differing attitudes of the texts. The hagiographies were addressing the concerns of the community networks through a dual strategy. First, the narratives placed Rāmānuja distinctively above the Advaitins, thereby underscoring the superiority of the Śrīvaiṣṇava ideology. Second, the narratives attempted to ensure royal patronage while projecting the Viśiṣṭādvaita as an intellectually profound doctrine, thereby reflecting their anxiety over acquiring royal patronage for the consolidation of the Śrīvaiṣṇava community. The *Yatirāja Vaibhavam*, while disparagingly referring to Yādavaprakāśa as monkey-like (*Yādavamarkaṭena*), however, focused on the intellectualism of Rāmānuja much more, rather than on his performance of miracles.[43] Hence the superiority of Rāmānuja's interpretation over the Advaita or Yādavaprakāśa's interpretations and narratives revolving around it are emphasized, while the other narratives like the story of *brahmarākṣasa* are only briefly described.

Besides demonstrating the polemics of Viśiṣṭādvaita and Advaita, these narratives of Rāmānuja's early life as a *śiṣya* projected the Śrīvaiṣṇava ideal of the *guru–śiṣya paramparā* structured on the principles of obedience and unflinching loyalty. Despite their detailed accounts of Rāmānuja's ideological protest against his *guru* Yādavaprakāśa (renowned for his expositions of Advaita), the hagiographies always projected Rāmānuja as a devoted disciple who never turned his back on his *guru*. He was depicted as ever respectful to his *guru*, serving him with great devotion despite knowing of the *guru*'s plans to kill him. The hagiographies lay the onus of anger, arrogance, and provocation on Yādavaprakāśa, while the dissenting Rāmānuja is shown as calm, humble and fully in line with the mandated *guru-śiṣya* code of behaviour. Even the dissent here was not strident but persistent. The hagiographies also highlighted his devotion to God. The saving of Rāmānuja's life by Lord Varadarāja, the daily *kainkarya* (service)

[43] *Yatirāja Vaibhavam*, *śloka* 32.

performed by Rāmānuja of bringing water from a roadside well for the *tirumañjanam* (holy bath) of Lord Varadarāja—all show the power of devotion, which recognized Viṣṇu as the supreme god.

The hagiographers' intent was obvious, their message to *bhaktas* unambiguous: follow Śrīvaiṣṇavism, follow Viśiṣṭādvaita, whatever the opposition, for in any situation of adversity the Lord would come to the rescue. It is the *guru* who was shown to be petty and narrow minded in his attitude towards his humble student. The hagiographers while depicting Yādavaprakāśa's behaviour attempted to highlight the intolerance of the Advaita interpretation and condemn it as incorrect and hollow. Finally, while the narratives denounce Yādavaprakāśa for his murderous impulse, they also underscored the compassion and flexibility of Śrīvaiṣṇava *bhakti* that accepted Yādavaprakāśa as a convert; the *guru* finally became a disciple of his former disciple, Rāmānuja.

All the four hagiographies narrate this conversion. We are told that finally, Yādavaprakāśa became Rāmānuja's disciple. This was on his mother's insistence who told him to become a *tridaṇḍin* like Rāmānuja and follow the latter's interpretation of the Vedas. Listening to this, Yādavaprakāśa decided to circumambulate the earth. God then appeared to him in a dream and told him that instead he should circumambulate Rāmānuja, for that action was equivalent to circumambulating the earth. However, Yādavaprakāśa was sceptical about this dream-instruction and went to Tirukacci Nambi (Kāñcīpurṇa), Rāmānuja's *guru*, and requested the latter to beseech the Lord that he would circumambulate the earth. However, the Lord told Kāñcīpurṇa that he had already appeared in Yādavaprakāśa's dream, and that Yādavaprakāśa should follow instructions without any fear. Finally, with profound respect and love, Yādavaprakāśa went around Rāmānuja, took *sanyāsa* under him, and then became his disciple. According to *Āṟāyirappaṭi*, the primary intention of Yādavaprakāśa was to renounce his *ekadaṇḍin* (one pointed staff) and the thread and do penance (*prāyaścitta*) by going around the earth. However, he realized that he was too old for it and lamented. It is then that the God appeared before him and asked him to circumambulate Rāmānuja.[44]

It should be noted that this narrative was inserted in the texts after Rāmānuja formally became a renunciate, a status that qualified him to have

[44] *Divyasūricaritam*, Ch.17, *ślokas* 72–6; *Yatirāja Vaibhavam, śloka* 53; *Āṟāyirappaṭi*, pp. 176–7; *Muāyirappaṭi*, pp. 91–2.

disciples. As described in the *Yatirāja Vaibhavam*, 'Then, Yādavaprakāśa who became purified by the gracious looks of Yamunācārya became the disciple of Yatirāja with the name "Govindayogin". He composed a work on the duties of the ascetics.'[45] The *Āṟāyirappaṭi* and *Muāyirappaṭi* tell us the text was composed at Rāmānuja's behest and was titled *Yatidharmasamuccaya*, and the *Muāyirappaṭi* further recounted that Rāmānuja glanced at it.[46] The *Divyasūricaritam* is silent on the subjects, namely the composition of the text by Yādavaprakāśa and the name of his work.

Interestingly, the narratives with themes of sectarianism exhibited certain biases. Advaitins were ideological opponents to be intellectually overwhelmed and finally to be converted to Śrīvaiṣṇavism, whereas the Śaivas or Jainas were eliminated and their religious identities erased. For instance, Yajñamūrti, a famous *advaitin* who lost to Rāmānuja in a polemical debate, converted to Śrīvaiṣṇavism.[47] It was the divine intervention of Peraruḷāḷa (form of Viṣṇu at Kāñcīpuram) that enabled Rāmānuja to achieve victory with great difficulty over such a formidable rival. Thereafter, at the behest of Rāmānuja, Yajñamūrti renounced his *ekadaṇḍa* (single-pointed staff)—the mark of an Advaitic renunciate and donned the saffron robe, sacred thread, tuft of hair, and the *tridaṇḍa*. Rāmānuja then initiated him through the rites of *pañcasamskāra*, taught him the meanings of the *Prabandhas*, and christened him as Aruḷāḷapperumāḷemberumānār after the God Peraruḷāḷa and inducted him amongst the inner coterie of his disciples.[48] The narratives inform us that Yajñamūrti functioned independently.[49] At a later stage we are told that he was finally overwhelmed and that his *maṭha* was subsequently assimilated into Rāmānuja's *maṭha*.[50] Thus, it is implied here that Rāmānuja had assigned Yajñamūrti the supervision of a *maṭha* and named it after him. Such a reference to the large-

45 *Yatirāja Vaibhavam*, *śloka* p. 53 *Āṟāyirappaṭi* also mentions this. According to it, after Yādavaprakāśa became Rāmānuja's disciple, the latter named him Govinda Jīyar.

46 *Āṟāyirappaṭi*, p. 178; *Muāyirappaṭi*, p. 92.

47 *Divyasūricaritam* provides a different name—Kāruṇyakār, See Ch. 18, *śloka* 6.

48 *Divyasūricaritam*, Ch.18, *ślokas* 6–9; *Yatirāja Vaibhavam, ślokas* 85–6; *Āṟāyirappaṭi*, pp. 203–7; *Muāyirappaṭi*, pp. 102–3.

49 *Āṟāyirappaṭi*, p. 207.

50 *Āṟāyirappaṭi*, pp. 220–1.

heartedness of Rāmānuja in the *Āṟāyirappaṭi* was an oblique way of exhibiting sectarianism.

On the other hand, hagiographies depict Rāmānuja as eliminating, through miracles and prayers, the Śaivas and the Jainas. The instance of rivalry with the Śaivas over the appropriation of the Venkatēśvara temple has been cited in the previous chapter. The story of persecution of Rāmānuja and his followers at the hands of the Cōḷa ruler who was a Śaiva is replete with sectarian overtones. In this story, apart from the Cōḷa ruler's highhandedness and the Śaivas' evil temperament, the unflinching devotion towards one's own *guru* at the cost of self-sacrifice as an important Śrīvaiṣṇava ideal is accentuated. The Cōḷa ruler compelled everybody to sign the palm leaf on which was written that nobody is greater than Śiva.[51] However, he was advised that Rāmānuja's signature was imperative; otherwise this exercise would be futile. So the king sent his soldiers to bring Rāmānuja. When Rāmānuja's disciples got to know, one of them, Kurattāḻvān, quickly wore Rāmānuja's robes as the latter was bathing. Posing as Rāmānuja, Kurattāḻvān, accompanied by Periya Nambi, went to the Cōḷa court. Meanwhile, Rāmānuja after much persuasion escaped to the Hoysala kingdom. Thereafter, the hagiographies describe at length Rāmānuja's sojourn in this region and establishment of a Śrīvaiṣṇava temple of Nārāyaṇasvāmī at Mēlkōṭe. The Cōḷa ruler is further demonized when the narratives inform us that he blinded both Kurattāḻvān and Periya Nambi as they refused to sign the palm leaf manuscript and the latter being old, finally died. Ultimately, the Cōḷa ruler was struck by a dreaded disease in which the worms had infected his throat and hence the narratives named him Kṛmikaṇṭha Cōḷa. He met a cruel end and the persecution of the Śrīvaiṣṇava was thus avenged.

Interestingly, while describing the persecution of one religious community by another that had political support, the narratives introduce another aspect of the sectarian trope, in which the agency of the Śrīvaiṣṇavas is recounted. While Rāmānuja was in Mēlkōṭle, he vanquished the local Jaina religious leaders in polemics and converted the people of Mēlkōṭe to Śrīvaiṣṇavism:

51 For the episode on the persecution by the Cōḷa ruler, see *Divyasūricaritam*, Ch. 18, *ślokas* 71–88; *Yatirāja Vaibhavam, ślokas* 94–5, 102; *Āṟāyirappaṭi*, pp. 239–41, 255; *Muāyirappaṭi*, pp. 112–13, 117.

> The Hoysala king, Vitthaladevarāyā, a Jaina, was unhappy that his daughter was afflicted by a spirit (*piśācha*) and nobody could cure her. Toṇḍanūr Nambi informed the king that his *guru* Rāmānuja was there and adviced the king that the latter should beseech Rāmānuja's help. Then Toṇḍanūr Nambi recounted the *brahmarākṣasa* episode. Vitthaladevarāyā promised that if Rāmānuja cured his daughter, he would submit to Rāmānuja forever. After much persuasion on the part of Toṇḍanūr Nambi, Rāmānuja finally came to the Hoysala court. The princess was given Rāmānuja's *śrīpādatīrtha* (water after washing the feet). After drinking it, she was cured and fell at Rāmānuja's feet, followed by her father. Thereafter, Rāmānuja renamed the Hoysala king as the Viṣṇuvardhanarāyā. Meanwhile, the priests of the king numbering 12,000 *Śravaṇas* were agitated and challenged Rāmānuja to prove his merit in a debate. Rāmānuja agreed, went to the *mandapa* behind a screen and like Ādiśeṣa with 1000 tongues answered all their questions and stunned them. Thereafter Rāmānuja made them grind the stone mill. Some of them changed and submitted to him.[52]

Thus, one notes a differential attitude of the hagiographers towards their sectarian rivals. Clearly, the Advaitins were important rivals than the Śaivas and Jainas. With regard to the former, the narratives emphasized the intellectual competition and arguments relating to metaphysics, and in the case of the latter, they focused on pragmatic matters of control over the temple and competition over attracting royal patronage. These two episodes that engaged with the Cōḷa and Hoysala rulers betrayed the anxiety of the hagiographers over the share in the royal patronage. Clearly, Śaivas had royal support and this was decried by the hagiographers when they disparagingly mentioned that some signed the palm leaf out of fear and some out of sheer greed for benefactions. Since the Śrīvaiṣṇava base was attenuated during the Cōḷa period, the story of persecution gave respectability to a relatively insignificant past. The narrative on the Cōḷa persecution receives an elaborate treatment in the *Divyasūricaritam*. Another theme that was recounted at length in the same hagiography was the Yādavaprakāśa-Rāmānuja episode. The historical period of both the Cōḷas and Rāmānuja were around the twelfth and the thirteenth centuries. Then do these narrative tropes support the argument that the *Divyasūricaritam* was composed between the twelfth and the thirteenth centuries? However, the conversion of the Hoysala

[52] *Āṟāyirappaṭi*, pp. 247–9; Also see, *Yatirāja Vaibhavam, śloka* 97; *Muāyirappaṭi*, p. 114.

ruler and the defeat of the Jainas are missing from the *Divyasūricaritam*, thus indicating a softer sectarian attitude. In fact, the *Divyasūricaritam* narrates the instrumentality of Veṅkateśvara of Tirupati in disabling the Cōḷa ruler by infecting the latter's throat with his divine weapons.[53] Thus, the persecution of the Jainas as recounted above was a symbolic depiction of the spread and expansion of the community network and fresh avenues of royal patronage. However, in one instance, the diatribe against Śaivism is rather muted. This was in the narratives on the conversion of Rāmānuja's cousin, Govinda Bhaṭṭar, who was a devout Śaiva residing at Kālāhasti, into Śrīvaiṣṇavism. The tone is not aggressive, rather persuasive and the hymns are sung to woo him. The hagiographies tell us that Govinda Bhaṭṭar was moved and extremely penitent and finally joined Śrīvaiṣṇavism, and after sometime, he became a member of Rāmānuja's *maṭha*.[54]

Finally, to conclude, it needs to be emphasized that perhaps no other theme received such an exhaustive treatment in the hagiographies than the one on sectarianism against other religious traditions. The narratives while dealing with Advaita, Śaiva, and Jaina traditions, referred to commonly as *kudriṣṭis*, were not only belittling towards them, but also had an undertone of symbolic violence that either attempted to erase the memories of the religious traditions, like in the case of Jainism in the Hoysala kingdom and the Śaivism in the case of Tirupati, or subjugate them like in the case of the Advaita tradition. In all the cases, the final result was the conversion to the Śrīvaiṣṇava faith at the behest of none other than Rāmānuja. Written between the twelfth and the fifteenth centuries, these hagiographies were probably not only building up strategies to compete with other religious traditions over patronage and disciples but were also trying to attract their respective followers to deflect from their original faiths and join Śrīvaiṣṇavism. In this context, the delineation of Rāmānuja as an exceptional religious leader became more significant and was often linked to the theology, thus eulogizing the Śrīvaiṣṇava ideas of devotion:

> Rāmānuja now confronts the Jainas, Sāṅkhyas and Liṅgatittapurāṇas and destroys the argument of the *māyāvādins* and people with narrow views

[53] *Divyasūricaritam*, Ch.18, *ślokas* 85–8.

[54] *Yatirāja Vaibhavam, ślokas* 70, 79. *Āṟāyirappaṭi*, pp. 185–90, 214–19; *Muāyirappaṭi*, pp. 91, 94. *Divyasūricaritam* does not give details. See *Divyasūricaritam*, Ch.18, *śloka* 35.

> opposing the correct views of the Vedānta. He states clearly that the by only following the path of *bhakti-jñāna upāsanā*, you will get *mokṣa*, the ultimate goal of Vedānta.[55]

This sectarian delineation is also evident on the narratives of Rāmānuja's travels to other Vaiṣṇava centres within and outside the southern regions, which will be discussed in the fourth section.

COMMUNITY, ORGANIZATION, AND TRADITION

The fundamental importance of the *guruparamparā* was its function as the carrier and transmitter of Śrīvaiṣṇava tradition and history including the lives and deeds of major spiritual preceptors. In this context, it was a crucial hagiographical exercise to present the organization of the community structure that would take the tradition forward and disseminate it. Since the hagiographies had acquired a scriptural status, the narratives were thus a template for future generations. There were three guiding principles discussed in the hagiographies on the basis of which the community organization evolved. One, the ideology of *Ubhaya Vedānta*, in which the *Nālāyira Divya Prabandham*, especially the *Tiruvāymoḻi*, assumed precedence. Two, the notion of an unbroken lineage that would establish the veracity of the tradition and its transmission. Three, was the organization of the lineage and the structure of the community for the perpetuation of the tradition. The ethos of these principles was the *guru-śiṣya paramparā* that forged an ideological bonding between the *ācārya* and his disciples.

Ubhaya Vedānta, Tiruvāymoḻi, and Rāmānuja

As earlier discussed in this study, along with depicting and celebrating a specific preceptor personified in Rāmānuja, the *guruparamparā*s also focused on the community, its identity, and its image and position vis-à-vis other religious and social groups. The textual tradition of which the *guruparamparā*s were a part had already canonized the Tamil hymns through the commentaries and through rendering the life story of Nāthamuni, credited with the recovery of the hymns, especially the *Tiruvāymoḻi* of Nammāḻvār. The Tamil hymns of the Āḻvārs, expressing

[55] *Āṟāyirappaṭi*, p. 222.

significant devotional themes such as the spontaneous praise of Viṣṇu, complete surrender to him (*prapatti*), a sense of community overriding caste considerations, and strong elements of mysticism were crucial to the Śrīvaiṣṇava identity. The hagiographers realized the importance of these themes in terms of reinforcing the organization of the community, perpetuation of a spiritual lineage, and expansion of the Śrīvaiṣṇava social base. The narratives by portraying the successful recovery of the Tamil hymns and also putting them to music, by the ninth-century preceptor Nāthamuni, created a crucial link between the life stories of Āḻvārs and the biographical accounts of the *ācāryas*. Hence, one of the hagiographical concerns was to associate Rāmānuja with the Tamil hymns of the Āḻvārs and the hagiographers consciously inscribed Rāmānuja's association with the Tamil hymns in order to project him as the charismatic central vehicle of the Śrīvaiṣṇava *bhakti* tradition.

The hagiographies also tell us that over time, the custom of singing the hymns as a part of worship in the temple became irregular, and it was Rāmānuja who revitalized the practice through re-institutionalizing the important temple festival called *Adhyayanōtsavam*, first at Śrīraṅgam (the centre of Śrīvaiṣṇava *bhakti* and community activities), and thereafter in other temple centres. In one account, Rāmānuja goes to visit the shrine of Āṇṭāḷ at Śrivilliputtūr. Āṇṭāḷ was the only woman Āḻvār said to have married symbolically Raṅganātha, the god at Śrīraṅgam. Āṇṭāḷ complains to Rāmānuja that the festival of *Adhyayanōtsavam*, that is, the singing of the hymns of the Āḻvārs, especially Nammāḻvār's Tiruvāymoḷi, was not being held properly anywhere:

> Rāmānuja promises that he would renew the singing festival in all temple centres with full honours ... Likewise, he installed the idols of those Āḻvārs and Āṇṭāḷ in the holy places of great glory and also had the *Adhyayana* festival conducted everywhere. The great Rāmānujācārya offered plentiful ghee; rice mixed with ghee, milk and jaggery for the delight of the Lord of Vṛṣbhāgiri (Tirumāliruñcōḷai or Aḻagar hills near Madurai) and was much honoured by the gracious looks of Āṇṭāḷ.[56]

The hagiographies not only bound together the Tamil and Sanskrit traditions, but also embedded this convergence in the life story of

[56] *Yatirāja Vaibhavam of Āndhrapūrṇa (Vaṭuka Nambi)*, V. Varadachariar (ed.), *śloka*s 105–6.

Rāmānuja. Further, by foregrounding the institutionalization of devotional practices in the form of the temple festival, the narratives were also creating a historical memory for the community. From the fourteenth and the fifteenth centuries onwards, the celebration of *Adhyayanōtsavam* is documented in numerous temple records, and up till today the festival is celebrated for twenty-one days. Its central activity is the recitation of the hymns of the Āl̲vārs (4,000 in number and compiled as a scripture called the *Nālayira Divya Prabandham*).[57] The recitation is performed in front of an array of images of the most important spiritual figures—the twelve Āl̲vārs, Tirukacci Nambi (the non-*brāhmaṇa* teacher of Rāmānuja), Rāmānuja, his spiritual successor Kurattāl̲vān, and some later Śrīvaiṣṇava *ācāryas*. Interestingly, images of Nāthamuni and Yāmuna, the two *ācāryas* immediately preceding Rāmānuja, are never included in this group of ceremonial audience, and the central role of Rāmānuja in the Śrīvaiṣṇava *bhakti* tradition is consciously reiterated. 'Finally, after all the hymns have been sung and the Āl̲vārs and *ācāryas* returned to their respective shrines, the image of the deity is taken to the shrine of Rāmānuja in order to thank him for arranging for the recitation.'[58]

Why has the connection between the Tamil and the Sanskrit traditions been so seminal for the Śrīvaiṣṇavas? Why did the *guruparamparās* choose to reinforce this crucial association through the biography of Rāmānuja when it was already established in Nāthamuni's life story? Why has this particular hagiographical narrative been institutionalized in such an impressive manner and made an integral part of the Śrīvaiṣṇava cultural memory? The answer to these questions can be found in the Śrīvaiṣṇava concerns relating to community identity and coherence, as well as in the social location and ideology of the hagiographers and the larger socio-political context from the twelfth to the fifteenth centuries that witnessed a significant emergence of the textual tradition to which the hagiographies and the *stotras* belonged.

The Śrīvaiṣṇava tradition articulated in these *guruparamparās* was the tradition of *Ubhaya Vedānta*, or the dual Vedānta, in which the Tamil hymns of the Āl̲vārs were given the appellation of the *Draviḍa Veda* and put at par with the Sanskrit Vedas. This represented both the linguistic

[57] Younger (1982), 'Singing the Tamil̲ Hymnbook in the Tradition of Rāmānuja', pp. 272–9.

[58] Ibid., p. 275.

and as the social sphere, which were the Tamil and Sanskrit domains of the Śrīvaiṣṇava community. These developments influenced the language of the texts in the fourteenth century, which began to be composed in a language which is today called the *Maṇipravālam*. In this so-called 'new' language, Tamil words were interspersed with Sanskrit words, just as gems of ruby (*maṇi*) and coral (*pravāla*) were strung alternatively in a necklace. For the first time, a 'vernacular' or a regional language (Tamil) was used alongside Sanskrit and both were accorded a scriptural status.

This new linguistic trajectory that evolved represented a radical innovation. Until the thirteenth century, the Tamil and the Sanskritic traditions were separate and had developed independently from each other. One has to be cautious as to not overstress the dichotomy between Tamil and Sanskrit as equivalent to popular and elite respectively. In fact, the records of the famous Raṅganāthasvāmī temple at Śrīraṅgam indicates that the singing of some of the Tamil hymns in the temples, particularly the *Tiruvāymoḻi* of Nammāḻvār, were associated with the *brāhmaṇa* community. Grants made for this purpose were always addressed to them. However, parallel to this tradition, though not necessarily opposed, was the autonomous textual engagements of Nāthamuni, Yāmuna, and Rāmānuja with the Āgamic and the Vedāntic traditions respectively. Yāmuna's treatise *Āgamapramāṇya*, a tenth-century text, theoretically argued for using the more ritualistic and integrative *Pañcarātra Āgama* over the austere and exclusive *Vaikhānsa Āgama* in the temple rituals. Rāmānuja's Vedāntic interpretation (later termed Viśiṣṭādvaita), also argued for a perception of God that was more integrative and his 'qualified monism' postulated divinity (in this case, Viṣṇu) with attributes. Clearly, these three *brāhmaṇa ācāryas* belonged to perhaps the same ācāryic lineage and scholastic tradition, and their works written exclusively in Sanskrit acknowledged each other's philosophical contributions. Rāmānuja's acknowledgement of Yāmuna in his *Gītābhāṣya* and the latter's composition *Stotraratna* illustrate this. Śrīvaiṣṇava hagiographers and the composers of the *stotras* and commentaries were also part of this genealogy. Interestingly, all the hagiographic texts analysed in this study were written by *brāhmaṇa* authors who claimed a staunch affiliation with Rāmānuja despite the difference in their lineages. For instance, Garuḍavāhana Paṇdita, the author of the *Divyasūricaritam*, said that he was the keeper of the *ārogyaśāla*, a kind of a hospital established by Rāmānuja at the temple in Śrīraṅgam. Similarly, Āndhra Pūrṇa, the author of *Yatirāja Vaibhavam*, documented his relationship to Rāmānuja as that of a 'humble servant', serving milk.

Since pre-thirteenth-century (which also includes Rāmānuja's time period), temple records do not document any relationship with Rāmānuja or his successors, it may be assumed that the Sanskritic intellectual tradition and religious groups affiliated with it had yet to establish an institutional foundation. On the other hand, the Tamil hymns and the temple *brāhmaṇa*s associated with them clearly had a temple base, however attenuated. It could be speculated that from the eleventh century onwards, when the region's major temples were sustained to a great extent by royal Cōḷa patronage, Vaiṣṇava supporters of the Sanskritic tradition and its *brāhmaṇa*s (some affiliated with the Āgama framework of rituals and others with the Viśiṣṭādvaita framework of devotion) began laying a dominant claim to the temple and its resources. As explained earlier in this study, the Śaiva temples were patronized heavily by the Cōḷa rulers and the Vaiṣṇava temples had to compete with them. Additionally, this was a period when powerful new non-*brāhmaṇa* political and social groups from a Tamil context were asserting themselves; the inclusion of Tamil devotional works in the Vaiṣṇava liturgy and the fact of these being accorded a status equal to that of the Sanskrit Veda was a strategy to attract these emergent social groups.

The hagiographers, therefore, delineated Rāmānuja, who by then had acquired a formidable reputation as a Vedāntist, as the epitome of this unique mingling of cultural streams that culminated in the creation of *Ubhaya Vedānta*. It might even be said that the *guruparamparā*s tended to inscribe Rāmānuja as the primary vehicle of the Tamil *bhakti* tradition, given their detailed accounts of how Rāmānuja was instructed in the learning of the Tamil *Prabandham*s. This strategy adopted was then engendered through various narratives regarding the *Tiruvāymoḻi* and the rest of the *Nālāyira Divya Prabandham*. Amongst the hymns, Nammāḻvār's *Tiruvāymoḻi* occupied the centre stage in all the narratives. Whether it was the institutionalization of ritual singing in the temples, or initiations of various Śrīvaiṣṇava leaders including Rāmānuja, or the process of the conversion from another religious tradition or a funeral or a festival, the efficacy of the occasion was established only by singing this *Prabandham* and simultaneously providing the explanations for it. Even Govinda Bhaṭṭar, a staunch Śaiva, on hearing Tirumalai Nambi (Śrī Śailapūrṇa) explaining the purport of some of the verses of this hymn, was so moved that he tore off his *rudrākṣa*.[59] In most cases, however, the explanations were predictably provided by none other than Rāmānuja. We are told that while learning the explanations of the *Tiruvāymoḻi* from his preceptors, Ṭiruvarangapperumāḷ Araiyar and Tirumalaiāṇḍāṉ (Mālādhara) in separate sessions, Rāmānuja provided a different explanation. Both the *gurus* were impressed by Rāmānuja's interpretations and after discussing with each other, they decided to accept them.[60] In another version, it is reported that at one point Rāmānuja's interpretation of a particular passage in the *Tiruvāymoḻi* annoyed his *guru* Mālādhara. Goṣṭhīpūrṇa who was present there intervened and told Mālādhara that Rāmānuja's explanation was correct and in line with Yāmuna's views which he had heard from Yāmuna himself. Thereupon, Mālādhara was surprised and, at the same time, he was impressed too and his son became the disciple of Rāmānuja.[61] The narratives hinted at different interpretations of the *Tiruvāymoḻi* that were circulating and Rāmānuja's was shown to be most influential amongst them. Such narratives established Rāmānuja firmly in the ācāryic lineage that was the medium of knowledge transmission. Further, Rāmānuja is said to have commissioned Piḷḷāṉ, one of his close disciples, to write a commentary on the *Tiruvāymoḻi*, and the tradition often considers Piḷḷāṉ's commentary to be a record of Rāmānuja's views regarding the Tamil Veda. This work of Piḷḷāṉ coupled with his being Rāmānuja's uncle, Śrī Śailapūrṇa's son qualified him to be the direct descendant of Rāmānuja. It is told to us that on one occasion, Rāmānuja was contemplating about a particular *Prabandham*. Piḷḷāṉ articulated the thoughts of Rāmānuja who was surprised as well as impressed on Piḷḷāṉ's insightfulness and declared him his intellectual descendant (*jñānaputra*).[62]

The *Muāyirappaṭi* states that apart from providing interpretations on the *Tiruvāymoḻi* and revitalizing the defunct *Adhyayanōtsava* festival, Rāmānuja also stabilized the structure of the ritual singing into an order.[63] The hagiography records that *Rāmānuja Nūṟṟandādi* was composed by Tiruvaraṅgamudanār in Tamil in praise of Rāmānuja and appended to the corpus of the *Nālāyira Divya Prabandham* at the *ācārya*'s behest.

59 *Āṟāyirappaṭi*, p. 188.

60 *Āṟāyirappaṭi*, pp. 198–200; *Muāyirappaṭi*, p. 97.

61 *Divyasūricaritam*, Ch. 18, *śloka* 66.

62 *Yatirāja Vaibhavam, śloka*s 81–2; *Muāyirappaṭi*, pp. 109–10.

63 *Muāyirappaṭi*, pp. 119–20.

Thereafter, Rāmānuja also decided in consultation with Piḷḷāṉ regarding the arrangement of *taṉiyaṉs* preceding and succeeding the ritual singing. This was accompanied by Rāmānuja's visits to various Śrīvaiṣṇava centres or the *divya desas*, including Kuḍandai, Āḻvār Tirunagari, and installation of the shrines in honour of the Āḻvārs, especially Nammāḻvār and Āṇṭāḷ.

The narratives thus became the ideological basis on which this particular group of *brāhmaṇas* allied to the Sanskritic tradition were reclaiming and appropriating the already existent Tamil base and consolidating themselves as an influential group within the temple organizations. The hagiographies also document tensions within the Śrīvaiṣṇava community. Rāmānuja is said to have faced opposition when he took over as the *Śrikāryam* or the manager of the temple, to the extent that there were attempts to poison him, as described earlier in this chapter. One can conclude that the conflict was between the new, Sanskritic-affiliated aspirants and the older established hymnal groups, already entrenched within the temple hierarchy.

Thus, within the framework of the *Ubhaya Vedānta* tradition and the language of *Maṇipravāḷa*, the hagiographies were both a record of the evolution of Śrīvaiṣṇava liturgy and of community history, sectarianism, and political expediency. Asserting a unified Śrīvaiṣṇava community on one hand and reflecting the claims of the different religious groups on the other, these texts encrusted the image of Rāmānuja with legends and stories that acquired immense popularity over the generations and circulated in the cultural sphere so effectively that they became a permanent and integral part of cultural memory. However, such a duality in the Śrīvaiṣṇava tradition could not sustain itself for long. The authors of the complex textual tradition were the *ācāryas* or the spiritual heads who were *brāhmaṇas* themselves. It is to be noted that this duality also crept into the names of the Śrīvaiṣṇava Āḻvārs, and *ācāryas*—all of whom, according to the textual tradition, had a Sanskrit as well as a Tamil name. The tensions between the Sanskrit and Tamil components were always evident in the texts, and the ensuing schism led to the community dividing itself into the Vaṭakaḷai (northern) and Teṉkaḷai (southern) sects of Śrīvaiṣṇavism.

Lineage: Continuity of Transmission

Historically speaking, Śrīvaiṣṇava religious leadership was not an unbroken sequence. The role of the hagiographers was to fill these gaps and create a sense of continuity, especially with regard to documenting the spiritual genealogy from the last Āḻvārs to the first *ācārya*, Nāthamuni, and from his successor Yāmuna or Ālavandar to Rāmānuja, and from Rāmānuja onwards to other *ācāryas*. For instance, the Śrīvaiṣṇava hagiographies state that the appointment of Rāmānuja as the *ācāryic* head of the community was divinely preordained. This was significant considering that he was not born into a Śrīvaiṣṇava lineage and, as stated before, he was a *smārta*. The texts further inform us that while Rāmānuja was a student, his fame as an intellectual countering the formidable Advaita philosophy with alternative interpretations spread far and wide. This reputation impressed Yāmuna, who was anxiously searching for a befitting successor at that point of time. This anxiety on the part of Yāmuna for a successor was clearly a manifestation of the hagiographers' concerns for a lineage to ensure the transmission of the tradition. We are further told that Yāmuna made repeated attempts to meet Rāmānuja, but failed. Along with his chief disciples, Yāmuna arrived at Kāñcīpuram to worship Lord Varadarājasvāmī. He saw Rāmānuja from a distance in the company of his *guru* Yādavaprakāśa and fellow disciples, and wondered as to how and when Rāmānuja would become his own student. He then prayed to Varadarāja that his wish should be fulfilled. However, he was unable to meet Rāmānuja and finally returned to Śrīraṅgam.[64] This narrative reflects the hagiographic intent to show that even before Rāmānuja was aware of it, the Śrīvaiṣṇava community with Yāmuna as its chief *ācārya* had decided to induct Rāmānuja as an *ācārya*, despite not being born as Śrīvaiṣṇava.

The hagiographies relate that after leaving Yādavaprakāśa's *āśrama* due to tensions with him, Rāmānuja then started worshipping Varadarājaswāmī, the Śrīvaiṣṇava deity at the temple in Kāñcīpuram and continued with his *kainkarya* or service to the God of offering water from the roadside well. Yāmuna rejoiced upon hearing this, and in order to bring Rāmānuja within the Śrīvaiṣṇava fold, he sent a learned man called Mahāpūrṇa (Periya Nambi) to Kāñcīpuram with his own composition *Stotraratna*. When Rāmānuja heard the *stotra*, he was moved but the hagiographies still did not show him embracing Śrīvaiṣṇavism.

Finally, it was at Yāmuna's funeral that Rāmānuja got the opportunity to learn about the three last wishes of Yāmuna: the veneration of Vyāsa

[64] *Divyasūricaritam*, Ch. 17, *ślokas* 12–15; *Yatirāja Vaibhavam*, *ślokas* 13–16; *Āṟāyirappaṭi*, pp. 148–50; *Muāyirappaṭi*, pp. 78–9.

and the composition of a commentary on the *Vedāntasūtra* of Vyāsa (i.e., the Sanskritic tradition); the propagation of the hymns of the Āḻvārs (i.e., the Tamil tradition) through a commentary on the *Tiruvāymoḻi*; and finally the remembrance of the Lord. Rāmānuja's promise to fulfil Yāmuna's wishes implied a philosophical synthesis which also served to consolidate the Śrīvaiṣṇavas into a single community with a particular a belief system.[65] It also established continuity between the two *ācārya*s, which is otherwise historically missing, and legitimized Rāmānuja as the next *ācārya* of the community. As Hardy has rightly pointed out:

> These hagiographers do not deceive us concerning the facts that Rāmānuja was never directly taught by Yāmuna, that the intellectual relationship between Yāmuna and Nāthamuni is a distant one, and that Nāthamuni's contact with the Tamil Viṣṇu *bhakti* tradition is very indirect indeed. What is done here is to establish an inner continuity *in spite* of chronological problems. That such problem is acknowledged and not simply wiped away by means of a truly fabricated and merely seemingly logical account, is the impressive feature I am commenting upon.[66]

The *Muāyirappaṭi* interestingly points out that Yāmuna stated his three desires before he died.[67] The *guruparamaparā* texts are peppered with references to Rāmānuja implementing a system perpetuated by Yāmuna. Since there was no direct *guru-śiṣya* relationship between Yāmuna and Rāmānuja, the site of Yāmuna's funeral became a crucial context to establish a connection. The hagiographies report that when Rāmānuja promised to fulfil these three desires, Yāmuna's three fingers which were bent till then signifying his three unfulfilled wishes straightened, seeing which everybody declared that Rāmānuja was the legitimate successor and establisher of the *Siddhānta*. On different occasions in these texts, it was clearly stated that Rāmānuja fulfilled the three wishes: he composed the *Śrībhāṣya*, a commentary of the *Brahmasūtra* (the first wish); he commissioned Parāśara Bhaṭṭar, son of Kurattāḻvān to compose the *Viṣṇusahasranāma Bhāṣyam* (commentaries, thousand names of Viṣṇu, the second wish); and

[65] *Divyasūricaritam*, Ch. 17, *śloka*s 35–44; *Yatirāja Vaibhavam*, *śloka*s 32–38; *Āṟāyirappaṭi*, p. 164; *Muāyirappaṭi*, pp. 86–7.

[66] Hardy (2001), 'The Formation of Śrīvaiṣṇavism', in Dalmia, et al. (eds), *Charisma and Canon*, p. 57, fn. 11.

[67] *Muāyirappaṭi*, pp. 83–4.

finally, Piḷḷān̲ wrote a comprehensive commentary of the *Tiruvāymoḻi* at his behest (the third wish).[68] However, while describing Yāmuna's funeral and Rāmānuja's bereavement, the *Divyasūricaritam* does mention the pose of Yāmuna's three fingers signifying his three unfilled wishes. But we are not informed as to what the three wishes were, except that on Rāmānuja's arrival at the funeral site, Yāmuna's three fingers straightened. Neither are we told anything about Rāmānuja's promise to fulfil these wishes nor the unanimous approval of the crowd about Rāmānuja being the legitimate successor.[69] The anxiety to link Rāmānuja to Yāmuna is undoubtedly there but muted compared to the other three hagiographies, especially the *Ār̲āyirappaṭi* and *Muāyirappaṭi*.

This textual anxiety over succession and lineage apparent in the hagiographies may be a reflection of the larger Śrīvaiṣṇava practice of remembering preceptors who may or may not have had any physical contact with the *ācārya* concerned. For instance, Yāmuna in his *Stotraratna* pays homage to Nāthamuni, the first *ācārya* and Nammāḻvār, the composer of the *Tiruvāymoḻi* (that was accorded the status of the *Dravida Veda)*, although he did not meet either of them. He even acknowledged Parāśara, the father of Vyāsa and author of the *Viṣṇu Purāṇa*, a purely mythological figure.[70]

To strengthen this link further, the narratives assigned more than one spiritual preceptor to Rāmānuja, who were the direct disciples of Yāmuna. These preceptors individually imparted five different tenets of Śrīvaiṣṇavism to Rāmānuja. Tirukacci Nambi (i.e., Kāñcīpūrṇa) also exercised tremendous influence over Rāmānuja and imparted the basic theology, as stated in the epigraph at the beginning of this chapter. Periya Nambi (i.e., Mahāpurṇa) performed Rāmānuja's *pañcasamskāra* and initiated him formally into Śrīvaiṣṇavism. Tirukkōṭṭiyūr Nambi (Goṣṭhīpūrna) imparted the *dvaya mantra* as well as the secret interpretations of *Tirumantaram.* Tirumalaiāṇḍān (i.e., Mālādhar) imparted the text of *Tiruvāymoḻi* and the traditional commentaries on this core text. Tiruvaraṅga Perumāl Araiyar (i.e., Raṅga) taught Rāmānuja the *stotras*

[68] *Yatirāja Vaibhavam, ślokas* 71–2, 80–4; *Ār̲āyirappaṭi*, pp. 223, 231–2; *Muāyirappaṭi*, pp. 105, 108–11.

[69] *Divyasūricaritam*, Ch. 17, *ślokas* 38–45.

[70] *Stotraratna of Śrī Yāmunācharya* (trans. from Sanskrit by Swami Adidevananda) (1950), pp. 1–6.

and other key ritual and liturgical elements, while Tirumalai Nambi (i.e., Śrī Śaila Pūrṇa) taught the *Rāmāyaṇa* to Rāmānuja at Tirupati.

The hagiographies were conscious that Rāmānuja had not met Yāmuna. Anticipating any objection to Rāmānuja's succession, they raised this question in their narrative and provided an answer that was encoded within the Śrīvaiṣṇava thought. So we are told that on one occasion, Rāmānuja asserted that his interpretations on the *Tiruvāymoḻi* were ratified by Yāmuna. Tirumalaiāṉḍān, who was instructing Rāmānuja, asked how he could make such a claim when both of them had never met. To this Rāmānuja replied that he was an Ekalavya to Yāmuna.[71]

This account of Rāmānuja's five preceptors had significant connotations for the Śrīvaiṣṇava community. First, it unified the different components—metaphysical, liturgical, and scriptural—into a single theistic framework of which Rāmānuja was the central authority. It also implied that he was the first to organize the community within this ideological structure. Second, the concept of more than one *guru* (since Rāmānuja officially had five) was significant. This continued in the post-Rāmānuja period, when Śrīvaiṣṇava leaders as well as devotees had more than one *guru*. This multiplicity of *gurus* enabled the formation of diverse religious identities within the community. Third, it established that the *guru* was mostly a *brāhmaṇa*. The *Āṟāyirappaṭi* provides a justification by raising a question as to why Rāmānuja had to go to more than one teacher, when Periya Nambi had already initiated him. The answer in the text provided by Tiruvaraṅga Perumāl Araiyar established the greatness of Rāmānuja:

> If you ask this question, the comparison is with the king who because of special affection for his son, entrusts his wealth with several ministers and instructs the ministers that when the son is worthy of it, he should get it. Ālavandar (Yāmuna) has distributed the knowledge to various *ācāryas*. He has graced Rāmānuja with his kind looks and instructed the *ācāryas* to divulge these secret meanings to Rāmānuja. Those *ācāryas* who were before Rāmānuja achieved because of him (became his teachers) and there were those who came after him,who became his disciples. Just as in a necklace the bright central gem makes it more beautiful,

[71] *Āṟāyirappaṭi*, p. 200. Ekalaya was a character in the *Mahabhārata* who had never met Droṇācārya, the teacher of the Kauravas and Pāṇḍavas, but acknowledged him as his *guru*. He made an image of Droṇācārya for a symbolic presence and practised archery in front of it.

similarly Rāmānuja was like this gem (is in the middle, the most important amongst the *ācāryas).*[72]

Śrīvaiṣṇava Community: Organization and Structure

The structuring and configuration of the Śrīvaiṣṇava spiritual genealogy into a cohesive organization further established the credibility of Rāmānuja as supreme *ācārya* of the community. Except the *Divyasūricaritam,* all the hagiographies provide the following details with regard to the organization of the community structure: Rāmānuja appointed 74 disciples, had a following of 700 (*jīyars*) ascetics, 12,000 *ekāṅgīs*, both *brāhmaṇa* and non-*brāhmaṇa* devotees, 300 *koṟṟiammais*, and countless kings.[73] The narratives further report that these disciples were of good conduct, followed meticulously the rules of the *Śāstras*, and therefore Rāmānuja entrusted them to carry on the tradition forward. *Yatirāja Vaibhavam* also mentions that according to Rāmānuja's instructions, these disciples installed his images in Śrīperumbudūr, Śrīraṅgam and Tirunārāyaṇapuram.

The hagiographies like *Yatirāja Vaibhavam* and *Muāyirappaṭi* pointed out that Rāmānuja was pleased that even his senior disciples like Kūreśa followed Piḷḷāṉ's instructions, who was otherwise junior in the *ācāryic* hierarchy. Perhaps the authors were aware of the contestations that arose or could have arisen, and therefore, establishing unanimity about Piḷḷāṉ as the immediate successor became crucial in assuaging any kind of doubts and apprehensions that could have existed or had the potential to develop. For instance, the *Muāyirappaṭi* invokes the divine sanction as well as Yāmuna's association to justify Piḷḷāṉ's succession:

> Uḍaiyavar (Rāmānuja) decided that *mudalis* who were within, were innumerable and there should be some order. He made 74 *śaṅkhas* and *cakras* which he installed and 4 *Śrībhāṣyas, Śrīkoṣas* and offered with the *Āṟāyirappaṭi* composed by Piḷḷāṉ before Peraruḷāḷa. He called the *mudalis* and gave 74 of them the *śaṅkhas* and the *cakras*.... He instructed that those who came later would be given *ubhayavedānta* and signet ring and thus 74 were given *simhāsanapāditya,* of them 4 had *Śrībhāṣya simhāsanapāditya,* 1

[72] *Āṟāyirappaṭi,* pp. 201–2.

[73] *Yatirāja Vaibhavam, ślokas* 109–10; *Āṟāyirappaṭi,* pp. 270–1; *Muāyirappaṭi,* pp. 121–4.

> *ubhayavedānta -ādhipatya*. Apart from this, there were 700 disciples, 12,000 *tiruvādya ekāntīs* and those who did *tirumañjanam* and other *kainkaryas* and many Śrīvaiṣṇavas who did their *kainkaryas* according to Rāmānuja's instructions. Because of Ālavandar's instructions, the title *jñānaputra* was given to Piḷḷāṉ and through him the *Āṟāyirappaṭi* was composed. Because he (Piḷḷāṉ) had the *ubhayavedanta*, all these seniors who were older than him, who were *dattaputras* obeyed Piḷḷāṉ born after them and did *kainkaryas* according to his instructions. Rāmānuja seeing that this was acceptable to the *Śāstras* and to himself was pleased.[74]

Interestingly, this anxiety over succession becomes accentuated when one finds that in the *Divyasūricaritam* and *Āṟāyirappaṭi*, Rāmānuja appointed Parāśara Bhaṭṭar as the successor:

> Rāmānuja took Bhaṭṭar to the *sanctum sanctorum* and made him receive the *tīrthaprasāda* (offering of holy water) and he also took the *prasāda*. He told Bhaṭṭar, 'there is a learned man who is a *Vedāntin* and lives in Mēlnāḍu. You go there and convert him to our ways.' Then he took Bhaṭṭar to the *maṭha* and called all the *mudalis* and made them touch his feet and gave them water and food.[75]

Though Bhaṭṭar was at the centre of the lineage, subsidiary lineages emerged with the narratives telling us that Rāmānuja entrusted different sets of disciples to Kaṇḍāḍaiāṇḍāṉ, Aruḷāḷapperumāḷemberumānār, Embār, Piḷḷāṉ, and Naḍavilāḷvāṉ (presumably his own closest disciples) respectively.[76]

Unlike the *Divyasūricaritam* and *Yatirāja Vaibhavam*, the specifications about the lineage are much more detailed in the *Āṟāyirappaṭi* and *Muāyirappaṭi*.[77] The latter two hagiographies were situated in a context when the issue of succession assumed significant dimensions in the post-Rāmānuja period (thirteenth century onwards) and the hagiographical texts attempted to establish the credibility of the

74 *Muāyirappaṭi*, pp. 121–2.

75 *Āṟāyirappaṭi*, p. 316. *Divyasūricaritam* merely mentions that Rāmānuja appointed Bhaṭṭar as his successor. See *Divyasūricaritam*, Ch.18, *śloka* 95.

76 *Āṟāyirappaṭi*, p. 316.

77 *Divyasūricaritam* though does not provide any such details, the narratives in it provide at length about the names of the disciples and their family background, in most cases, the sons of the *gurus* of Rāmānuja.

various groups they were representing. These texts thus emerged as the ideological basis for the subsequent sectarian identity/conflict. Since the group of 74 who were called *simhāsanapatis*, meaning heads of various thrones (apostolic throne) was supposed to have been personally chosen by Rāmānuja, an association with their lineage would automatically bestow legitimacy to any claims of socio-religious space made by the sectarian leaders. Interestingly, the early preceptors of both the Vaṭakaḷai and Teṉkaḷai lineages belonged to this group of seventy-four. Further, the powerful sectarian families in the Vijayanagar period (for instance, the Kanḍāḍai family and the Tatācārya group) also traced their descent from one of the seventy-four claiming an honorable lineage that would entrench them dominantly within the Śrīvaiṣṇava community. The political prototype of these seventy-four religious heads in Śrīvaiṣṇavism may have its source in the thirteenth and the fourteenth centuries, when the practice of the 'seventy-two', that is, *bahattara-niyoga* was instituted in the temples of the Telugu country. Legend has it that when the Vijayanagara chief Kumāra Kampana conquered the southern regions, he or one of his chief *nāyakas* established the institution of the seventy-two *nāyakas*.[78]

Both the hagiographies provided a comprehensive list of disciples (*mudalis*). Despite variations, the details of the disciples in both the set of narratives comprised *brāhmaṇas*, non-*brāhmaṇas*, and women, thus marking out a broad-based community, a point that will be taken up in the next chapter for discussion. The *Āṟāyirappaṭi* even documents the various activities that Rāmānuja allotted to each of his disciples.[79] For instance, Vaḍuga Nambi, the author of *Yatirāja Vaibhavam*, was allotted the duty of anointing the Lord with oil; Kiḍāmbiāccān Piḷḷai and Kiḍāmbi Perumāḷ were responsible for the kitchen, the food that was to be cooked, and so on. The concept of succession was so crucial to the community identity that the *Āṟāyirappaṭi* and *Muāyirappaṭi* have details about the important disciples of Rāmānuja, commending their achievements and delineating them as befitting successors.

[78] Without providing specific references, Jagadeesan speculates that Rāmānuja was probably inspired by the Jainas, who had seventy-two religious *samasthānas*. He also suggests that the Śaiva canon with its sixty-three *nāyanārs* is a precedent for the framework of sixty-three Jaina *ācāryas*. See Jagadeesan (1977), *History of Srivaishnavism*, p. 47.

[79] *Āṟāyirappaṭi*, pp. 271–2.

Intending to ascribe an impressive organizational capacity and network to Rāmānuja, the narratives registered three concerns. First, was the identity of a Śrīvaiṣṇava. Amidst such diversity, this had to be settled so as to provide a reference point. We are told that Rāmānuja ordained five tasks or *kainkarya* that a Śrīvaiṣṇava must perform as long he lived: reading and propagating the *Śrībhāṣya*; if for some reasons he is unable to do so, then he should attend the discourses that explain the *Śrībhāṣya*; further he could not listen to the discourses, then he should serve in the various Śrīvaiṣṇava temple centres (*divyadesas*), performing duties like lighting the lamps, making flower garlands, offering food to the Lord, and so on; if he still was unable to do this, then he should listen to the meaning of the *dvaya mantra*; finally, if even this was not possible to do, then he should take refuge with a Śrīvaiṣṇava who honored Rāmānuja, implying that it should be the *ācārya*s chosen as successors by Rāmānuja.[80]

Second, was the status of the Śrīvaiṣṇava tradition amongst other religious tradition, which the narratives tried to establish by documenting the benedictions of various forms of Viṣṇu and the extraordinary spiritual and devotional acts of the *ācārya*s, especially Rāmānuja who by now was delineated as acceptable to everybody as someone 'who had corrected the whole world'.[81] Third, was the issue of perpetuation of the tradition through the lineage. *Muāyirappaṭi* narrates:

> In order that his *siddhānta* should withstand the passage of time, Uḍaiyavar told his disciples, 'Since Lord had decided that this *siddhānta* should be propagated by you, give the *siddhānta* to those who deserve to receive this.' He gave the image of Hayagriva and Peraruḷāḷa whom he worshipped everyday to Piḷḷāṉ. Looking at Piḷḷāṉ kindly in front of the temple, laid his head on Piḷḷāṉ's lap and placed his feet on Kiḍāmbiāccān's lap and closed his eyes … Rāmānuja went to heaven…. Piḷḷāṉ and other *mudalis* were sad and consoled themselves and Piḷḷāṉ performed the last rites. According to Rāmānuja's instructions he gave lectures on the *siddhānta* (*siddhānta pravacana*) and installed Rāmānuja's image in the temple and continued worshipping in that form….[82]

Therefore, the structure and organization of the community became an important strategy in the hagiographies to create a religious space that

[80] *Muāyirappaṭi*, pp. 130–1.

[81] *Muāyirappaṭi*, p. 127.

[82] *Muāyirappaṭi*, pp. 132–3.

would further generate community consciousness. Often reflecting the Śrīvaiṣṇava reality, these narratives also created a normative ideal that would form a pattern for future structuring of the community lineage.

PILGRIMAGE AND PEREGRINATIONS: RĀMĀNUJA AND THE EXPANSION OF COMMUNITY NETWORK

Another factor which led to the dissemination of the Śrīvaiṣṇava *bhakti* was Rāmānuja's travels to various religious centres within and outside south India, described in detail in the hagiographies. The traditional sacred geography of the Śrīvaiṣṇavas included 108 centres, some located in northern part of India. During the course of his tours, Rāmānuja is supposed to have impressed upon the people of other faiths to voluntarily convert to Śrīvaiṣṇavism. This systematic, mission-oriented travel extended the regional supremacy of the Viśiṣṭādvaita faith at a pan-Indian level and enlarged community influence beyond the geographical boundaries delineated by the Āḻvārs. While visiting these sacred centres, the narratives depicted Rāmānuja setting up the shrines of the Āḻvārs, introducing temple festivals and instituting the ritual singing of the *Nālāyira Divya Prabandham*.

Thus, the hagiographical narratives highlighted the notion of sacred journeys through the depiction of Rāmānuja's visits to these sacred sites and their revival into vibrant centres of Śrīvaiṣṇava activities. Such a concept of pilgrimage as a devotional practice was aimed to construct and consolidate community consciousness.[83] On one hand, pilgrimage was expected to provide an arena for group/community interaction and present collective consciousness as the Śrīvaiṣṇava followers would be expected to converge to these centres or *divyadesas*. On the other, it would provide a single context for the assertion of multiple identities within the overarching community paradigm. Such a notion was emphasized upon as the journey to sacred Śrīvaiṣṇava shrines within a well-defined area strengthened territorial presence of the community. Pilgrimage and its associated activities implied not only the movement and relationship of diverse sets of people, but also the transmission, exchange, and circulation of ideas and beliefs, a flow that influenced and enriched community ideology.

[83] For details, see Dutta (2010), 'Pilgrimage as a Religious Process', pp. 17–38.

A comprehensive pilgrimage network comprising 108 sacred centres was charted out in the hagiographies. Out of these 108, two, namely Tirupāḍkaḍal (the Milky Ocean) and Vaikunṭham (Abode of Lord Viṣṇu), are other worldly. A visit to the remaining 106 appeared prominently in Rāmānuja's life-story. The hagiographers clearly marked the route he took, starting from Śrīraṅgam, the major Śrīvaiṣṇava centre.[84] In general, he visited Tirukkōvalūr, the meeting place of the first three Āḻvārs, Kāñcīpuram, Tirumala-Tirupati, Tirukuḍandai, (Cōḷa country, Tañjāvūr district), Aḻagarkōyil, Śrīvilliputtūr, Madurai, Tirukkuruṅguḍi (Pāṇḍya country), Tiruvānpariśāram, Tiruvattānu, and finally Tiruvananthapuram (Malaināḍu). He also travelled towards north along the western coast to reach Dvāraka, Mathurā, Vṛndāvana, Govardhana, Naimśāraṇya, Badrikāśrama, and Śālagrama (Nepal). His journey also took him through Kāśi (Uttar Pradesh), Jagannātha Puri (Orissa), Śrīkurmam, Simhācalam, Tirumalai (Andhra region), and finally he returned to Śrīraṅgam.[85] Pilgrimage did emerge significantly as a religious practice from the fourteenth century onwards as reflected in the epigraphical records that clearly stated the sectarian statuses of the donor and donee to the temples and their affiliation with a particular shrine.

The narratives on Rāmānuja's peregrinations had political overtones. Referring to his journeys as *digvijaya* (victory in all directions) or *vijaya*, his spiritual victories over other traditions were depicted as analogous to political victories The narratives termed these other traditions disparagingly as *kūdṛṣtis* (bad ideas). Further, the narratives clearly stated that Rāmānuja converted the rulers of various places to Śrīvaiṣṇavism, thereby revealing the Śrīvaiṣṇava desire for political patronage:

> Then the king of the place came and fell at his feet. The *vidwāns* (scholars) full of jealousy tried to abuse Rāmānuja who said, 'I shall see this.' Then the *vidwāns* became mad and clashed one against the other and were scattered all over the place like spirits. King prayed to Rāmānuja that he should not do this and make them normal and not mad like this. Rāmānuja obliged the king and the king came with his retinue and bid him farewell. After that, Rāmānuja came to Vāranasī, bathed in Ganges, worshipped the god at

84 *Yatirāja Vaibhavam*, *śloka*, 87; *Āṟāyirappaṭi*, p. 223.

85 *Divyasūricaritam*, Ch.18, *ślokas* 11–48; *Yatirāja Vaibhavam*, *ślokas* 87–93; *Āṟāyirappaṭi*, pp. 222–9; *Muāyirappaṭi*, pp. 106–7.

> Kadinagari and then went to Śrī Purśottamam, worshipped Jagannātha and conquered the *pracanḍa* and *bhanḍa vidwans*, established a Rāmānujam *maṭha* there, went to Śrīkūrmam and worshipped there. Then he went to Simahādrī, worshipped there, met other scholars, agrued with them and conquered them ...[86]

The hagiographies focused on four main ideas that influenced the sacred geography of the Śrīvaiṣṇavas in the post-Rāmānuja period:

(1) Accounts of the pilgrimage to the northern sites were characterized by descriptions of Rāmānuja's successful assertion of Viśiṣṭādvaitic philosophy through various debates with the Advaitins on metaphysical subjects, and his assertion of a distinct Śrīvaiṣṇava identity. This was further magnified in the portrayal of Rāmānuja's exceptional ability to undertake intellectual debates with the divine personalities. Hagiographies provide several instances. The episode of interaction between Sarasvatī, the goddess of learning, and Rāmānuja and the latter acknowledging his intellectual abilities, presenting him an idol of Hayagriva, and conferring on him the title of *Bhāṣyakāra* has already been cited earlier.

(2) Descriptions of the pilgrimage within the southern boundaries always centred on the organizational aspects of Śrīvaiṣṇava religious practice. At all these sites Rāmānuja was credited with the establishment of a new temple organization and community reform in terms of a significant new aspect—the introduction of non-brāhmaṇical participation in temple worship. At Tirupati, Rāmānuja was supposed to have accepted Viṭṭhaladeva, the local ruler as his disciple and got the place settled with thirty Śrīvaiṣṇava.

(3) The emergence of Śrīraṅgam as a major centre of Śrīvaiṣṇavism is clearly documented, and the site is depicted as the starting and the culminating point of the journey. In fact, the entire pilgrimage narrative is punctuated with references to Rāmānuja's organizational and intellectual activities at Śrīraṅgam, especially the institution of the singing of the *Prabandhas*, composition of his works, and delivering of discourses in which crucial theological issues were expounded upon. By combining the liturgical and

[86] *Āṟāyirappaṭi*, pp. 226–7.

intellectual characteristics at Śrīraṅgam, a focal point of pilgrimage network emerged.

(4) The narratives describe the inclusion in the pilgrimage network of new sites which otherwise do not figure in the 108 established shrines but became significant due to their association with Rāmānuja. Mēlkōṭe in Karnataka is one such example. Rāmānuja's migration from Toṇṇūru to Mēlkōṭe in the Karnataka region during Hoysala rule in the twelfth century generated a new pilgrimage route in that region, linking it to the larger pilgrimage network. This was also the case with the areas of Śrīkākulam and Simhācalam in the Andhra region. Jagannātha Puri in Orissa was also inducted into the pilgrimage network as Rāmānuja was attributed with the establishment of a *māsa* there.

Very often the reason for travel or journey was also the context of religious persecution that accidentally and incidentally culminated in the establishment of a temple centre and hence a pilgrimage site. The story of the persecution of Rāmānuja and his fellow Śrīvaiṣṇavas by the Cōḷa ruler, described in this chapter before, further offshoots into the narrative of the establishment of the Nārāyaṇasvāmī temple at Mēlkōṭe. After spending time in the Hoysala kingdom, the narratives in the *Divyasuricaritam* tell us that Rāmānuja discovered the god Sampatkumāra (a form of Viṣṇu) near a lake in Yādavagiri and installed it there, providing for the services of 52 Śrīvaiṣṇavas in the temple. Thereafter, at the request of the devotees there, he installed his own idol and, with a heavy heart, departed from Yādavagiri.[87] The *Yatirāja Vaibhavam*, *Āṟāyirappaṭi*, and *Muāyirappaṭi* also give similar details; the *Āṟāyirappaṭi* and *Muāyirappaṭi* even provide a date, Śaka 1012, Bahudānya *samvatasara*, *Paṅguṇi māsa* or month (according to *Muāyirappaṭi*) and *Tai māsa* (according to *Āṟāyirappaṭi*), *śukla caturdasi*, Thursday, in Purnarvasu *nakṣatra* (star) when the god at Yādavagiri was discovered near the water tank.[88] However, all of them provide an account—though with variations—of Rāmānuja's recovery of the festival image (*utsavamurti*), Rāmapriya, at Mēlkōṭe that was looted in the past by the ruler of Delhi during his invasion of the Karnataka region. The *Muāyirappaṭi* has a detailed narrative, a summary of which is presented below:

87 *Divyasūricaritam*, Ch. 18, *śloka*s 89–90.

88 *Āṟāyirappaṭi*, p. 251; *Muāyirappaṭi*, p. 115.

> One day, Viṣṇu appears before Rāmānuja in a dream and reveals that I am in the snake-pit under a bakula tree which is in the south west corner of Yadugiri's lake (*kalyāṇasaras*). The myth informs us that Yadugiri was already a Vaiṣṇava centre due to the presence of the *tirumaṉ*, the holy white clay used by the Śrīvaiṣṇavas. With the help of Viṣṇuvardhana, the converted Hoysala ruler, Rāmānuja clears the forests at Yadugiri, builds a temple, and installs the god in it. However, he finds that the festival image or the *utasava murti*, Rāmapriya is missing and the festivals of the temple cannot therefore resume. Viṣṇu appears again before Rāmānuja and reveals that the deity is in the palace of the *Turuṣka* (Turkish) king in Delhi. Then along with the other Śrīvaiṣṇavas, Rāmānuja reaches Delhi and meets the Sultan. The Sultan impressed by Rāmānuja's radiance, honours him and asked him what he wanted. Rāmānuja replied that he wanted Rāmapriya back. At the ruler's behest, the royal treasury is searched but the image is not found. He is told that the idol is being worshipped by the princess. He informs the king about this and the king grants the permission. When Rāmānuja invokes the god, the *utsava murti*, walks out of the princess's bedroom, comes to him and sits on his lap. Rāmānuja is delighted, embraces him and calls him Śelvapiḷḷai, my little boy.The princess who is sleeping, wakes up and says that I cannot live without Śelvapiḷḷai. The king sent his men to get back the idol. Rāmānuja quickly took Śelvapiḷḷai secretly and the people of that area wanted a reward and he installed Śelvapiḷḷai in Yādavagiri. The princess follows the god, braving many hardships on the way. On reaching the temple site, the *Turuṣkarāja putrī* (daughter of *Turuṣka* king), prostrated before the god and disappeared. Meanwhile, the news of the Cōḷa ruler's death reaches Mēlkōṭe. Rāmānuja decides to leave. At the request of his devotees, he makes an idol of himself, infused it with power and gave it to them.[89]

The *Yatirāja Vaibhavam* documented this episode succinctly in two *śloka*s stating that 'the daughter of the Delhi king, having arrived there passed out of sight'.[90] However, the hagiography does not refer to the Tulukkan (Turkish) identity of the king and his daughter, merely calling them as *Dillīśa* (king of Delhi) and *Dillīśaputrī* (daughter of the king of Delhi).[91] Interestingly, the *Āṟāyirappaṭi* while recounting this episode merely referred to daughter of the Delhi ruler in context of the idol

[89] *Muāyirappaṭi*, pp. 115–18.

[90] Krishnaswami Aiyangar 1909 [1985], *The Yatirājavaibhavam of Āndhrapūrṇa (Life of Rāmānuja), śloka* 101.

[91] Ibid., *śloka*s 100–1.

of Rāmapriya found in her bedroom (*sajjāgṛha*). The narratives of the princess' bereavement when Rāmānuja took away the idol, the king's soldiers chasing the Śrīvaiṣṇavas with the princess following them and finally her merging with the god at Mēlkōṭe are absent. Stating that the king (*Turuṣkarāja*, *Dillipurendra*) repeatedly fell at Rāmānuja's feet, first apologizing for not being able to trace the idol and, second, impressed with Rāmānuja's spiritual powers that could beckon the Lord; the *Āṟāyirappaṭi* also stated that the king honoured Rāmānuja with all the royal paraphernalia, on the latter's departure from Delhi.[92]

In relation to this north Indian 'Tulukkan' element featuring in Rāmānuja's hagiographies, it should be noted that while Rāmānuja lived from c.1017–1137 CE, the invasions of Alauddin Khalji took place between 1296 CE and 1310 CE, and the next set of northern Turkish invasions were by Muhammad bin Tughlaq in the fourteenth century. Therefore, under no circumstances, could the invasions have preceded Rāmānuja. While the hagiographic descriptions in this regard are anachronistic and without historical validity, they mirror vital Śrīvaiṣṇava concerns about the need for increased presence. The hagiographies drew upon political narratives, the first accounts to introduce the invasion motif as a means of portraying a successful dominant ideology, which became significant against the background of an unstable political situation in south India after Cōḷa decline in the thirteenth century. The ignominious defeat of the chiefs and petty rulers, by the Delhi Sultans referred to as '*Yavanas*', '*Tulukkas*', and '*Turuṣka*', and the establishment of political and moral order by various local chiefs became the theme of several court chronicles and political biographies from the fourteenth century onwards. These texts projected an exalted notion of kingship, in which the ruler was an ideal hero and an embodiment of the combined virtues of chivalry and benevolence. The subjugation of an external enemy and benefactions made to temples that were supposed to have been ravaged during Tulukka attacks buttressed this image of the ruler as the upholder of the moral order.[93] However, such an imaging of an

92 *Āṟāyirappaṭi*, pp. 251–3.

93 See Chattopadhyaya (1998), *Representing the Other? Sanskrit Sources and the Muslims* (*Eighth to Fourteenth Centuries*); Talbot (1995), 'Inscribing the Other, Inscribing the Self: Hindu-Muslim Identities in Precolonial India', in *Comparative Studies in Society and History*, 37 (4): pp. 692–722; and Wagoner (1996), 'Sultan among the Hindu Kings: Dresses, Titles and Islamicization of Hindu Culture at Vijayanagar', in *The Journal of Asian Studies*, 55 (4): pp. 851–80.

external enemy did not tally with the political reality. The reversals suffered by the Vijayanagar rulers at the hands of the Bahamani for the control of the Rāichūr Doāb and the final defeat of the Vijayanagar ruler in the sixteenth-century battle of Tālikota tell a different story.

These accounts of valour and victory strongly influenced Śrīvaiṣṇava hagiographical narratives between the late thirteenth-fourteenth and seventeenth centuries. The late thirteenth and early fourteenth centuries were the time period of both the *Āṟāyirappaṭi* and *Muāyirappaṭi*. However, these narrative do not feature at all in the *Divaysūricaritam* which, though, describes in detail Rāmānuja's persecution by the Cōḷas and his subsequent sojourn in Karnataka. The invasion motif in the hagiographies signified Śrīvaiṣṇava vulnerability and its chequered development. The decline of the Pāṇḍyas and the Hoysalas, especially in the Tamil region, resulting in suspension of the patronage by these prominent dynasties, also aggravated the community instabilities. Thus, the exaggerated accounts of plunder, destruction, and the apparent breakdown of the Śrīvaiṣṇava moral order (which was reflected in the Cōḷa persecution story) validated their position vis-à-vis the Vijayanagar rulers and the elites. By projecting a shared past when both (rulers and the Śrīvaiṣṇavas) had to confront a common enemy (Tulukkas, king of Delhi), the texts conveyed an impression of a collective historical experience to regain the patronage which the Śrīvaiṣṇavas claimed they had lost. Hence, the hagiographies only offer a general treatment of the theme of invasion within the larger chronicling of community history—they do not discuss any specific incursion, nor do they specify the name of the Delhi Sultan. In this context, it should be noted that the *Yatirāja Vaibhavam* written by Vaṭuka Nambi is in all probability a thirteenth-century text as discussed in Chapter 2. So, how did the motifs of *Dillīśvara* and his daughter become a part of the hagiography? Was this a later interpolation by those who considered this hagiography significant for their identity? Or was the text written in the last four years of the thirteenth century when Alauddin Khalji invaded? Or was this text written in the fourteenth or fifteenth century and ascribed to Vaṭuka Nambi, whose reputation as a close disciple was established?

Such narratives associated with Rāmānuja and his activities during his peregrinations became the model for the hagiographical narratives on the subsequent *ācāryas*, especially those who were associated as preceptors of various sectarian affiliations. This became important for legitimizing the claims over the temple resources, disciples, and patronage, where both the traditions with their respective spiritual preceptors claimed to be the legitimate successors of Rāmānuja and his ideas. For instance, the Vaṭakaḷai hagiographies refer to their *guru* Vedāntadeśika's pilgrimage journey to all the centres, including the northern sites. His escape to Satyamangalam near Mysore and Mēlkōṭe following the Turkish invasions from the north are reminiscent of Rāmānuja's sojourn in the Karnataka region. Similarly, the *guruparamparās*, especially *Yatindrapravanaprabhāvam* gives a lengthy account of the Turkish invasions and the flight of Piḷḷai Lokācārya, the Teṉkaḷai leader from Śrīraṅgam with the idol of Raṅganātha to Mēlkōṭe and Mysore. According to the narratives, Piḷḷai Lokācārya, due to old age, could not bear the strain and died on the way. Thereafter, the followers continued with their flight and carried the idol to Tirumala-Tirupati and were finally successful in reinstalling it in Śrīraṅgam after peace was established.

While concluding this discussion on Rāmānuja's journeys, it needs to be emphasized again that the hagiographies asserted that Rāmānuja systematically undertook progressive and visionary measures for the consolidation and spread of the Viśiṣṭādvaitic faith. Particularly noteworthy were his temple reforms and the establishment of a strong organization to carry on the tradition after him. Introduced at Śrīraṅgam, these reforms were made mandatory in other temple centres. This had two important implications. First, Rāmānuja's base, that is, the Raṅganāthasvāmī temple at Śrīraṅgam, became the institutional core of the community. According to Śrīvaiṣṇava tradition, Rāmānuja gave discourses and performed ceremonial functions at Śrīraṅgam but was never considered within the regular category of priest (*arcaka*); he was always regarded as supreme *ācārya* of the community. Second, the pattern of worship and the temple organization at Śrīraṅgam was replicated in other Vaiṣṇava centres, thereby integrating the otherwise dispersed religious groups into one community organization, with Rāmānuja as its spiritual head and the Raṅganāthasvāmī temple as its institutional base.

V. REMEMBERING RĀMĀNUJA

A key liturgical method of simultaneously eulogizing and memorializing Rāmānuja was through the oral genre of *stotras* (praise poems) intended for daily recitation during temple as well as domestic worship.

The tone in these *stotras* was generally self-denunciatory, beseeching God or Rāmānuja to deliver the composers who projected themselves as misguided, humble, and foolish devotees mired within the bondage of earthly vices. Thus, highlighting the notion of *bhakti*, *mokṣa*, and *guru–śiṣya* relationship, these *stotras* also underscored the hagiographical reflections on Rāmānuja. For instance, *Śrīraṅganātha Stotra* composed by Parāśara Bhaṭṭar confirms Rāmānuja's sacred journeys:

> The sage Rāmānuja enjoys [himself] worshipping
> At Śrīraṅgam, Kariśaila, Ajñanagiri,
> Tarksyādri, and Siṁhācala,
> At Śrīkūrma, and Puruśottama,
> Badrinārāyaṇa and Naimīśa
> At Śrīmaddvārka, Prayāg, Mathurā, and Ayodhyā,
> And at Gayā, Puśkara and Sālagrāmagiri.[94]

Similarly, the *Āṟāyirappaṭi* informs us that *Varadarāja Stava* was composed by Kūreśa (Kurattāḻvān) at Rāmānuja's request, who wanted that through this *stotra*, Kūreśa, whose eyes were blinded by the Cōḷa ruler, should ask for vision from the Lord. Kūreśa composed the *stotra* and sang it. Since Rāmānuja was preoccupied elsewhere, Kūreśa sang in his absence and pleased the Lord, who then asked him about his wish. Kūreśa pleaded for the redemption of the Cōḷa minister, Nāluraṉ, who was responsible for his blinding. When Rāmānuja heard this, he came running and complained to the Lord about ignoring his prayers. The diety pacified Rāmānuja and told him that he was granting Kūreśa spiritual vision (*divyacakṣu*). Thereafter, the Lord assured Rāmānuja that Kūreśa could see the world with the Lord's eyes, and finally Rāmānuja was satisfied after Kūreśa identified the Lord's jewels with the help of the Lord's vision.[95]

The *stotras* of Kūreśa and Parāśara Bhaṭṭar, composed mostly in Sanskrit, while praised the three most popular Śrīvaiṣṇava deities—Raṅganāthasvāmī of Śrīraṅgam, Varadarājasvāmī of Kāñcīpuram, and Sundara of Aḻagarkōyil near Madurai, they also validated their close relationship with Rāmānuja:[96]

[94] Parāśara Bhaṭṭar, *Śrīraṅganātha Stotra*, Nancy Ann Nayar, trans. (1994), *Praise-Poems to Viṣṇu and Śrī*, Verse 8, p. 313. Also see Nayar (1992), *Poetry as Theology: The Śrīvaiṣṇava Stotra in the Age of Rāmānuja*, pp. 76–104.

[95] *Āṟāyirappaṭi*, pp. 265–6.

[96] Nayar, trans. (1994), Praise–Poems to Visnu, pp. 1–3.

> I take refuge at the feet of my illustrious preceptor Rāmānuja the sole ocean of compassion who because of passionate attachment to the gold of Acyuta's lotus feet eternally considers all else as straw![97] I have obtained wisdom from the chief of ascetics Rāmānuja and have taken refuge with the auspicious feet of Hari....[98]

While Kūreśa and Parāśara Bhaṭṭar, Rāmānuja's close disciples, did not compose any *stotras* dedicated to Rāmānuja, Tiruvaraṅgatta Amudanār composed the *Rāmānuja Nūṟṟandādi* dedicated exclusively to him. Appended to the *Nālāyira Divya Prabandham*, it is recited till day, thus invoking on regular basis the memories of Rāmānuja. By thirteenth century, Rāmānuja as a figure of authority and the most important *ācārya* seems to have been well entrenched, for now *stotras* exclusively dedicated to him were composed. Vedāntadeśika and Maṇavāḷamāmuṉi composed *Yatirāja Saptati and Yatirāja Vimśati* in Sanskrit respectively, dedicated exclusively to Rāmānuja. Since both of them were influential ideologues of the Śrīvaiṣṇava community, the *stotras* composed by them were crucial in memorializing Rāmānuja.

Apart from extolling Rāmānuja's virtues, the emphases in all these *stotras* were on his status as *Yatirāja* (the king of ascetics), which bestowed upon him authority, his exposition of both the Sanskrit and the Dravida Vedas, and finally, lineage that connected Rāmānuja to the Āḻvārs, especially Nammāḻvār and to the composers of the *stotras* themselves, namely, Kūreśa, Parāśara Bhaṭṭar, Vedāntadeśika, and Maṇavāḷamāmuṉi. For instance, in Parāśara Bhaṭṭar's *Śrīraṅgarāja Stava* that describes the temple at Śrīraṅgam and lampoons other religious traditions, Bhaṭṭar provides a lineage starting from his father Kūreśa, followed by his *ācārya* Embār, Rāmānuja, Yāmuna, Nāthamuni, Nammāḻvār, Śrī, and finally Viṣṇu.[99] The *stotras* of Vedāntadeśika and Maṇavāḷamāmuṉi also provide a lineage glorifying the Āḻvārs and *ācāryas* before them. For instance, in *Yatirāja Vimśati*, Maṇavāḷamāmuṉi clearly outlines the lineage associating Nammāḻvār, Periyāḻvār, Tirumangaiāḻvār, Yāmuna, Kūreśa, and Piḷḷāṉ, Parāśara Bhaṭṭar with Rāmānuja.[100]

97 Kūreśa, *Śrīvaikuṇṭha Stava*, Nayar, trans. (1994), verse 1, p. 18.
98 Ibid., (1994), verse 1, p. 84.
99 Parāśara Bhaṭṭar, *Śrīraṅgarāja Stava*, Nayar, trans. (1994), pp. 175–276.
100 Maṇavāḷamāmuṉi, *Yatirāja Vimśati*, verses 1–3, p. 15.

Since Tiruvaraṅgatta Amudanār's *Rāmānuja Nūṟṟandādi* was a part of the canon and was recited along with liturgical exposition of the *Nālāyira Divya Prabandham*, the delineation of Rāmānuja in this *stotra* composed in Tamil becomes significant. It appears that Tiruvaraṅgatta Amudanār was a Śrīvaiṣṇava and probably a disciple of the disciples of Rāmānuja, for he repeatedly described himself as 'serving their feet'. The poet made direct reference to Kūreśa and Parāśara Bhaṭṭar known to be the contemporaries and closest disciples of Rāmānuja, as his own preceptors.

Presenting Rāmānuja as a *guru*, and endowing him with significant attributes and virtues, Tiruvaraṅgatta Amudanār also described the notion of a tradition through a continuous lineage, linking Rāmānuja with the Āḻvārs. The *stotras* highlighted the Āḻvārs hymns as the Tamil rendering of the Vedas that made the religious knowledge comprehensible to everyone. In this context, the *Rāmānuja Nūṟṟandādi* depicted Rāmānuja as the central vehicle of the Tamil Veda and as both establisher and embodiment of the Tamil *bhakti* tradition:

> Rāmānuja firmly established the *bhakti* path, in which the famed Tamil Vedas—the sweet songs of Southern Kurugūr city's King—are the means of union with the divine and see the bands of devotees who realise the truth in this![101]

The *stotra* forcefully asserted that Rāmānuja was the legitimate successor of the Āḻvārs:

> Madurakavi (Nammāḻvār disciple) only desired to enjoy in his heart his master Saṭakopan (Nammāḻvār) who took birth on Earth for the sole purpose of rendering the hard-to-comprehend Vedas into sweet Tamil songs. Rāmānuja showed us the way to the Āḻvār's feet. He alone is our refuge.
>
> The Tamil Veda, *Tiruvāymoḻi*, sung by Māṟaṉ Saṭakopan (Nammāḻvār) is the proper path to enjoy the lord's bliss, it is the only wealth to be attained, mother, father, the high teacher—even the lord of the lotus lady Lakṣmī himself. Rāmānuja who taught this to the world is our ambrosia.[102]

Further, *Rāmānuja Nūṟṟandādi* also depicted Rāmānuja as an interpreter of the Vedas. Rāmānuja's interpretations were valorized over

[101] *Rāmānuja Nūṟṟandādi*, verse 29.

[102] Ibid., verses 18–9.

those of other preceptors, for his exegesis of both the Tamil and the Sanskrit Veda and the new trajectories that arose from their liturgical fusion was considered unparalleled. Further, *Nūṟṟandādi* reiterated that widespread moral/ethical benefits accrued through Rāmānuja's ideological interventions:

> By the knowledge imparted by Rāmānuja, the contradictions of the *Upaniṣads* have been resolved, the lives of the polemics have ended, the Vedic seers have become elevated, the world has received much good, the twin *karmas* of faulty lives have been destroyed.[103]

The text indicated a strong presence of sectarianism; clearly, the milieu in which Tiruvaraṅgatta Amudanār composed was one of aggressive intellectual debates on the Vedas in which different traditions offered competing interpretations, all of which supposedly finally submitted to and were overcome by Rāmānuja's masterful analysis. Energized by the spiritual force of his asceticism, Rāmānuja was described as a warrior and the poet used metaphors of violence to underscore the *ācārya*'s impact on dissenters and opponents:

> O Polemics! Watch out! The rutted elephant called Rāmānuja—with the ichor of sweet Pāṇṇ Paṉ based Māṟaṉ's Tamil *Tiruvāymoḻi* and the hefty tusks of Vedic truths—is running amuck everywhere. Your lives are ended.[104]
>
> When the tigers of heretic thoughts roamed everywhere freely, Rāmānuja came as a lion unto them, strengthened at heart by the Paṉ based songs of fertile Kuraiyaḷūr's king Kalinkaḷũi. I bow to him.[105]
>
> Drawing out his shinning sword called grace; the great *tapasvi* Rāmānuja came to me and cut asunder the overgrowth of *karma* by root. Is he not also our lord who silences the babble of the wicked ones, who pass off bad *Śāstras* in the name of Vedic literature?[106]

Interestingly, the *stotra* also showed that while Viṣṇu was intolerant of those who did not follow the interpretations of the Vedas prescribed by Him, Rāmānuja, on the other hand, was ever patient with devotees, winning them over with his benevolence and converting them to

[103] Ibid., verse 65.
[104] Ibid., verse 64.
[105] Ibid., verse 88.
[106] Ibid., verse 93.

Śrīvaiṣṇavism. In some places, the poet actually considers him superior to Viṣṇu. A definite sense of community, with the Śrīraṅgam temple as its spiritual node, emerges in the poem. Although the canonical *stotra* was an integral part of the daily liturgy, neither issues of caste nor those of pilgrimage and temple reform figured in the text.

This chapter taking hagiographical accounts as a basis for analysis attempted to disucss the earliest Śrīvaiṣṇava perceptions of Rāmānuja, his philosophy of the Viśiṣṭādvaita and his role as the *ācārya* of the community. Through the incorporation of certain ideas and motifs, within the context of the larger textual tradition of an integrated Tamil-Sanskrit liturgical framework, the *guruparamparā*s offered a highly charismatic delineation of Rāmānuja, and this depiction mediated the normative canon and institutional practices. These texts and the textual tradition at this stage were setting the tone for future elaborations of Rāmānuja's image, especially that of a compassionate *guru*. It is stated that the texts selected for analysis here, presented an image that was, to use A.K. Rāmnujan's phrase, 'context-specific' or particular to their respective textual concerns and the composer's intentionality; they were also part of the complex processes of community identity and the building and augmenting of a canon at that point of time. However, such an image of Rāmāṇuja was also intended to be 'context-free', that is, have a universal appeal that transcended temporality and the specific historical context in which they were written.[107] This becomes evident over time when the Rāmānuja of the twelfth- to fourteenth-century texts becomes an ideological fulcrum of the Śrīvaiṣṇava textual tradition from the fifteenth to the seventeenth centuries, over the next three centuries, and subsequently in the modern period too.

[107] Ramanujan (1999), 'Is there an Indian Way of Thinking? An Informal Essay', in Vinay Dharwadker (ed.), *The Collected Essays of A.K. Ramanujan*, pp. 34–51.

CHAPTER FIVE

Devotion and Dissent*

Rāmānuja as a 'Social Reformer'

....Then Tirukkōṭṭiyūr Nambi told Iḷaiāḻvār (Rāmānuja), 'I will tell you the meaning and you should not tell anybody other than these two (Mudaliāṇḍāṉ and Kurattāḻvān, the disciples of Rāmānuja). Thereafter Tirukkōṭṭiyūr Nambi teaches the meaning of the *aṣṭākśara mantra* and *periyatirumantra*. Next day, Rāmānuja goes to the temple courtyard (*tiruvōlakkattilē*) and tells the meanings to many Śrīvaiṣṇavas (*anekam Śrīvaiṣṇavagaḷukku*). Tirukkōṭṭiyūr Nambi called Rāmānuja and said, '[D]id I not tell you to not to reveal this very secret meaning to anybody else?' Rāmānuja said, 'Yes, this is true. Keeping your divine feet in my mind, I told the *mantra*.' Nambi said, 'Do you realize the consequences (*phala)*. Rāmānuja said, 'Since I disobeyed the *ācārya*s order, my fruit is that I will go to hell.' Nambī thereafter asked, 'Knowing this, why did you

*This chapter is a revised version of an article titled 'Devotion and Dissent: The Biographical Process of *Ramanuja* in Shrivaishnava Tradition and History', in Ramswamy (ed.) *Devotion and Dissent in Indian History*, pp. 54–77.

> do it?' Rāmānuja said, 'Only I will go to hell. But since I had your divine feet in my mind, the people would be saved (with the knowledge of the meanings of the secret *mantras*). Nambi thereafter relented and told himself, 'He has *parasmriti*, I do not....' Nambi embraced Rāmānuja and said, 'From now onwards you will now be called Emperumānār (our lord). Up to this time this *darśana* was called *paramavaidika-darśanam*. From now on it will be called *Emperumānār darśanam*.'
>
> *Āṟāyirappaṭi Guruparamparāprabhāvam*[1]

This episode of sharing the knowledge of the sacred *mantras* with all the Śrīvaiṣṇavas, otherwise exclusively confined to the renunciate *brāhmaṇa ācāryas* of the community, has positioned Rāmānuja in modern period as a 'social reformer'. He is revered as unique, for despite his brāhmaṇical status, he dared to defy the brāhmaṇical orthodoxy of his times and dissented against the established social norms. His large-heartedness, especially in connection with this episode, has been considered as 'one of the most spectacular actions' and finds resonance in the contemporary issues of social exclusion.[2]

The hagiographies narrate that as a part of the training in the Śrīvaiṣṇava scriptures, Rāmānuja at the behest of his *guru* Periya Nambi at Śrīraṅgam, accompanied by his disciples, Mudaliāṇḍāṉ and Kurattāḻvān, came to Tirukkōṭṭiyūr to learn the meaning of the exclusive *mantras* from Goṣṭhīpūrṇa, also called Tirukkōṭṭiyūr Nambi, who was an intimate disciple of Ālavandār. Tirukkōṭṭiyūr Nambi, deciding to test Rāmānuja's will and patience, refused to teach him. Despite the insistence of the deity in the temple and his disciples, it was only on the eighteenth visit by Rāmānuja that Tirukkōṭṭiyūr Nambi agreed to impart the secret meanings, on the condition that Rāmānuja comes alone with his *daṇḍa* (staff) and *pavittra* (ring), the insignias of a renunciate. As the *mantra* was highly covert, Nambi was unhappy to see that Rāmānuja was accompanied by Mudaliāṇḍāṉ and Kurattāḻvān, and thus refused to teach him. At this point, the narratives introduce the crucial concept of transmission and the *guru–śiṣya* tradition by reporting that Rāmānuja convinced Nambi that Mudaliāṇḍāṉ was equivalent to *daṇḍa*

[1] *Āṟāyirappaṭi*, pp. 193–5.

[2] Seshadri (1996a), 'Ramanuja: Social Influence of His Life and Teaching', p. 294. See also, Gōvindāchārya (1906), *The Life of Rāmānujāchārya*, pp. 93–9; Parthasarathy (2008), *Ramanujar*, pp. 28–32.

and Kurattāḻvān was his *pavittra*, implying that he would learn in their presence. Thereafter, Nambi taught him the secret meanings which Rāmānuja shared with everybody.

The patience and persistence of Rāmānuja, the arduous process through which he acquired this knowledge and sharing it at the risk of his damnation, along with other such catholic acts of democratizing the religious ideas and social practice have made his modern biographers compare him to Jesus, Buddha, and to bestow the epithet of 'Periyar who wore the *janeyū*' or Ambedkar who wore the twelve *nāmams*.[3] Such delineations of Rāmānuja as a social pioneer have also placed him as an important influence on the medieval *bhakti* movement, especially on Kabīr in the sixteenth century, who was well known for his strident protest against the social norms of hierarchy and religious rituals. This idea of devotion institutionalized in the worship and participation of the marginalized social groups supposedly at Rāmānuja's initiatives in the temple and its organization is also closely associated with his philosophy of Viśiṣṭādvaita. Thus, it follows that Viśiṣṭādvaita is a progressive system of thought that emphasizes upon the accessibility to the divine grace by any devotee, irrespective of his caste status.

The narratives in the *gururparamparā* texts, *stotra*s, and the commentaries that have interpreted and reinterpreted the exegetical ideas of Rāmānuja have been the basis of such delineations. Since all these genres of texts are regarded as sacred with a scriptural status for the Śrīvaiṣṇavas, their presentation of Rāmānuja assumes significance. The narratives focusing on his exemplariness in general and his compassionate attitude in particular have generated unmitigated devotion towards him. This has been especially crucial for the Śrīvaiṣṇava identity that articulated itself especially by continuously engaging with the Advaita philosophy of Śaṅkara. These scriptural representations have been the source of claiming the distinction of being egalitarian and, thus, liberal in outlook, making the advaitic tradition to appear as exclusive and limited.

Interestingly, these narratives on Rāmānuja's liberalism, while endorsing the inclusivistic attitude, qualify it with the notion of differential access and hierarchical placement of different social groups by assigning the *brāhmaṇa*s the superior status. Thus, they do not reject and

[3] Seshadri (1996a), 'Ramanuja: Social Influence of This Life and Teaching', p. 294; Kavingnar Vaali (2008), *Rāmānuja Kaviyam*, pp. 4.

rather incorporate the *Dharamaśāstric* norms of the *varṇāśramadharma* and redefine it within the Śrīvaiṣṇava social framework. This point is acknowledged by some of the biographers and scholars of Rāmānuja and they justify this as follows:

> One must not stretch Ramanuja's general attitude towards suffering and caste inequality too far. He was not completely for abolition of the caste system or untouchability. That would have been too much to expect given the times in which he lived. In fact, even today these evils persist and have taken firm political roots for greater bargaining power by the socially oppressed.[4]

One tends to agree that modern ideals of equality cannot be applied to a medieval worldview. However, it needs to be emphasized that the discourse on social hierarchy in the hagiographies was complex and varied. The narratives on the tropes of Rāmānuja's social outlook have never been unanimous in their representations at any point of time. Even during the twelfth and the thirteenth centuries, following Rāmānuja's death, the narratives that circulated in oral as well as in written forms varied. These variations were influenced by the form of the particular genre of religious literature and the intentions of the authors and the social groups they were representing. When analysed closely, it seems that these different versions not only registered the diverse perceptions of Rāmānuja's attitude towards the *varṇāśramadharma* but also reflected the varying social attitudes of the hagiographers and authors and the frameworks within which they operated.

Further, it also needs to be pointed out that the tropes discussed in these texts with reference to Rāmānuja and *varṇa* hierarchy were a part of the larger ongoing Śrīvaiṣṇava discourse on the relevance of the social status for achieving salvation. These discussions were debated upon in the commentaries that often attempted to trace the genealogy of their interpretations to the ideas of Rāmānuja himself. Consequently, there were diverse elucidations of Rāmānuja's Viśiṣṭādvaita and these then emerged as frames of reference. Therefore, neither do the hagiographical narratives have a unilateral, unitary approach to the delineation of Rāmānuja's activities with reference to the issues of *varṇa* hierarchy nor do the commentaries register a homogenous, undivided opinion about

[4] Seshadri (1996a), 'Ramanuja: Social Influence of This Life and Teaching', p. 298.

Rāmānuja's ideas of grace and salvation that is *prapatti* and *mokṣa*. Interestingly, none of these complexities are discussed or represented in the modern biographies, films, plays, and newspapers, and even if they do, they are expressed in an unproblematic and simplistic manner subordinated to the linear discourse of 'social reforms' and the association of Rāmānuja with it. The seamless continuation of these ideas reflects the ways in which the cultural memory of a particular religious community is shared, acquires a universal dimension, and enters the realm of the popular.

This chapter will attempt to analyse the ways in which the hagiographical narratives of the Śrīvaiṣṇava community on Rāmānuja in relation to the issue of social hierarchy developed and travelled through many layers of history to enter the modern biographical domain, thus collapsing the distinction between the hagiographies and biographies and merging the sacred and secular that have often been viewed as mutually exclusive categories. The first section will deal with the variant episodes on social hierarchy and highlight the fact that these variations reflected the social attitude of the hagiographies and their writers. The second section will discuss the ground situation by analyzing the epigraphical evidence on social inclusion in the arena of temple and discuss the ramifications of these aspects on the Śrīvaiṣṇava ideas and identities. The third section will attempt to look at the delineations of Rāmānuja that crossed the Śrīvaiṣṇava and the southern boundaries and will examine some of the modern notions reflected in the biographical genres of texts, plays, films, and comics against the relatively modern notion of caste and politics of caste discrimination.

SOCIAL ATTITUDE AND ITS VARIANT RAMIFICATIONS IN THE ŚRĪVAIṢṆAVA HAGIOGRAPHIES

It should be remembered that the textual tradition of the Śrīvaiṣṇavas, of which the hagiographical texts were an integral part were composed by the *brāhmaṇa*s and despite its avowed attempt to expand the social base, the brāhmaṇical orientation always predominated. That Rāmānuja and other Śrīvaiṣṇava *ācārya*s as well as the *maṭhādhipati*s were *brāhmaṇa*s was no coincidence. In fact, till day, the *ācārya*s and the heads of the *maṭha*s, *jīyar*s are always *brāhmaṇa*s and continue to wear the sacred thread despite being a renunciate. This is unlike the Śaiva tradition in which the heads of the *maṭhas* were the powerful non-*brāhmaṇa Vēḷāḷas* and the Advaita tradition in which the heads of the *maṭhas*, though *brāhmaṇas*, did not wear the thread, thus symbolically renouncing all earthly insignias.

One cannot help noticing that the majority of the narratives in the hagiographies focus on Rāmānujas engagements with other religious traditions and his organization of the community. The tenor is undeniably brāhmaṇical and sectarian with heavy emphases on Sanskritic learning, brāhmaṇical rituals, and avowed superiority against the Advaitic and Śaivite traditions. Within this frame, at various moments the hagiographers have introduced the questions of social hierarchy. Thus, inclusion of the episodes that questioned the established social hierarchy, especially in the life story of Rāmānuja, was a conscious attempt to project an open-mindedness that would popularize the tradition, community, and Rāmānuja himself. The positioning of these narratives in the structure of the texts was a strategy on the part of the hagiographers to create a memory around those moments, remembering which was crucial for the transmission of the tradition and community identity. For instance, we are told that the catalyst behind Rāmānuja's renunciation was the discriminatory attitude of his wife towards his non-*brāhmaṇa guru*, Kāñcīpūrṇa/Tirukacci Nambi, and *brāhmaṇa guru* belonging to a lesser brāhmaṇical order, Māhapūrṇa/Periya Nambi, and an ordinary Śrīvaiṣṇava. Therefore, the remembrance of these episodes would not only memorialize the compassionate and large-heartedness of Rāmānuja, but revoke the Śrīvaiṣṇava ideas that Rāmānuja's *gurus* expounded, highlight the *guru–śiṣya* relationship, and finally tell us how and why Rāmānuja became a *sanyāsin*, a crucial factor in his becoming the most important and exemplary *ācārya* of the community. Similarly, at the conclusion of the episode of reciting aloud the *mantra*, incurring the wrath of Tirukkōṭṭiyūr Nambi and finally the reconciliation between the two, the narratives recounted that Tirukkōṭṭiyūr Nambi declared that from then onwards, Rāmānuja's *darśana* or *Hari darśana* would be named after him, as *Emperumānār darśana*, *Lakṣmaṇa darśana*, *Rāmānuja siddhānta*—a significant moment that concretized the theological and philosophical orientation of the Śrīvaiṣṇava community.[5]

[5] *Divyasūricaritam*, Ch. 18, *śloka* 3; *Yatirāja Vaibhavam*, *śloka* 59; *Āṟāyirappaṭi*, p. 195; *Muāyirappaṭi*, p. 96.

Thus, this section will analyse the textual patterns in the narratives popularly perceived as anti-caste and draw attention to the fact that the hagiographical discourse on the *varṇa* and social hierarchy was complex, implying that protest against the *varṇa* hierarchy was not missed out, but was highlighted within the brāhmaṇical framework, according to the ethos of the context in which the hagiographies were situated. This point is often overlooked by the modern biographers whose frame of reference are the modern ideas of caste, its discriminatory structure, and clamour for an equal socio-religious space for the marginalized communities. Such ideas imposed onto the hagiographical narratives, read meanings into them where none probably existed.

The *Divyasūricaritam*, *Āṟāyirappaṭi*, and *Muāyirappaṭi* highlighted the accessibility of Viṣṇu through *arcavatāra* concept or the incarnations. As explained in Chapter 2, this *arcavatāra* frame was far more expansive than the traditional ten forms of incarnations of Viṣṇu and included his various forms in the temples. In addition, the hagiographies inform us that his weapons, insignias, and celestial accompanists took the form of the *āḻvār*s and *ācārya*s or *divyasūri*s in this mundane world. Thus, the hagiographies at the onset distinguished themselves with ideals of universalism and accessibility. However, only the *Divyasūricaritam* and *Āṟāyirappaṭi* further expanded the reach of these ideals by stating that Viṣṇu commanded that all his incarnations would take birth in different *varṇa*s and become the instruments of salvation.[6] The opening chapter of the *Muāyirappaṭi* explained the *avatāra* concept, but, strangely enough, has no reference to the god's command to his incarnations to be present in different *varṇa*s. On the basis of such an elucidation, it is difficult to conclude that the *Muāyirappaṭi* was circumspect in its universalistic delineation of Viṣṇu and in its orientation, lending itself easily to the conservative Vaṭakaḷai orientation. The narratives of social dissent that appeared in the *Āṟāyirappaṭi* also appeared in the *Muāyirappaṭi*, though often concise in their content. It needs to be pointed out that such details as in the *Āṟāyirappaṭi* and sometimes in the *Muāyirappaṭi* were not a part of the *Divyasūricaritam* and *Yatirāja Vaibhavam*, but both the texts have never been appropriated by any sectarian affiliations.

The first instance of Rāmānuja's discomfort with *varṇa* hierarchy was introduced in his pursuit of making Tirukacci Nambi—a non-*brāhmaṇa*,

[6] *Divyasūricaritam*, Ch. 1, *śloka* 86; *Āṟāyirappaṭi*, p. 7.

his *guru*. The narratives tell us that after he left the tutelage of the famous *advaita* teacher Yādavaprakāśa due to irreconcilable differences, Rāmānuja took upon himself to perform the *kainkarya* (service) of bringing water daily from a roadside well for Lord Varadarājasvāmīs *tirumañjanam* (holy bath). This was an act of gratitude to the Lord who had saved his life from Yādavaprakāśa. The texts at this juncture inserted the motifs of Yāmuna attempting to pursue Rāmānuja to come to Śrīraṅgam and take over as the *ācārya*, arrival of Periya Nambi at Kāñcīpuram and his interaction with Rāmānuja, Yāmuna's funeral, the three-finger episode and Rāmānuja's promise to fulfil the three wishes of Yāmuna. At this point, the narratives tell us that Rāmānuja came back to Kāñcīpuram, requested Tirukkaci Nambi to be his *guru*, but Nambi declined. The *Divyasūricaritam* reported that since an *ācārya*'s *kula* or family (clan) status was immaterial, Rāmānuja asked Nambi to be his preceptor. Nambi replied that though he had the blessings of Varadarājasvāmī, he could not transgress the *laukika karma* (the order).Thereafter, Rāmānuja beseeched Tirukacci Nambi to take his queries to the Lord and get answers from Him.[7] *Āṟāyirappaṭi* stated that acceding to Rāmānuja's request would result in the transgression of *vaidikamaryāda* and the principles of *varṇāśramadharma*; hence, Tirukacci Nambi's reservation in granting it.[8] Interestingly, *Āṟāyirappaṭi* introduced Tirukacci Nambi much earlier in the text, when Ālvandār came to Kāñcīpuram to see Rāmānuja.[9] Further, we are told that since the ties with Yādavaprakāśa were severed, Rāmānuja's mother told him to go to Tirukacci Nambi who then advised Rāmānuja do the *kainkarya* (service) of bringing water from the well daily for the Lords bath.[10] However, *Āṟāyirappaṭi* did not reveal the social status of Tirukacci Nambi, till Rāmānuja asked him to be his preceptor.

The *Muāyirappaṭi* made Tirukacci Nambi give a longer explanation to Rāmānuja's request:

> Nambi asked, 'Can Ālvandārs *śrīpādam* (disciple) transgress the *varṇāśramadharma* like this? At one time Nāthamuni followed the king and Uyyakōṇḍār tried to prevent him as it was against the *Śāstras*. Nāthamuni agreed and said that one should not go against the *Śāstras*. Tirukaṇṇamaṅgai

[7] *Divyasūricaritam*, Ch. 17, *ślokas* 46–7.

[8] *Āṟāyirappaṭi*, p. 166.

[9] Ibid., p. 149.

[10] Ibid., p. 153.

> Aṇḍāṉ had rejected food and sleep and therefore he could leave the *sandhyā kainkaryas*. But you have accepted the *deh dharma* (rules of this world), such as taking food, you should not transgress the *Śāstras*.'[11]

Did this imply that for a renunciate, rules of the *Śāstra*s did not apply? In all these narratives there is a suggestion that non-*brāhmaṇa*s were a part of the Śrīvaiṣṇava community, had important status, performed ritual duties, had special access to god like Tirukacci Nambi did, and interacted with *brāhmaṇa*s as seen in the case of Tirukacci Nambi interacting with Ālvandār and Rāmānuja. So what was special that the narratives wanted to convey through Rāmānuja's request? Were the narratives trying to emphasize that a *guru* can never be a non-*brāhmaṇa*? It should be noticed that the hagiographies hesitated to elevate Tirukacci Nambi to the status of a traditional Śrīvaiṣṇava *guru*. He was never shown to be initiating Rāmānuja and imparting the knowledge of the sacred *mantras*. He merely carried Rāmānuja's queries to the Lord who revealed the crucial tenets of Śrīvaiṣṇavism through him (as has been discussed in the previous chapter). Therefore, through the agency of Tirukacci Nambi, the narratives cited the rules of *varṇāśramadharma* that disqualified him from becoming a *guru*, emphasizing that a preceptor had to be a *brāhmaṇa*. Interestingly, *Yatirāja Vaibhavam* did not provide any such explanation. We are told that Rāmānuja came to Kāñcīpuram to Lord Varadarājasvāmī who had laid down the rules of *varṇāśramadharma* and orders of life, and Rāmānuja merely asked Tirukacci Nambi/Kāñcīpūrṇa to take his queries to the Lord. Further, *Yatirāja Vaibhavam* narrated that Tirukacci Nambi /Kāñcīpūrṇa declined due to differences with Rāmānuja regarding the approach to salvation. The text depicted Tirukacci Nambi's views in favour of *prapatti* as the best way for salvation and not conscious volition. Eventually, Nambi advised Rāmānuja to take Mahāpūrṇa as his preceptor.[12]

The hagiographies related accounts of Rāmānuja's wife who was socially conservative and behaved in a discriminatory manner towards Rāmānuja's *gurus*, Tirukacci Nambi (Kāñcīpūrṇa) and Periya Nambi (Mahāpūrṇa). The former was not a *brāhmaṇa* and the latter was a *brāhmaṇa* of a lesser denomination. The *Āṟāyirappaṭi* and *Muāyirappaṭi*, however, further narrated that Rāmānuja invited Tirukacci Nambi for

[11] *Muāyirappaṭi*, p. 88.

[12] *Yatirāja Vaibhavam, śloka*s 39–40.

a meal to his home. However, Nambi had to eat alone as Rāmānuja was delayed due to the *kainkarya* of bringing water from the well. On his return, he was upset on finding that his wife had bathed, was cleaning and purifying the place on account of a non-*brāhmaṇa* eating in their house.[13] Undoubtedly, Rāmānuja's catholicity is explicit, but one cannot help noticing the limited and reluctant manner in which the principle of commensality was introduced by the hagiographers by making Rāmānuja unavailable at that crucial moment. The *Āṟāyirappaṭi* and *Muāyirappaṭi* narrated yet another episode where again Rāmānuja's wife refused to serve food to a hungry Śrīvaiṣṇava of a marginalized *varṇa* which made Rāmānuja extremely angry.[14] All the hagiographies were unanimous that the breaking point came when Rāmānuja's *guru* Periya Nambi who had initiated him and Periya Nambi's wife were treated shabbily by Rāmānuja's wife and, consequently, Rāmānuja became a renuniciate. It seems Periya Nambi along with his wife was staying in Rāmānuja's house for six months as the latter wished to know the special meanings of various *mantras*. Except *Yatirāja Vaibhavam*, all the hagiographies recounted that once Rāmānuja's wife and Periya Nambi's wife were simultaneously drawing water from the well and both their utensils clashed against each other much to the annoyance of Rāmānuja's wife, who then insulted Periya Nambi's wife. Thereafter, Periya Nambi, along with his wife, quietly left Rāmānuja's house for Śrīraṅgam.[15] *Yatirāja Vaibhavam* did not provide these details but merely reported that when Rāmānuja had gone to Śrīperumbudūr, Mahāpūrṇa's wife and Rāmānuja's wife quarrelled with each other, where the latter insulted her. Mahāpūrṇa then, along with his wife, left for Śrīraṅgam. When Rāmānuja came to know about it, he was upset that his wife had committed *bhāgvad apacāra* (insulting a Śrīvaiṣṇava) and took his wife to her mother's house, left her there, and consequently became a renunciate or a *sanyāsī* in front of Varadarāja:[16]

> ... held the triple staff, had the tuft, sacred thread and saffron-robe and muttered the best *Mantra* (*Mūlamantra*). He became well known as the

[13] *Āṟāyirappaṭi*, pp. 166–7; *Muāyirappaṭi*, p. 88.

[14] *Āṟāyirappaṭi*, p. 172 ; *Muāyirappaṭi*, p. 90.

[15] *Muāyirappaṭi*, p. 90.

[16] *Divyasūricaritam*, Ch. 17, *ślokas* 69–71; *Yatirāja Vaibhavam*, *ślokas* 48–51; *Āṟāyirappaṭi*, p. 174; *Muāyirappaṭi*, pp. 90–1.

practioner of the conduct of (enjoined for) (his) caste and order (in life) (*varṇāśramācāraparaśravakāśe*).[17]

We are told that thereafter, Rāmānuja came to Śrīraṅgam, was given a grand reception, and became the manager or *Śrīkāryam* of Raṅganāthasvāmī temple there. According to the *Divyasūricaritam*, he introduced institutional reforms in the temple to incorporate non-*brāhmaṇa*s or the *śūdra* participation in the ritual as well as the organizational aspects of temple worship by creating ten divisions of duties for the *śūdra*s and ten divisions of work for the *brāhmaṇa*s.[18] The narrative mentioned that the nature of duties for the *śudra*s was that of *bhṛtya*s or servants.[19] This detail did not find any mention in the *Yatirāja Vaibhavam* or in the *Āṟāyirappaṭi* and *Muāyirappaṭi*.

One of the most crucial episodes that described the broad mindedness of Rāmānuja has been his chanting aloud the *mantra*s to a large crowd. The hagiographical accounts depicting nonchalance on Rāmānuja's part for being condemned at making an exclusive knowledge public was indeed an effective strategy to underscore the broad base of the Śrīvaiṣṇava community and the purported large-heartedness of the most important *ācārya* of the community. All the versions clearly stated that Rāmānuja shouted out the *mantra* to everybody so that even the ordinary people could achieve salvation from the miseries of this world. The words used in the narratives for the crowd who had gathered are *jagadbhirakṣhitu jagād* (for the upliftment of everybody), *anekān*, *anekam Śrīvaiṣṇavas* (all the Śrīvaiṣṇavas), *ellārum* (everybody), *ellārukum*.[20] Thus, none of these terms denoted any specific *varṇa* identity. Representing clearly a Śrīvaiṣṇava effort to reach out to the general non-brāhmaṇical community, through this narrative, the hagiographers also highlighted the irrelevance of social status for access to devotion. The unanimity with which the narratives reported this episode exhibited the realization on the part of the hagiographers and the Śrīvaiṣṇavas, the importance of the temple as an arena for community interaction, and an all-inclusive community consciousness that expressed itself beyond the

[17] *Yatirāja Vaibhavam*, *śloka* 16.

[18] *Divyasūricaritam*, Ch. 17, *ślokas* 84–5.

[19] Ibid., *śloka* 85.

[20] *Divyasūricaritam*, Ch. 18, *śloka* 2; *Yatirāja Vaibhavam*, *śloka* 58; *Āṟāyirappaṭi*, p. 194; *Muāyirappaṭi*, p. 95.

exclusive Vedāntic brāhmaṇical identity. This idea was further exhorted in the narratives that ascribed to Rāmānuja the intention behind the composition of some of his works:

> During the *Paṅguṇi Uttiram* festival, when the Lord and his consort were bathed and appeared together, Emperumānār (Rāmānuja) decided that the *pāsura* (poem) which the divine couple had given to him should be known to everybody, so that their lives would be enriched. Wishing thus, he composed the *Gadyatraya*. Also he composed the *Nityagrantha*, so that the *kainkarya* could be done everyday in proper order by those who had observed the *Gadyatraya*, since the latter was a means of attaining salvation ...[21]
>
> In some places, Emperumānār rejected the *varṇa-utakarṣa* and made everybody know the *Śrīvaiṣṇava lakṣaṇa* which is the truth given in the *Vedapramāṇa* (proofs in the Veda).[22]

Compared to *Divyasūricaritam* and *Yatirāja Vaibhavam*, *Āṟāyirappaṭi*, and *Muāyirappaṭi* were more expressive and detailed in their narratives with regard to the discourse on *varṇa* hierarchy and the relevance of social status for devotion. In fact, some of the episodes in the *Āṟāyirappaṭi* did not figure in the *Muāyirappaṭi*. For instance, *Āṟāyirappaṭi* recounted an episode of one of Rāmānuja's non-*brāhmaṇa* disciple, Uraṅgavillidāsar:

> When Emperumānār would go to the river to bathe, he would hold Mudaliāṇḍāṉ's hands and while coming back, he would hold Villidāsar's hands. His disciples asked the reason for this. Emperumānār (Uḍaiyavar) replied, 'There is a general opinion that by birth you do not become great. You may be born great but you may be lowly in your demeanour. Those born high have the pride of birth, but this person has no pride.'[23]

Extolling the greatness of Viṣṇu, the *Āṟāyirappaṭi* further asserted:

> Rāmāvatāra is great because Lord treated Guha as his friend. He did the *samskāra* (last rites) for Periyauḍaiyar (Jatāyu) and ate the half eaten fruits of Śabari and considered Hanumān and himself as one. This equality

[21] *Muāyirappaṭi*, p. 105, See also, *Divyasūricaritam*, Ch. 18, *śloka* 10; *Yatirāja Vaibhavam ślokas* 73–4.

[22] *Āṟāyirappaṭi*, pp. 295–6.

[23] Ibid., p. 236.

> (*sahabhojanam*) gave Rāma the greatness. In Kṛṣṇāvatāra, he gave the Gītā *upadeśa* and *Carma śloka* and left the mansions of Bhīṣma and Droṇācārya and had a meal at Vidura's house. He made himself famous in the group of enemies by rejecting the food given by Duryodhana. The reason why Kōyil (Śrīraṅgam) is great for it showed Tiruppāṇāḻvār as one. The greatness of Tirumalai is because Toṇḍaimāṉ Cakravarti and Kurumbarattu Nambi had a dialogue with each other. Perumāḷ Kōyil (Kāñcīpuram) is famous because he was one with Tirukacci Nambi and always smiling at him ...[24]

However, the narratives in the *Āṟāyirappaṭi* also reflected a discomfort in rejecting the hierarchy of *varṇāśramadharma*. One of the narratives, in this context, expressed some reservations by depicting Rāmānuja having inhibitions on flouting the norms of *varṇāśramadharma*. The accounts inform us that Māranēr Nambi was the disciple of Ālavandār. When Māranēr Nambi fell ill and died, Periya Nambi had no hesitation in performing his last rites according to the brāhmaṇical norms. However, the accounts tell us that Rāmānuja was uncomfortable with Periya Nambi's actions and objected:

> 'When I am establishing the fence to observe and protect the *samsāra* so that it not broken, you are taking off the fence.' Periya Nambi replied, 'Am I bigger than the God (Rāma) who took birth in the Ikśvāku *vamśa* (lineage) and displayed *samānyadharma* (religion for all)? Is Māranēr Nambi lower than Periyauḍaiyar (Jatāyu)? Am I bigger than the Dharmaputra who observed the *samānyadharmaniṣtha* (duties for all)? Is Māranēr Nambi lower than Vidura? Is the noise of the ocean a slave to the great effulgence of the God who is sleeping? When Māranēr Nambi died, he declared that his saviour was the feet of Periya Perumāḷ and Ālavandār'.[25]

Significant variations can be seen in the narratives on Rāmānuja's sojourn in Karnataka. While the *Divyasūricaritam* provided information only about Rāmānuja establishing the Nārāyaṇasvāmī temple, instituting the festivals, and introducing the services of 52 Śrīvaiṣṇavas at Tirunārāyaṇapuram (Mēlkōṭe), *Yatirāja Vaibhavam* in addition to this, recounted the conversion of kings, *brāhmaṇas*, and Jainas to Śrīvaiṣṇavism and Rāmānuja recovering the festival idol of Tirunārāyaṇapuram, Rāmapriya, from the king of Delhi. However, it did not mention the 52

[24] *Āṟāyirappaṭi*, p. 294.
[25] Ibid., pp. 237–8.

Śrīvaiṣṇava's and Rāmānuja's association with them. There was a general reference to the disciples who informed Rāmānuja that the annual recital of the hymns of Nammāḻvār had stopped. Thereafter, Rāmānuja instituted the festival of *Adhyayanōtsava*, installed the images of Nammāḻvār, Āṇṭāḷ, and other Āḻvārs.[26] The *Āṟayirappaṭi* and *Muāyirappaṭi* provided a detailed account on Rāmānuja and his stay in the Karnataka region. Woven into these lengthy narratives were the tropes of devotion, service, and, significantly, the non-*brāhmaṇas* participation in fulfilling the commitment towards Śrīvaiṣṇavism. According to narratives, after escaping the persecution of the Cōḷa ruler, Rāmānuja came to the Hoysala kingdom in Karnataka and took refuge in a forest. The hunting community there welcomed him enthusiastically and provided the much-needed hospitality to him and his disciples who were exhausted after their flight from the Cōḷa king's harassment. The hagiographies inform us that the hunters already knew about Rāmānuja, as their *guru* Tirumalai Naḷḷān (presumably a hunter too) in the course of his discourses had told them that Rāmānuja was their *dharmācārya*.[27] The hunters offered Rāmānuja and his disciples honey and uncooked millet and told them to prepare the food and eat, and they did so. The following morning, the hunters took them to another hunter's house who thought that since the *brāhmaṇas* were fasting, he would also not eat. He then took them to a *brāhmaṇas* house in a nearby village and instructed that *brāhmaṇa* to cook for them and serve them. Thereafter, Rāmānuja and his disciples had their meals and left.[28]

Is there an allusion to the adherence of the principles of *varṇa* where commensality is concerned? From the narratives it appears that Rāmānuja and his *brāhmaṇa* followers prepared their own food and did not eat with the hunters. While delineating the humility and devotion with which the hunters extended their hospitality to Rāmānuja, the narratives here underlined the relevance of hierarchy within the community. The tone was clearly brāhmaṇical, insisting on unflinching service by the laity to its *brāhmaṇa* order that controlled the religious leadership. The anxiety on the part of the hunters to locate a *brāhmaṇa* who could feed

[26] *Divyasūricaritam*, Ch. 18, *ślokas* 89–90; *Yatirāja Vaibhavam*, *ślokas* 96–101.

[27] *Āṟāyirappaṭi*, pp. 241–2; *Muāyirappaṭi*, pp. 112–13.

[28] *Āṟāyirappaṭi*, pp. 241–2.

the *ācārya* and his followers emphasized that the rules of *varṇa* had to be followed. In fact, the episode of a woman who was once initiated by Rāmānuja and was eager to cook for the *ācārya* and feed him and his disciples revealed the social attitude of the hagiographers themselves. The narratives in this case tell us that after a thorough examination of the woman's devotion to Rāmānuja and ascertaining her social status, Rāmānuja and his disciples ate the food cooked by her.[29]

The reference to the 52 as in the *Divyasūricaritam* appeared in the *Āṟāyirappaṭi* during the installation of the temple at Yadugiri (Mēlkōṭe). But the *Āṟāyirappaṭi* informed us about the social status of the 52. The *Āṟāyirappaṭi* relayed that after all the festivals are introduced, Rāmānuja established the Yatiraja *maṭha*, appointed the 52, taught them the services (*kainkarya*) to the God, and gave them the title of the Śrīvaiṣṇava. He enjoined that they would be called Śrīvaiṣṇavas in public but *Dāsyanāma* in private.[30] Brief information of the social groups that comprised the 52 disciples was provided in the narratives. Ranging from women (*Koṟṟiammaimārgaḷ*) to guards (*Tirumcēṇikāval, Tiruveṇaikāran*) to disciples who did not wear the thread (*Śāttāda mudaligals*), this eclectic group of 52 appeared to be consisting largely of non-*brāhmaṇas*. Thus, the expansion of the Śrīvaiṣṇava network which Rāmānuja's sojourn in Mēlkōṭe indicated was to be understood mostly in terms of the incorporation of the non-brāhmaṇical elements into the temple organization. The modern biographies state that the *guruparamparās* mentioned that Rāmānuja took the bold step in Mēlkōṭe to declare the outcastes as *Tirukkulattār*, meaning people belonging to the family of Lakṣmī, the Divine mother and accommodated them in the temple organization. Though Rāmānuja's flight to Mēlkōṭe is mentioned in the *Divyasūricaritam, Yatirāja Vaibhavam,* and *Āṟāyirappaṭi*, none of them referred to a group of devotees, known as the *Tirukkulattār*. However, though *Muāyirappaṭi* did not refer to 52 Śrīvaiṣṇavas, it refers to *Tirukkulattār*, explicitly stating that they were the *Caṇḍaḷās*:

> Rāmānuja installed Śelvapiḷḷāṉ with Tirunārāyaṇa in Yādavādri, conducted the daily *utsavas* (festivals) and named the *Caṇḍalās* who had helped in adversity as *Tirukkulattār* and gave them the right for *tīrthotsava* (offering of water), bathing in the holy pond (*kalayāṇa-tīrtha*),

[29] *Āṟāyirappaṭi*, pp. 243–6.

[30] Ibid., pp. 253–4.

> circumambulate the *bhagavad sannidhi* (shrine of the Lord) and receive the holy water (*tīrtha*).[31]

Epigraphical evidence does record indirectly Rāmānuja's presence in the Karnataka region and his interactions with the population comprising primarily of the non-*brāhmaṇas*. An inscription of twelfth century from Toṇṇūru informs that a certain Bēṟṟaḍiyān Trivaraṅgadāsan, a servant of Iḷaiāḻvān (Rāmānuja), received from the ruler Narashimadeva the village of Yādavanārāyaṇa-caturvedimangalam. Bēṟṟaḍiyān Trivaraṅgadāsan, in turn, gifted the village to the god Vīṟṟirunda-Perumāḷ of Kūttāṇḍi-viṇṇagara.[32] Was it the association with Rāmānuja that made Bēṟṟaḍiyān Trivaraṅgadāsan influential enough to receive a *brahmadeya* in donation? By fourteenth century, the hagiographical narrative about Rāmānuja going to the hill of Mēlkōṭe in search of white clay, *tirumaṇ*, recovering the god and installing him, and unearthing a huge amount of *tirumaṇ* soil seems to have been widely accepted. An inscription dated to 1319 CE stated that an official of Vīr Ballāḷa III, *Immaḍi Rāvuttarāya* Mādappa-daṇṇanāyaka, made over the title of land noticed by Emperumānār as *tirumaṇṇu* (holy earth), to god Tirimaṇṇa-Perumāḷ as charity.[33] Interestingly, references are made to the 52, as Śrīvaiṣṇava *mahājanas*, donating villages, issuing sale deeds, receiving land grants.[34] One of the inscriptions dated to perhaps fourteenth century describes the 52 as: ... worshippers of the lotus feet, first disciples of Rāmānujāchārya, and establishers of path of Veda.[35] This inscription from Mēlkōṭe recorded a land grant to the 52.

Thus, one may conclude that despite variations, the Śrīvaiṣṇava hagiographies were engaging with the issues of social hierarchy and inclusion of the non-brāhmaṇical groups within the community structure that eventually was reflected in the real Śrīvaiṣṇava realm of the temple. In addition, contradictions within the Śrīvaiṣṇava brāhmaṇical community were also brought out in the hagiographies. The Periya Nambi episode in which Rāmānuja's wife is said to have humiliated Periya Nambi's wife because Rāmānuja's family belonged to a higher denomination of

31 *Muāyirappaṭi*, p. 117.

32 Gopal (1983), *Sri Ramanuja in Karnataka*, no. 3, pp. 45–6, 118–19.

33 Ibid., no. 25, p. 126. Also see pp. 64–5.

34 Ibid., nos. 27, 28, pp. 66–8, 126–7.

35 Ibid., nos. 34, 35, pp. 131–4. Also see pp. 76–81.

brāhmaṇas has already been discussed. Similar tensions appeared in the narratives regarding the marriage of Parāśara Bhaṭṭar, Kurattāḻvān, and Āṇṭāḷ's son. It is recounted that Kurattāḻvān consulted Rāmānuja for a suitable bride for Parāśara Bhaṭṭar and the latter proposed the name of Periya Nambi's daughter as she was a *Śrīvaiṣṇava santānikā* (daughter of a Śrīvaiṣṇava). The import was that even if Periya Nambi's family belonged to a lower brāhmaṇical denomination, the expected kinship relations based on matrimony would still conform to the Śrīvaiṣṇava tradition. Kurattāḻvān agreed and, along with his wife, went to Periya Nambi's place and asked for his daughter's hand in marriage. Periya Nambi and his wife were happy, we are told, but did not reply immediately. This reluctance introduced at this point in the narrative was an indication of the awareness of the social differences and the apprehensions in contravening the *varṇa* norms. However, the matter was resolved by divine intervention, when Kurattāḻvān prayed to Raṅganātha for the match to be successful and the Lord appeared in the dream of the girl's parents and enjoined them to accept Parāśara Bhaṭṭar as their son-in-law.[36]

The narratives reflected a complexity in the social attitudes of the hagiographers themselves. Belonging to the Vedāntic tradition whose primary articulation was influenced by intellectualism in scholastic aspects of soul, matter, consciousness, and Brahman, engagement on the part of the hagiographers with devotion and equitable access to it was bound to create ferment in their ideological disposition. While on one hand, the hagiographers realized that to broaden the scope of a religious community, devotion had to be accentuated at the cost of ascribed social status, on the other hand, they were not willing to undermine the brāhmaṇical values altogether. The narratives in the hagiographical texts attempted to adopt and incorporate both the social attitudes without going to the 'extremes either of dismissing caste structures entirely or of entirely subordinating devotion to caste. New values were to take primary place while old norms were to be reinterpreted and given new meanings.'[37] Thus, while trying to maintain a balance between devotion and caste, the narratives celebrated Rāmānuja's protest against the *varṇāśramadharma* as the triumph of Vaiṣṇava *bhakti* without foreclosing the relevance of

[36] *Āṟāyirappaṭi*, pp. 235–6.

[37] Clooney (2002), 'Fierce Words: Repositionings of Caste and Devotion', p. 399.

the caste status altogether.[38] This approach was also reflected in the rest of the textual tradition that attempted to articulate the normative ethics of devotion by prioritizing the community affiliation over caste status.

Another aspect of the complex nature of dissent and devotion was that it was gendered. The hagiographies, while discussing the theme of unflinching devotion to god and surrender, used the motif of marriage and association in a complex way. Any male devotee aspiring to be a disciple of Rāmānuja and a Śrīvaiṣṇava was given a place in the temple organization and other community activities. But the devotion for a woman had to be reconciled within the marital structure of the household. Any deviant religious attitude on the part of a woman led to her being deprived of her marital status. This is best reflected in the accounts of Rāmānuja's life itself. The narratives repeatedly point out that Rāmānuja's compassion towards his teachers like Tirukacci Nambi and Periya Nambi was not appreciated by his wife who insulted his teachers and their respective wives and justified her attitude as adherence to the *varṇa* norms. Her elitist attitude and arrogance of being a *brāhmaṇa* became the basis of subsequent marital discords. Finally, a tired Rāmānuja was compelled to leave his wife at her parents' house, never to bring her back, and then he became a renunciate. The language in the *Āṟāyirappaṭi* is laced with gendered overtones:

> Rāmānuja said, ... There is a saying that women instigate sin—you have proved it. In the matter of Tirukacci Nambi and the Śrīvaiṣṇava you have erred and now you quarrel with Periya Nambi's wife. 'So get out this moment.' He gave her some money and sent her to her maternal home and said, 'For us this *samsāra* has to be renounced.' He goes to Tiruvanathasāras, bathes there and resolves to become a *sanyāsin* and goes to the sanctum sanctorum of Varadarājasvāmī and prays to the God, 'I am sick of this *samsāra* where there is a repeated scope of committing transgression, give me the *tridaṇḍa* and *kāśāya* (robe) and make me accept the *sanyāsa* (renunciation).'[39]

One of the important qualifications of an *ācārya* of a Śrīvaiṣṇava *maṭha* is that he should have been a householder, but on acquiring office, he must be a *sanyāsin*. Could it be that this qualification of a renunciate was

[38] Ibid.

[39] *Āṟāyirappaṭi*, pp. 173–4.

to compete with the established Śaiva and Advaita orders that were based on strict celibacy? Could it be that the transgression of this brāhmaṇical norm of adhering to *gṛihasta āśrama* had to be legitimized, and what better way could it be than through an agency of a cantankerous wife who came in the way of her husband's devotion? Rāmānuja's wife's attitude is constantly contrasted with Kūreśa's wife Āṉṭāḷ whose unflinching devotion to her husband is expressed in the narratives with appreciation. Perhaps, through the narratives of two women the hagiographers were trying to convey to the followers that deviance meant excommunication from the faith and devotion implied accommodation within the community and its institutional structures.

Therefore, it should be noted that dissent remained largely within the framework of brāhmaṇical tradition and did not transgress significantly. The hagiographical narratives, while treating the themes of caste and *bhakti*, attempted a departure from the erstwhile organization of the community that was conservative and put forth the basis of a new organization through the figure of Rāmānuja that attempted at a broader social base. However, while using the motif of dissent, they created their own orthodoxies that further consolidated the brāhmaṇical norms of caste and gender.

CASTE, COMMUNITY, AND DISCOURSE

The *Divyasūricaritam* and *Yatirāja Vaibhavam* did not engage intensely with the concerns of caste and devotion. In fact, the entire narrative of the *Yatirāja Vaibhavam* is silent on Rāmānuja's protest against caste hierarchy. Since it was written in a highly brāhmaṇical philosophical framework, the text was probably attempting to carve out an intellectual identity appealing to the elite brāhmaṇical section within the Śrīvaiṣṇava community or to the Advaitas, for whom such issues were not significant. The detailed discussion on devotion and caste figured in the *Āṟāyirappaṭi* and *Muāyirappaṭi*. Composed in the fourteenth and the fifteenth centuries, these hagiographies reflected the historical context of that period that has already been discussed in chapters two and three. However, it needs to be emphasized again that the rise of non-*brāhmaṇa* landed class, emergence of the merchants, and the migration of the Telugu warriors and landed magnates to the Tamil region led to the evolution of a distinct Śrīvaiṣṇava non-*brāhmaṇa* identity. As powerful and influential groups, they emerged as major benefactors of the temples and patrons of the sectarian leaders. A network of redistribution and exchange between the non-*brāhmaṇa* and *brāhmaṇa* elite groups developed, which brought into the temple arena the former and provided a regular channel for patronage to the latter.[40] This interactive/productive relationship in which the powerful sections of both the caste groups came together influenced the Śrīvaiṣṇava discourse on society. The theological dialogue took cognizance of these changes and new concepts like the *Ubhaya Vedānta*, that is, dual Vedas (the Tamil *Prabandhas* and the Sanskrit Vedas), and *prapatti* were evolved and Tamil came to be emphasized along with Sanskrit as the sacred language. The notion of a *guru–śiṣya* relationship also came to be highlighted in this respect, where the *guru*, invariably a *brāhmaṇa ācārya*, was indispensable in forging a link between the divine and an ordinary devotee. Therefore, different orders with distinct lineages emerged within the Śrīvaiṣṇava community with *brāhmaṇa ācāryas* as their heads and the non-*brāhmaṇas* comprising a large section of the laity.

The *Āṟāyirappaṭi* and *Muāyirappaṭi* responded to this socio-religious context by including narratives on caste and devotion (as shown in the previous section). They attributed Rāmānuja with a large following from all sections of the society. Rāmānuja's followers were said to have comprised 700 *sanyāsins*, 1,200 *ekāṅgis* (non-*brāhmaṇa* renunciates), and 300 *Koṟṟiammai* (i.e., women followers).[41] The *Āṟāyirappaṭi* even provided an exhaustive list of Rāmānuja's non-*brāhmaṇa* disciples who belonged to different places and social groups and included chieftains, *brahmarāyas*, and temple trustees, *sthānattārs*.[42] Similarly, the *Muāyirappaṭi* also presented a list of disciples that included the *brāhmaṇa* disciples of Rāmānuja and various non-*brāhmaṇas* belonging to different social groups:

> *Ekāntis* like Alaṅkāra Veṅkaṭavara, Nambi Kuḍendeva, 12,000 *kainkaryaparas* (servants) like … *kāval adhikāris* (guards) like Tiruvaraṅga Māyōṉ, Nāṭṭatta *mudalis* and so on who had the knowledge of *bhakti*, Śāttāda Śrīvaiṣṇavas like Uraṅga Villidāsar, women … all these people obeyed Rāmānuja and involved in their respective *kainkarya*.[43]

40 Appadurai (1981), *Worship and Conflict*, pp. 63–104.

41 *Āṟāyirappaṭi*, pp. 270–1.

42 Ibid., pp. 267–9.

43 *Muāyirappaṭi*, p. 125.

Some of the brāhmaṇical religious leaders at Śrīraṅgam, Tirupati, and Kāñcīpuram had non-*brāhmaṇa*s as their disciples. These non-brāhmaṇical groups referred to as *ekāki*s, *ekāṅgi*s, and Śāttāda Śrīvaiṣṇavas, figured prominently as the recipients of several shares in temple offerings.

Amongst the non-brāhmaṇa groups, the Śāttāda Śrīvaiṣṇavas emerged prominently. Epigraphical evidence from Śrīraṅgam, Tirupati, and Kāñcīpuram highlight their presence in the temple administration and service. The first recorded instance of the presence of the Śāttādas at Śrīraṅgam was in 1427 CE issued during the reign of Vijayanagar ruler Devarāya II and it recorded a grant of land to the temple by a Śāttāda Śrīvaiṣṇava from Pratāpgiri in Uttaradeśa.[44] An epigraph at Tirupati dated to 1442 CE reported that Karuṇākaradāsar, a Śāttāda Śrīvaiṣṇava, made a donation of 100 *pon* for daily offerings to the Lord Gōvindapperumāḷ during the worship. It was enjoined that he would get a particular amount as a share in the offering and 'likewise it shall continue throughout the succession of his descendants and shall be effective as long as the moon and the sun endure'.[45] According to some scholars, the Śāttādas were previously *brāhmaṇa*s who had renounced their sacred thread, removed their top knot, and stopped performing Vedic rites in favour of temple services.[46] It has also been pointed out that there were two types of *śūdra*s groups that participated in the Śrīvaiṣṇava temple administration: the Śāttāda Śrīvaiṣṇavas or non-*brāhmaṇa* householders and the *Śāttāda ekāki*s

[44] South Indian Inscriptions, vol. XXIV, no. 320.

[45] *Tirumala-Tirupati Devasthanam Epigraphical Series* (1933), vol. I, no. 211, pp. 212–13. (Henceforth, *TTDES*)

[46] Lester (1994), 'The Śāttāda Śrīvaiṣṇavas', p. 39. In the same article Lester (p. 42) says, 'It can also be argued, as many non-Sāttādas do and some Sāttādas concede, that the latter are śūdras, mixed castes, or both, who established themselves as "pure" (at least, *purer* than other non-brahmins), either or both by once having control of major temples or by reason of inspiration by the Piḷḷai Lokācārya/Maṇavāḷamāmuni theology and *pañcarātra dīkṣā*. With respect to either of these scenarios, Sāttāda Śrīvaiṣṇavism may have arisen during or just after the time of Maṇavāḷamāmuni (1370–1445), or it may represent the continuation of a very old *bhāgavata* (*sātvata* corrupted to *sāttāda*?) Vaiṣṇavism inspiring and inspired by the Āḻvārs, and progressively "taken over" by certain *smārta* brahmins.'

and *Śāttāda mudali*s or non-*brāhmaṇa*s renunciates at Tirupati and Śrīraṅgam respectively.[47]

Since the *Śāttāda ekāki*s and *Śāttāda mudali*s had become renunicates, the regular caste injunctions of an ordinary *śūdra* did not apply to them. They had to follow the rules of their respective orders.[48] Subsequently, they became prominent under their leader Kanḍāḍai Rāmānuja Dāsar or Kanḍāḍai Rāmānuja Ayyaṅgār (c. 1430–96 CE).[49] The inscriptional evidence referred to him for the first time in 1456 CE at Tirupati, describing him as the disciple of Aḻagiyamaṇavāḷa Jīyar and the trustee of *Rāmānujakūtams* (feeding houses within the temple premises).[50] The Vijayanagar ruler Sāḷuva Narasimharāya, in whose period the inscription was recorded, appeared to have constructed the *Rāmānujakūtams* and, as stated in this epigraph, conferred certain rights to Kanḍāḍai Rāmānuja Ayyaṅgār:

> A quarter of the offered *prasādam*, viz., 3 (*marakkāl* of) *prasādam*, 13 *appa-prasādam* and 1 *nāḻi akkāḻi prasādam*, these being the share of the donor will be delivered, as stipulated to the *Rāmānujakūtams* constructed by you as your charity both at Tirumala and Tirupati and managed by Kanḍāḍai Rāmānujayyan, the disciple of Aḻagiyamaṇavāḷa Jīyar, in order that they may be served to the Śrīvaishṇavas in these *Rāmānujakūtams*; and this practice of delivering the donors share of the offered *prasādam* to the *Rāmānujakūtam* shall continue to be in force through the succession of the disciples of Rāmānujayyan, till the lasting of the moon and the sun.
>
> This is the writing of the temple accountant, *Tiruninṟa-ūr-uḍaiyān* with the permission of the Śrīvaishṇavas. May these the Śrīvaishṇavas protect.[51]

Subsequently, Kanḍāḍai Rāmānuja Ayyaṅgār seems to have emerged as a powerful person who supervised the temple repair works at Tirupati, was the trustee of the gold treasury there, and built and managed the

[47] Burton Stein (2004). 'Social Mobility and Medieval South Indian Hindu Sects', in David Lorenzen (ed.), pp. 95–7.

[48] Ibid., p. 96.

[49] Lester (1994), pp. 43–7, for a discussion on the avowed brahmanical status of Kanḍāḍai Rāmānuja Ayyaṅgār.

[50] *TTDES*, vol. II, no. 4, pp. 7–8.

[51] Ibid.

Rāmānujakūtams in Śrīraṅgam and Kāñcīpuram.[52] In the inscriptions of the Raṅganāthasvāmī temple at Śrīraṅgam, he was referred to as Ayodhyā Kanḍāḍai Rāmānuja Ayyaṅgār, a *Śāttāda-parama ekāṅgi* of Tiruvaraṅgam-Tirupati, indicating that he was influential in both the temples at Śrīraṅgam and at Tirupati.[53] One of the records registered that he donated two villages in Toṇḍaimaṇḍalam to Lord Raṅganātha 'for offering during the Rāmānujayan *avasaram* and to feed the Śrīvaishṇava Brāhmaṇas with the donor's share of the offering in the *Rāmānuja-kūtam* situated in the west of Pallavarāyar maṭha, on the eastern portion of the southern row of the Vikrama-chōḷan-tiruvidi'.[54] The influence of Kanḍāḍai Rāmānuja Ayyaṅgār seems to have increased by the end of the fifteenth century, as important political officials like *mahāmaṇḍaleśvaras* and their families donated generously to his *Rāmānujakūtam* for feeding the Śrīvaiṣṇavas.[55] Śāttāda *Ekāki* Śrīvaiṣṇavas were his disciples and they looked after the administration of the feeding houses and after his death were entitled to his share of benefactions.[56] However, it seems that his *brāhmaṇa* disciple, Kanḍāḍai Mādhvayyaṅgār, inherited his office in the beginning of the sixteenth century as the *dharmakartā* of the *Rāmānujakūtam* at Tiruvaraṅgam-Tirupati.[57]

The Śāttāda *Ekāki* Śrīvaiṣṇavas seemed to have gained prominence under their leader, Kanḍāḍai Rāmānuja Ayyaṅgār, and were granted shares in the temple offerings, participated in the singing of *Tiruvāymoḻi*

[52] Lester (1994), p. 44 and fn. 18; *TTDES Vol. II*, no. 128, pp. 289–91; no. 134, pp. 310–18.

[53] South Indian Inscriptions, vol. XXIV, no. 346.

[54] Ibid., No. 346.

[55] Ibid., No. 355; Also see, Vasudha Narayanan (2007), 'With the Earth as a Lamp and the Sun as the Flame', *International Journal of Hindu Studies*, vol. 11, no. 3, pp. 227–53. In this work, the achievements of Kanḍāḍai Rāmānuja Ayyaṅgār are described. It is stated here that apart from being the chief manager at the temple at Tirumala-Tirupati, he also created the performative tradition for the singing of the Tamil hymns, their preservation and institutionalization not just at Tirupati, but in other temple centres of the Tamil region.

[56] Robert C. Lester, pp. 46–7.

[57] South Indian Inscriptions, vol. XXIV, no. 357: This record tells us that Kanḍāḍai Mādhvayyaṅgār constructed a temple and consecrated the image of Viṭṭhaleśvara and Madurakaviāḻvār, arranged for their worship, and also constructed a kitchen.

and so on.[58] This becomes evident as their rights and honours in the temple documented in one of the inscriptions dated 1464 CE is as follows:

> ... with the year 1386 of the Śaka era, the following *śilāśāsanam* was executed in favour of Kaṇḍāḍai Rāmānuja Ayyaṅgār, the manager of *Rāmānujakūtams* (free feeding house)....
>
> In accordance with the directions issued by you to your disciples, the Śāttāda *Ekāki* Śrīvaiṣṇavas, in the matter of offering, as your *kainkaryam* (service), of *meditta śāttuppaḍi* (*chandanam*, sandal paste), turmeric paste, the paste of the fruit of..., musk, refined camphor, a small cloth, these, and 25 areca-nuts and 25 betel leaves, supplied from the *Rāmānujakūtams* (situated) on Tirumala. These (disciples) shall bring the above articles (to the temples) daily at the time of the *Alagappirānār-tirumanjaṅam*, shall cause the small cloth and the *śāttuppaḍi* to be put on and smeared and the areca-nuts and betel leaves to be offered to the deities, and out of the offered *prasādam* shall receive back 4 areca-nuts and 4 betel leaves for the *Rāmānujakūtam* with the mention of your name and present them to you.
>
> In this manner the service shall be carried on through the succession of your disciples, till the lasting of moon and the sun ...[59]

The hagiographies took note of these developments and the *Āṟāyirappaṭi* and *Muāyirappaṭi* included the names of several Śāttāda Śrīvaiṣṇavas, Śāttāda *mudali*s, and *ekaṅgi*s as disciples of Rāmānuja. However, it appears that in the course of the sixteenth century, the status of the *Śāttāda ekāki*s and *Śāttāda mudali*s declined as there were hardly any references to their administrative involvement in the temples. Similarly, Śāttāda Śrīvaiṣṇavas who were householders and officiated with the *brāhmaṇa*s in the ritual matters in temples also met a similar fate.[60] In fact, the *Kōil Oḷugu*, the chronicle of the Raṅganāthasvāmī temple at Śrīraṅgam compiled around seventeenth-eighteenth century, noted that the non-*brāhmaṇa*s were not accorded any ritual duties; rather they functioned as ordinary temple servants:

[58] *TTDES*, vol. II, no. 68, pp. 129–38; no. 81, pp. 154–5 and no. 22, pp. 35–6.

[59] *TTDES*, vol. II, no. 22, pp. 35–6.

[60] Stein (2004), 'Social Mobility and Medieval South Indian Hindu Sects', pp. 96–7.

> Decorating with flowers the *tirumaṇḍapas* during festivals and the *Aḻagiyamaṇavāḷan tirumaṇḍapa* daily; making garlands and offering them for the starting of procession; raining (sic) flowers (on special occasions); proceeding in two rows holding ceasors, two folded cloths, eight gold torches and twenty silver torches and waving two pieces of cloth; forming a rear batch, with hands folded behind the row by the waists reciting the last two lines of each stanza; bearing the Rāmānuja sword and acting as the bodyguard of the *Jīyars* and the Śrīvaiṣṇavas.[61]

Some scholars are of the opinion that the gradual decline in the marginalization of the *śūdra* participation, in this case, the Śāttādas, was due to two reasons. One, Kaṇḍāḍai Rāmānuja Ayyaṅgār, the leader of the *śūdras* was an agent of the Vijayanagara ruler Sāḻuva Narasimha and was, therefore, influential. Thus, it is argued that the *śūdra* participation and control in the temple administration at Tirupati and Śrīraṅgam increased, directly challenging the brāhmaṇanical order, which, sensing an impending crisis, asserted itself.[62] Besides, pressures within the Śrīvaiṣṇava community to contain the differences between the Vaṭakaḷais and Teṉkaḷais over the temple honours led to the restructuring of the brāhmaṇanical resources.[63] Consequently, the brāhmaṇanical interest asserted itself and was consolidated at the expense of the Śāttādas. Another reason cited for the decline of the *śūdra* participation was the assertion of the *Vaikhānasa Āgama* (temple manuals) in the case of the Veṅkateśvarasvāmī temple at Tirupati. Although there was a textual advocacy of the *Pañcarātra Āgama* that was broader based and inclusivistic regarding the participation in the temple rituals, it was the *Vaikhānasa Āgama* in the ritual practices that was more conservative, exclusivistic, and brāhmaṇical in its outlook that prevailed at Tirupati, marginalizing the Śāttāda participation in the temple services.[64]

Two, it has been suggested that the political ideology of the Vijayanagara rulers in an attempt to articulate against Islam was based on orthodox brāhmaṇical norms, enjoinment of caste duties, and avowed protection of brāhmaṇical institutions with extensive patronage to the *brāhmaṇas*. Therefore, it follows that the non-*brāhmaṇas* warrior elite

61 *The Kōil Oḻugu*, p. 46.

62 Stein (2004) 'Social Mobility and Medieval South Indian Hindu Sects', p. 99.

63 Ibid., pp. 97–101.

64 Ibid., p. 100.

supported the *brāhmaṇas* and gained legitimation, and this enhanced the importance and indispensability of the *brāhmaṇas* in the political dispensation at the expense of the *śūdras* in the temples.[65]

While it is not incorrect to conclude that after twelfth century, the social base of the Śrīvaiṣṇavas expanded, involving more social groups within the arena of temples, but that did not imply that they were always effective. The rise and decline of the Śāttādas should be seen along with the rise and decline of various groups within the temples. Since the orientation of the Śrīvaiṣṇavas was always brāhmaṇanical and the *brāhmaṇa* base was never marginalized, understanding the temple society through the frame of the *Vaikhānasa* and *Pañcarātra Āgamas* is too simplistic. For such binaries do not apply in reality as both had elements of conservatism as well as liberalism entrenched within them. Despite the fact that the Raṅganāthasvāmī temple at Śrīraṅgam followed the *Pañcarātra Āgama*, the Śāttāda Śrīvaiṣṇavas were gradually marginalized within this temple too. It also needs to be emphasized that the Vijayanagar state did not posture as a Hindu state against Islam. There is a large body of work that has convincingly demonstrated the influence of the Islamicate culture in the Vijayanagar court, political rituals, dress, and warfare technology. The Vijayanagar rulers employed Muslim soldiers in the army and adopted titles like *Hindu Rāya Suratrāṇa*, that is, Sultan amongst the Hindu kings, indicating that the Islamicate world was a part of their reference framework.[66]

Although the issues of *varṇāśramadharma* and the community, especially in the hymns of the Āḻvārs from seventh century, were always a major ideological concern, these issues evolved as the markers of the religious community identities with the assertion of the *varṇā* order as a norm as well as practice within the Śrīvaiṣṇava community in the thirteenth century.[67] The textual tradition expounded on these subjects and generated a dialogue which had ramifications on the Śrīvaiṣṇava theology and social practice. The *guruparamparās* and commentaries

[65] Ibid., pp. 100–1.

[66] Eaton (2000), *The Articulation of Islamic Space in Medieval Deccan*, in Eaton (ed.), pp. 159–75; Wagoner (1996), 'Sultan Among the Hindu Kings', *The Journal of Asian Studies*, 55 (4), pp. 851–80; Wagoner (2000), 'Harihara, Bukka and the Sultan: The Delhi Sultanate in the Political Imagination of Vijayanagar', in Gilmartin and Lawrence (eds), pp. 300–26.

[67] Champakalakshmi (2012), *Religion, Tradition and Ideology*, pp. 236–9.

discussed the relation of the *varṇa* with the community, in which both were adjusted and accommodated in accordance with the Śrīvaiṣṇava religious values. The central concern of the hagiographers was to explicate the Śrīvaiṣṇava tradition not only from a theological point of view, but also expound it as the ideological basis of the organizational and institutional networks of the temples and the *maṭhas*, both of which provided an arena of interaction for the community. Thus, the notion of a community was of foremost significance and the *guruparamaparās* developing as scriptures of the community, despite their differing orientations reiterated the normative concept of a single homogeneous uniform community in the charismatic portrayal of Rāmānuja. Uniformity became the dominant theme in all the hagiographies that provided the respective sects with a lineage. The origin of the lineage in most of the cases was traced to Rāmānuja. In this manner, each sect with its lineage claimed to represent the uniform Śrīvaiṣṇava community. Projection of a uniform community became important for establishing claims in the competitive spheres of resource control in the temples. It represented an integrative framework, whereby devotees could be from any section of the society. Therefore, the concept of uniformity made the caste ascription secondary to that of a community.

Nevertheless, on the one hand, there was an emphasis on the irrelevance of birth status in access to devotion, and on the other, the social reality of the *varṇa* hierarchy was not ignored and thus incorporated within the Śrīvaiṣṇava ideological frame in the institutional structures of the community. It should be noted that in the Śrīvaiṣṇava hagiographies taken up for analysis, the word *śūdra* rarely occurs for caste, except in Chapter 17 of the *Divyasūricaritam* in *śloka* 85 that stated that since Rāmānuja took care of everybody, therefore he gave an opportunity to the *śūdras* (*śūdraṇama*) in the temple services by allotting ten sets of duties for them. The terms used are usually generic: *varṇa*, *kula*, and *jāti*. Only the term Śāttāda used in the hagiographies denoted specific social identity. The commentaries also applied the terms *varṇa*, *kula*, and *jāti* to denote the social hierarchy.[68] Understood largely as religious class, birth status, and clan respectively, these terms assumed theological significance. It has been pointed out that in dialogues amongst the Śrīvaiṣṇava ideologues, commentators like Periyavāccāṉ Piḷḷai

[68] Clooney (2002), 'Fierce Words', p. 401.

(thirteenth century), while commenting upon the hymns of the Āḻvārs, explained that difference in birth status should not be an obstruction to religious knowledge and promote hierarchical behaviour within the community, with a qualification, however, that marriage could not take place within families of different ranks.[69] Both the hagiographies and commentarial texts, while engaging with the discussions on the caste question, devotion, and service to the community, cited cases from the epics to substantiate their arguments. For instance, the righteous king, Yuddhiṣṭhira, a *kṣatriya* from the *Mahābhārata* who on advice of none other than Lord Kṛṣṇa, performed the last rites of Vidura, a low born; Rāma, a *kṣatriya*, the hero of the *Rāmāyaṇa* who performed the last rites for Jatāyū, a bird and ate the fruit tasted by a tribal woman Śabari Similarly, Vibhīṣaṇa, a *brāhmaṇa* by birth but from the clan of demons, left his brother Rāvaṇa and came into the fold of Rāma. All these were used to illustrate the irrelevance of birth status to devotion.[70] Later commentators based their views on Periyavāccāṉ Piḷḷai's ideas and used these illustrations to present different interpretations. Piḷḷai Lokācārya in his work *Śrīvacanabhūṣaṇam* and Aḻagiyamaṇavāḷa in his commentary *Ācāryahṛdyam* and Maṇavāḷamāmuṉi argued that 'differences in the birth status ought not to divide the community and that pride in birth status has no place in the Śrīvaiṣṇava community'.[71] However, all of them accepted the inevitability of distinctions based on birth and existence of religious classes and argued that though a manifestation of divine creation, they should not be given importance beyond a certain point for spiritual achievements. According to these *ācāryas*, it was not high birth but humble behaviour and negation of the egoistic self that determined one's status.[72] This idea was also

[69] Ibid., pp. 401–5.

[70] In addition, the commentaries also used other examples of the wise *brāhmaṇas* willingly learning the wisdom of *dharma* from Dharmavyādha, a low born trading in meat, an impure occupation and the redemption of a *brāhmaṇa* who had turned into a demon by listening to the *kaiśika* song from the low-born Pāṭuvāṉ. Ibid., p. 406

[71] Ibid., p. 408. Also see, Hardy (2007), 'A Radical Reassessment of the Vedic Heritage: The Ācāryah-dayam and its Wider Implications', in Dalmia and Heinrich von Stietencron (eds), pp. 29–49.

[72] Ibid., p. 410.

reflected often in the hagiographical narratives, for instance, in the episode of Uruṅgavillidāsar and Rāmānuja's views on it. The narratives through the agency of Rāmānuja repeatedly emphasized a humble behaviour that withstood the arrogance of even the greatest scholars like Yādavaprakāśa.

The views of Vedāntadeśika differed, privileging the observance of the rules of *varṇāśramadharma* while serving the Lord. The examples from the epics, according to Vedāntadeśika, were not exceptional but circumspect in observing the traditions:

> when this one [i.e., Vidura], who was learned in Brahman, gave up his life by the power of *yoga*, Dharmaputra felt it his duty to perform Vidura's funeral rites in the special form of the *brahmamedha*.... But [the funeral rites] may have been performed in silence, or were justified in the case of this exceptional individual. But this should not be considered a precedent in the case of other individuals.... Otherwise, it would follow that because the virtuous Pāṇḍavas shared a common wife due to exceptional circumstances others too might do likewise. Each individual should stand firm in his birth status and render service to the Lord in accord with what is prescribed as suitable to that birth status.[73]

The views of Piḷḷai Lokācārya and Vedāntadeśika have been considered as the Teṉkaḷai and Vaṭakaḷai worldviews on caste respectively. Often posited in contradiction to each other, with the former supposed to be radical and later conservative, it has been rightly observed that these two theological responses have more in common and less in contradiction.[74] Both attempted to strike a balance between birth status and devotion and accepted the prior legitimacy of the *varṇāśramadharma*, though undermining it for religious purpose. Therefore, the caste question was resolved not by eradicating it and expounding an egalitarian society in a modern sense, rather it was reconciled within the Śrīvaiṣṇava theological framework of devotion and community.

73 Vedāntadeśika, *The Śrīmad Rahasya Trayasāra* (Tr. by Rajagopala Ayyangar, Salem: Literary Press, 1956), pp. 303–4 in Clooney (2002), 'Fierce Words', pp. 412–13.

74 Clooney (2002), 'Fierce Words', pp. 399–419; Mumme (1988), *The Theology of Maṇavāḷamāmuṉi*; Mumme (1993), 'Rules and Rhetorics: Caste Observance', *Journal of Vaisnava Studies*, 2 (1): pp. 113–38.

The hagiographies, as stated above, while reconciling the caste question within the community paradigm, also reiterated the tradition. The episode of Rāmānuja requesting Tirukacci Nambi to be his *ācārya* and the latter's denial on the grounds of rules of *varṇāśramadharma* has already been recounted. Thus, the hagiographers were informing the devotees that although *yogis* and spiritual men are born amongst all castes and caste injunctions do not apply in such a case, they are to be followed in the external social circumstances, and though Tirukacci Nambi was wise, he would never become the *guru* of Rāmānuja. Similarly, Rāmānuja would take shelter in the abodes of the hunters but would not eat the food cooked by them.

The discourse on *varṇā* assumed complexities for the hagiographers as well as for the theologians as Rāmānuja in his writings advocated adherence to it. Rāmānuja's highly intellectual writings never intended to address the lay devotee. Rather his concern was to evolve a coherent theological base for Śrīvaiṣṇavism, thereby making it ideationally significant for the community, through an intellectually well-articulated and emotionally more appealing philosophy and theology vis-à-vis others, particularly the Advaitins. The principles of *varṇāśramadharma* were never questioned in any of his works. Neither did Rāmānuja intend to do so. For the caste identity was the primordial identity and a complete rejection of it implied the disruption of the social order. The philosophy of Viśiṣṭādvaita by its association with the Vedic texts was structured within a highly Sanskritized framework, not comprehensible to the common man. Thus, it was left for the later-day Śrīvaiṣṇava hagiographers and theologians to evolve a Tamil tradition through the structuring of the canonical literature and finally attempting to merge the Tamil and Sanskritic traditions, in the personality of Rāmānuja.[75] However, a careful observation would reveal that Rāmānuja's *bhakti* was more intellectual than popular.

In Rāmānuja's *Śrībhāṣya*, a commentary on the *Brahmasūtra*, while answering who is to be permitted salvation, it is stated clearly in the comments on the first *sutra* that a *śūdra* is not qualified for knowledge of Brahman. In fact, Rāmānuja accused the Advaitin for permitting a *śūdra* to gain knowledge of the Supreme Being.[76] He explained:

[75] For instance, see Jagadeesan (1977), *History of Srivaishnavism*, pp. 175–83; Venkatachari (1978), *The Manipravala Literature*, pp. 16–21.

[76] Hardy (2001), 'The Formation of Śrīvaiṣṇavism', in Dalmia et al., p. 52.

> Śūdras cannot have competence [for the study of the *Upaniṣads* and consequent knowledge of Brahman] since they lack the capability. Persons who do not know the proper form of Brahman and the mode of meditation on it, and who are not competent for knowledge of the requisite subsidiaries of that meditation, i.e., recitation of the Veda, sacrifices, etc., cannot be capable of integral meditations. Even if such persons who are not capable desire such knowledge, it is still not possible for them to be competent. They are incapable because they do not study the Veda....
>
> The epics and purāṇas become useful means only insofar as they confirm the Veda, but not independently. That śūdras gain knowledge in accord with hearing the epics and purāṇas is meant only to destroy their sins, and not for the sake of meditation. A few [śūdras] such as Vidura were established in Brahman due to knowledge 'stolen' by them from previous lives, while they have [inferior] births due to the force of karmic merits already operative [but not yet exhausted].[77]

Though Rāmānuja was credited with the temple reforms that were radical in nature, some scholars have been sceptical about the agency of Rāmānuja in the temple reforms, concluding that Rāmānuja's so-called temple management policy was more liberal than what had existed before and it was this *relative* liberalism with reference to caste differences within the Śrīvaiṣṇava community that was emphasized in the stories.[78]

One of the important aspects of devotion was the notion of *prapatti*, that is, unconditional surrender to god by a devotee whose caste status was of no consequence. The catholicity of Rāmānuja in the hagiographies was further highlighted by showing that *prapatti* was an integral part of his philosophy. According to Hardy:

> While in Rāmānuja it is the *bhakti-yoga*, which includes meditation that allows a person to achieve liberation, among the later authors this *bhakti yoga* is either contrasted as an extremely difficult method—of which only the privileged few are capable—with the easy means of *prapatti*; or it is rejected outright as a sign of human arrogance vis-à-vis the availability of divine grace. By virtue of being human, every one has access to *prapatti*. This now has the potential of being turned into most radical and revolutionary

[77] Rāmānuja, *Śrībhāṣya, Sūtra* 1.3.33. Tr. by Clooney in Clooney (2002), p. 402.

[78] Carman (1981), *The Theology of Rāmāyana*, p. 37.

> social programme. Indeed the outlines of such a programme were produced in the *Ācāryahṛdyam*, by Aḻagiya Maṇavāḷa Perumāḷ Nāyaṉār. Here the religion of *prapatti* presents itself as a total replacement of the Vedic tradition. Of course such an extreme position found few followers, at least in practice.[79]

A social revolution was not what Śrīvaiṣṇavism needed. It required a strong base with a legitimizing force of the *brāhmaṇa*s and a community structure that was socially heterogeneous. In fact, the attribution of *prapatti* to Rāmānuja was a reaction to the viewpoint that *prapatti* has been marginalized in Rāmānuja's scheme of religious doctrine. The Śrīvaiṣṇava theologians in their own way resolved this controversy by showing that *prapatti* as a concept was central in Rāmānuja's *Gadyatrayam*.[80]

Whether Rāmānuja addressed the theological concept of *prapatti* and what were his views on it and how he saw it vis-à-vis the *bhakti-yoga* became a major issue of contention in the schism of the Śrīvaiṣṇava community into the Vaṭakaḷai and Teṉkaḷai. According to the Vaṭakaḷais, *bhakti* and *prapatti* were two different goals. Status by birth, knowledge, and capability were pre-requisites for *bhakti*. *Prapatti* did not require any qualifications and could be attained by any ordinary human being. *Kainkarya* or service to the God and community was to be performed according to the rules of the *Śāstras*. According to the Teṉkaḷais, since *bhakti* required individual effort, it was inferior to *prapatti*, which was effortless and depended on total surrender to god. The Teṉkaḷais did not give importance to the Śāstric injunctions for performing the *kainkarya*.

Thus, enmeshed with the idea of *prapatti* was the issue of caste and a particular religious attitude based on the sectarian orientations. The Vaṭakaḷais represented the Sanskritic tradition. They were considered brāhmaṇical and conservative in their outlook. The Teṉkaḷais, on the other hand, represented the Tamil tradition. Since the Teṉkaḷais regarded the *Dravida Veda*s as their scriptures, they were considered to be more broad-based than the Vaṭakaḷais and had a large non-brāhmaṇical following.

[79] Hardy (2001), 'The Formation of Śrīvaiṣṇavism', pp. 52–3.

[80] Venkatachari, 1978, pp. 99–103; Lester (1966), 'Rāmānuja and Śrivaiṣṇavism: The Concept of Prapatti or *Śarṇāgati*', in *History of Religions*, 5(2), pp. 266–82.

MODERN REPRESENTATIONS AND PERCEPTIONS OF RĀMĀNUJA AS A SOCIAL REFORMER

By sixteenth century, the perception of Rāmānuja at the pan-Indian level was that of a thinker and commentator of the Vedānta tradition who belonged to the Śrīvaiṣṇava or the Śrī Sampradāya community. His ideas were called *Rāmānuja darśana*. As we have seen in Chapter One, the Ramanandīs regarded him as the propounder of the *saguṇa* (devotion to a personalized God with attributes) *bhakti*. However, the impression of Śrī Sampradāya as a conservative religious tradition that admitted only twice born males into its fold and the Sanskritic orientation of Rāmānuja were always present in the Rāmānandi sub-consciousness. As discussed in Chapter One, in the early eighteenth century and finally in early nineteenth century, the association with Rāmānuja and Śrī Sampradāya became controversial. One section amongst the Rāmānandis found his canonization irrelevant on the grounds that Rāmānuja's teachings and the Śrīvaiṣṇava community had a Sanskritic/Vedic theological orientation. Those followers who continued to identify Rāmānanda as a part of Rāmānuja's lineage were called Rāmānujīs, while those who advocated an independent status of Rāmānanda were called Rāmānandis.

The narratives in the hagiographies represented Rāmānuja as an exegete whose sphere of interaction was limited to the select intellectuals with a Sanskritic orientation. Simultaneously, they also projected him as socially liberal and accessible to the common masses. Such a dualistic representation reflected, in fact, their own perceptions of the community that had theological moorings in the ideas of Viśiṣṭādvaita and simultaneously provided a ritual and social space for everybody but within the framework of *varṇāśramadharma*. In this manner, caste and community were balanced without upholding one at the expense of the other. Though the *varṇā* hierarchy was critiqued but in the secular Śrīvaiṣṇava domain the caste hierarchies continued. This was justified by insisting that caste status, though relevant in the external world of social interaction, had no application in the inner world of spirituality and devotion. This was the sum of ideas that comprised the medieval Vaiṣṇava *bhakti* in south India. It has been rightly pointed out that the meaning of *bhakti* changed with the changing context. It may have had somewhat anti-caste sentiments to begin with, but adapted itself to the historical reality and evolved a new value system that did not outrightly challenge the social equation, rather accommodated it.[81]

It is evident from the analysis that the hagiographies delineated Rāmānuja as an exceptional *ācārya* who was a great intellectual and organizer of the community. Rāmānuja's engagement with the caste question was a part of this larger narrative and was not the grand narrative itself. However, a separate discussion on the caste question is required as the contemporary structure of identity politics and social configuration rooted in pigeon-holed notions of discrimination and egalitarianism read into the hagiographies primarily the large-heartedness of the twelfth-century *ācārya*, marginalizing the larger discourse of an exceptional philosopher, whose interpretation of the Vedanta was considered path-breaking in the pre-colonial intellectual world. In addition, it needs to be emphasized that in the narratives themselves, inequity and justice existed not in contradiction but in agreement with each other, which is an unthinkable proposition for the modern worldview. Therefore, the subsequent discussion in this section will analyse the modern views of Rāmānuja as a liberal religious figure. However, even in this case, there have been variations. While on one hand, some regarded unquestioningly Rāmānuja as a social reformer, on the other hand, some have been more circumspect and have felt that given the medieval context, a radical revision of the *varṇa* hierarchy was too much to expect from him. However, both the viewpoints situated in their socio-intellectual contexts nevertheless assumed the hagiographical narratives as Rāmānuja's actual social philosophy, hesitating to break away from this compelling image of a social reformer.

The Orientalist discourse in the nineteenth century proposed a particular perception of *bhakti* that generated a scholarship for several decades to come.[82] The Orientalists like George Abraham Grierson

[81] Van Der Veer (1987), 'Taming the Ascetic', p. 682.

[82] The writings of H.H. Wilson, Albrecht Weber, Lorinser, Monier Williams, and George Abraham Grierson appeared in various issues of the *Journal of Royal Asiatic Society* and in monographs and finally under different entries in various volumes of the *Encyclopedia of Religion and Ethics*, James Hastings (ed.). These works have been analysed for researches on the nature of religion in general and *bhakti* in particular in the pre-colonial as well as colonial periods. For details, See Sharma (2004), 'Towards a New Perspective', in Lorenzen (ed.), pp. 291–332; Hawley (2007), 'Introduction', pp. 209–25; Dalmia (1997), *The Nationalization of Hindu Traditions*, pp. 338–429.

(c.1851–1941 CE), while attributing a unitary character to '*bhakti marg*', characterized it as a religion of 'devotional faith' based on the emotional outpourings through prayers and adoration to a personalized God, Viṣṇu (his incarnations) in order to achieve salvation. This monotheism was opposed to the 'works path' (*karma mārg*) and knowledge of the Supreme (*jñāna mārg*) in Sankara's Advaita, which, according to Grierson, was monism.[83] Further, it was held that this '*bhakti* religion', primarily a Vaiṣṇava religion, possessed strong reformist tendencies to purge the polytheistic and monistic trends and was characterized by 'four churches of reformation', or *Sampradāyas* 'viz., *Śrī -sampradāya* founded by Rāmānuja, the *Brahma-sampradāya* founded by Madhva, the *Rudra-sampradāya* founded by Viṣṇusvāmin, the *Sanakādi-sampradāya* founded by Nimbāditya'.[84] According to Rudolph Otto, a well-known German Orientalist (c.1869–1937 CE), the 'School of Rāmānuja' was like the Lutheran Church with its own sets of rituals, place of worship, and hymn book. It therefore followed that Rāmānuja was a reformer like Martin Luther and this Church of Rāmānuja had, at some point of time, had difference of opinion over the doctrine of Grace and split into the sects of the Vaṭakaḷais and Teṉkaḷais. Thus, for Rudolph Otto, Ramanuja's school was analogous to the Christian church with its doctrine of Grace and the Vaṭakaḷais and Teṉkaḷais groups were equivalent to the two sects of the Roman Catholics and Protestants.[85]

Concomitant with the Orientalist discourse, there was a vibrant discussion amongst Indian scholars during this period on the notion of *bhakti*, religion, and religious philosophies.[86] The terms of debates and discussions in the Tamil intellectual environment were not only informed by Orientalism, but also by the ideas of reforms, the Dravidian movement, and the national movement. As discussed in Chapter One, the ideas of reform in general were initiated primarily by the *brāhmaṇas*.

[83] Grierson (1907), 'Bhakti Marg', p. 539.

[84] Ibid., p. 544.

[85] Raman (2007), *Self Surrender (Prapatti) to Gods*, pp. 12–13.

[86] There were vibrant writings in the Hindi literary sphere about the *bhakti* movement, especially the works of Hazariprasad Dvivedi and Ram Sharan Shukla. The scholars have argued about the provenance of the term '*bhakti* movement', the ubiquitous influence on Vaisnavism for medieval *bhakti* that ignored the Advaitic and *dasanāmī* traditions. See, for details, Sharma (2004), 'Towards a New Perspective', pp. 291–332; Stratton Hawley (2007), 'Introduction', pp. 209–25; Dalmia (1997), *The Nationalization of Hindu Traditions*, pp. 338–429.

It has been rightly pointed out that '[t]he names that more frequently "appear" in the nineteenth century Hindu reformist discourse are those of Śaṃkara, Rāmānuja, Caitanya, the Buddha or the Maharashtrian poet saints-men mostly belonging to the upper castes'.[87] It needs to be highlighted that by drawing from the religious reserves and projecting the idea of Rāmānuja as a reformer, the scholars, mostly *brāhmaṇas* were using a conservative medium whose perception of egalitarianism was confined merely to the experiential aspects of devotion and maintaining the traditional social balance. However, though it is important to consider the consequences of the encounter with the West and the new equations that the colonial state and colonialism posed, the role of the Theosophical Society in the redefinition of Hinduism and its influence upon a specific delineation of religious leaders of the pre-colonial period, such a study is beyond the scope of the present research.

This upper caste initiative of projecting religious leaders as reformers was countered by the non-Brāhamaṇa movement during the same period. It has been pointed out that Periyar rejected the reforms.[88] The ideas of the non-Brahmana movement focusing on the language issue impacted the cultural and intellectual sphere which had consequences for the Tamil literature.[89] The Tamil literary canon, comprising religious and didactic texts including the commentaries, hymnal corpus, and hagiographies, was contested with the influence of the Dravidian movement and was restructured. A modern literary canon emerged based on the notion of antiquity in secular, historical terms spanning more than a millennium.[90] The old Cankam texts now replaced the religious texts as classics with the exception of *Tevāram* and the *Nālāyira Divya Prabandham* that were retained on account of their aesthetic and literary merit.[91] The older canon was now reduced to the category of *bhakti* literature with mere religious significance and was secondary to the secular Cankam literary tradition with love, war, and heroism as important literary tropes. The development of printing technology and the concomitant print culture made several of these old Cankam texts readily

87 Sen (2007), 'The Idea of Social Reforms', p. 109.

88 Ibid., p. 128.

89 Venkatachalapathy (2006), *In Those Days There Was No Coffee*, pp. 89–113.

90 Ibid., p. 97.

91 Ibid., p. 110.

available. The underlying principle of the new canon, now purged of religious texts, was the assertion of Tamil as an ancient language and castigation of Sanskrit and the caste structure, both now considered as alien to the southern context and, therefore, irrelevant. It was emphasized that 'ancient Tamil Nadu' was 'an egalitarian society where caste and religion did not exist—if they did, it was the beginning of incursions from the north/Aryans/Sanskrit ... Caste and religion accompanied them thus turning the Tamil society into an unequal one'.[92]

Thus, amidst the background of the Orientalist discourse, ideas of social and religious reform and Dravidian movements, the ideas of Rāmānuja as a social reformer evolved. Interestingly, the Orientalist discourse, while attributing *Śrī Sampradāya*/Śrīvaiṣṇavism as a 'reformist church', did not focus on the social aspect. Even the entry in the *Encyclopedia of Religion and Ethics* under 'Rāmānuja' never highlighted his quality as a liberal. None of these narratives on the questioning of the social hierarchy in this chapter find a mention in that essay that primarily focused on Rāmānuja's philosophy. According to the essay:

> The essential contribution of Rāmānuja to the Indian thought was the effort to develop in a complete system, in opposition to the uncompromising Advaitism of Śaṅkara, a philosophical basis for the doctrine of devotion to God which was presented in the poetical forms in the hymns (*prabandhas*) of the Ālvārs—a task for which his training under a teacher of Advaitism rendered him specially fit.... The *Śrībhāsya*, his commentary on the *Brahmasūtra*, conveys an impression of no mean philosophical insight, and it is fair to assume his work in substantial merit and completeness far outdid any previous effort to find in the *Brahmasūtra* a basis for monotheism.[93]

Similarly, R.G. Bhandarkar did not mention Rāmānuja's catholicity but had a discussion on his ideas with a brief account of his life in a matter of fact manner.[94]

Thus, clearly, it was not the Orientalist influence so much as the influence of the ideas of reform that seemed to have highlighted the notion of a progressive liberal. In addition, the attack on religion for perpetuating

[92] Ibid., p. 104.

[93] Keith (1918), 'Ramanuja', in James Hastings (ed.), p. 572.

[94] Bhandarkar (1965) [reprint], *Vaisnavism, Saivism and Minor Religious Systems*, pp. 50–7.

caste and inequality also could have led to a reassertion of the past to counter the accusation of inequity. Interestingly, while on the one hand the biographies on Rāmānuja projected him as a great social revolutionary, on the other, they upheld the caste values as essential for the moral order of the universe. In this connection, Ālkondaville Gōvindāchārya's *The Life of Rāmānujāchārya. The Exponent of Viṣishṭādvāita Philosophy*, written in 1906, becomes important. While calling Rāmānuja a great revolutionary, Gōvindāchārya's comments on the hagiographical narratives on contestation of the *varṇāśramadharma* did not jettison it, rather justified its existence for the preservation of the universe. On the episode of Rāmānuja beseeching Tirukacci Nambi to be his teacher, Gōvindāchārya commented: Ramanuja *admitted the legality and expediency of the caste system*, and yet he felt it ought to be disregarded in special cases where such spiritually advanced souls as Kanchi-puṟṇa's were concerned.[95]

He then went to provide a long footnote, quoting from the speech of Mr. N.N. Ghosh at the Hare Anniversary Meeting in 1904 on the vexed question of caste in India, which the Christian will not understand:[96]

> He said—-The division into castes cannot be understood by any one who does not realise that all Hindu institutions were inspired by one principle. It was not political expediency, not social convenience, not the happiness of the greatest number, not the development of fighting capacity. Material good was a subordinate end. The ruling principle was the spiritual evolution of man, the perfection of character, realisation of the self. For the purposes of spiritual evolution, a segregation of classes and occupations was considered necessary....[97]

Further, Gōvindāchārya's own comments to this quote in the same footnote were as follows:

> The warning voice against promiscuous intercourse and admixture of castes is found in the *Bhagavad- Gita*, I, 40 to 44; which may be read by all the devotees of this Holy Bible, and laid to heart before venturing to anathematize the caste-institution of India ...[98]

95 Gōvindāchārya (1906), *The Life of Rāmānujāchārya*, p. 60. Italics mine.
96 Ibid., p. 59, fn 2.
97 Ibid.
98 Ibid.

Why was Gōvindāchārya so defensive about the validity of caste system? Was he also reacting to the Christian missionaries who critiqued this social order? Interestingly, the modern biographers provide different terms for Tirukacci Nambi's social status. Gōvindāchārya labelled him as a *vaiśya* and Swami Ramakrishnananda, another of Rāmānuja's biographer (whom we will discuss soon), called him a *śūdra*.[99] Some others did not deviate from the hagiographic narratives and remained ambiguous about this aspect.

Swami Ramakrishnananda (1863–1911 CE), a noted biographer of Rāmānuja, shared the same viewpoint on his social philosophy.[100] Swami Ramakrishnananda can be credited with perhaps one of the earliest writings on the life of Rāmānuja in Bengali. He was the disciple of Swami Vivekanada and was also the President of the Ramakrishna Mission in Chennai. Writing within the reformist frame of the nineteenth and the twentieth centuries, his comments on Rāmānuja's life abounded with details on mass consciousness and reaching out to ordinary people. While recounting Rāmānuja's shouting of the *mantra* from the temple to everybody, he reported:

> As he walked towards the high gates of the Vishnu temple at Goshthipura, he invited whomsoever he met on the way, 'Please come near the temple. I will give you a priceless jewel.' Attracted by his joyous countenance, his eager words and his effulgent beauty, men, women and children followed him spell-bound as it were. Gradually a rumour spread in the town that a prophet had descended near the temple and was giving away to men whatever they wanted. Within a short time a large number of men and women of the town and the suburbs assembled there. At the sight of this vast congregation of people being swept by the wave of joy, the boundless ocean of love in Ramanuja's heart swelled and heaved. He shared his joy with the two disciples, Dasarathi and Kuresa, who had come there, by embracing them. Then he climbed to the top of the temple tower and in a mighty voice addressed the gathering.

[99] Gōvindāchārya (1906), *The Life of Rāmānujāchārya*, p. 59; Swami Ramakrishnananda (trans. from Bengali by Swami Budhananda) (1986), *Life of Sri Ramanuja*, p. 101.

[100] Swami Ramakrishnananda (trans. from Bengali by Swami Budhananda) (1986), *Life of Sri Ramanuja*.

'Brothers and sisters, you that are dearer to me than my life, if you want to get liberation from the torments and afflictions of this world for ever, then pronounce three times along with me the gem of the Mantra which I have procured for you. Do this and be blessed.'

At this all spoke out in a chorus, 'Please tell us the mantra; make us blessed; we are ready.' Then Ramanuja, the incarnation of Lakshmana, the only knower of the innermost feelings of the heart of Yamunamuni, the master of both the superhuman powers (Ubhayavibhutipati), the dispeller of afflictions, the beloved of all people, the ocean of the milk of kindness, the sun that destroys the darkness of despair-pronounced, in a stentorian voice from the depth of his joyful heart, the great Mantra 'Om Namo Narayanaya' (Om, Salutation to Narayana). This great assemblage received the Mantra as eagerly as hungry men receive the dole of food, and pronounced it all together in a thunderous voice. They uttered the Mantra twice more in unison with Sri Ramanuja and then became all quiet. At that time, the earth appeared like Vaikuntha!

The faces of children, men and women, were all flushed with joy. It seemed as if all misery had left the earth forever. Those who came with the hope of gaining money or fulfilling their worldly desires, forgot all about it and the world. In their joy, they felt like one who suddenly got a diamond, having come to gather pieces of glass. As the crowd began to melt away, men and women prostrated themselves towards Ramanuja, in profound thankfulness and took leave of him deeming themselves blessed.[101]

Such stirring of mass consciousness interned in the spirit of this biography was in conformity with the ideas of Swami Vivekanada whose disciple the author was. According to Swami Vivekanand, Śaṅkara was intellectual and advocated strict adherence to caste rules. His Advaita had no scope of emotional outpouring. On the other hand, according to him, Rāmānuja's philosophy was emotional, appealed to ordinary masses, disregarded caste rules for the attainment of spiritualism and was successful in bringing back common masses to the Vedic religion.[102]

Most of the modern biographers of Rāmānuja identify him as a 'social reformer' in his supposed attempts to make the otherwise limited brāhmaṇical access to the knowledge of Brahman available to people

[101] Ibid., pp. 152–54.

[102] Swami Vivekanand 'The Historical Evolution of India', as quoted in 'Preface' in Swami Ramakrishnananda (1986). Also see, Indra 'Hagiography Revisited', p. xxxvii in Parthasarathy (2008), *Ramanujar*.

from all castes. It is a wonder that nobody has ever cross-checked this perception with his actual writings in which he upheld the *varṇa* rules in this matter, as quoted in the previous section of this chapter. Some of the biographers do recognize that to apply modern notions of equality to his life story would be misplaced.[103] With regard to the famous narrative of Rāmānuja shouting the *Mantra* from the temple top, some scholars feel that only those people could enter the temples who were not outcastes.[104] They have rightly observed that '[t]he event, however, was so appealing to the imagination of the latter day biographers and chroniclers that they presented a larger than life image of Ramanuja ...'[105] However, whatever may be the rationale in analyzing Rāmānuja's life, the biographies did not deviate from the larger image of his being a compassionate *ācārya*.

The community's perception of Rāmānuja that has always been a part of the Śrīvaiṣṇava received tradition has impressed upon the modern secular genres of biographies and various writings. Ranging from the modern period of nineteenth century to the contemporary period of the twenty-first century, these writings have often unquestioningly replicated the sacred exaltation of Rāmānuja in their respective analysis of religion and philosophy. In most of these works, the comparison with Śaṅkara and his philosophy is invariable and inevitably Śaṅkara's Advaita is always referred to as more intellectual and Rāmānuja's Viśiṣṭādvaita appeal is perceived as comprehensible to an average devotee. In the nineteenth-century context of the social reform movement, this juxtaposition of Śaṅkara and Rāmānuja projected the latter as a precursor of modern social reforms.

In an article that featured on the Entertainment page of a national daily of great repute, the following was written about Rāmānuja:

> How does one describe Sri Rāmānuja? Scholar nonpareil? Ideal disciple? Sterling leader? Intense bhakta? The very personification of humility? Friend of the marginalised? Bold reformer far ahead of his times? Hero of the spirit? The great Vaishnava Acharya transcends all such compartmentalisations. In fact, the very fort walls of Srirangam echo his words; the streets remain sanctified by his touch, long, long after he has withdrawn from the physical. His dedication to temple ritualism went hand in hand

103 See, for instance, Indra (2008) in Parthasarathy, *Ramanujar*, pp. xxxvi–xlv.

104 Ibid., p. xl.

105 Ibid.

> with his intensely practical outlook. He was the one who brought about a complete integration of people belonging to various castes and creeds. The manner in which he functioned while looking after the Srirangam temple reveals the ideal administrator as well.[106]

Articles such as these have often been printed in various national dailies, clearly indicating a wide readership. Cast within the framework of the *bhakti* movement that has often been regarded simplistically as a protest against the caste hierarchy, the portrayal of Rāmānuja's unflinching devotion to god, in this case Viṣṇu, inspired his dissent against the brāhmaṇical domination and shaped his worldview towards the marginalized caste, has an appeal in the Indian society in general and the Tamil society in particular, where caste identities still dominate and influence social interactions and political configurations.

In conclusion, three things need to be stated. One, while there has been a discussion on the caste question in the hagiographical narratives, these discussions were not predominant and were interwoven with the larger depiction of Rāmānuja as a great exegete and an *ācārya*. Two, the hagiographies at no point of time claimed to be radical in their approach. Nor were they keen to represent Rāmānuja in such progressive terms. Their ideology was in synchrony with the larger community exegesis that incorporated the *varṇāśramadharma* within the community, not even for a moment marginalizing the former. Therefore, these aspects were ignored by the modern chroniclers. The inclusion of complexities and contradictions in the representations of Rāmānuja was avoided or not taken cognizance of, thereby creating an impression of an unproblematic monolithic received tradition. Though sometimes the alternate discussions manifest, but within the text itself these are evened out with an explanation that is always in congruence with the delineation of Rāmānuja as a 'social reformer'. Three, it needs to be pointed out that whatever may be the social attitudes of the various religious traditions including Śrīvaiṣṇavism, they were not reformist in the modern sense. Therefore, the term 'social reform' is anachronistically applied to the precolonial religious traditions. It has been rightly pointed out that these religious traditions situated themselves within an unbroken continuous

[106] Kumar (2005). 'Administrator par excellence', in *The Hindu*: Friday, May 13. Entertainment Page.

tradition, and 'the modern paradigm of reform put greater faith in the instrumentality of human intervention and projected this as some kind of moral responsibility that individuals had towards community at large'.[107] Past was invoked to project a historical continuity and exemplification of progressive traditions that the Indian social system was accused of lacking. Thus, the idea of Rāmānuja as a social reformer was a combination of individual social responsibility and projected historicity to highlight a glorious tradition of social progressiveness.

[107] Sen (2007), 'The Idea of Social Reform', p. 128.

CHAPTER SIX

From Hagiographies to Biographies

Some Concluding Remarks

One of the significant aspects of the religious identity of a community is the representation of a particular past that legtimizes the status and authority of the concerned community, justifying its claims in the contemporary socio-political context. Further, associated with the notions of an antiquated past is the concept of a tradition that is important for the development of a specific religiosity and religious ideals that become central to the evolution of a community. Thus, the representation of the past, while providing a sense of history and cultural continuity to the community, gives legitimacy and credibility to the tradition. In many ways this past and the tradition that it transmits become representative of the community ideology, enabling the building up of the community identity vis-à-vis the 'other'.

Therefore, this work has attempted to analyse the hagiographical representations from the twelfth to the fifteenth centuries and the influence of these representations on the modern biographies of Rāmānuja. Such a study becomes relevant for understanding the historical process in which a religious tradition develops and is transmitted over several generations, influencing and, in turn, getting influenced by its followers and external milieu. An intensive study of the early representations is crucial as somehow with the passing of time, the complexities in the narrative tradition get lost and the handed down tradition that we receive seems to be a seamless and simplistic product of the historical time. Therefore, the biographies on Rāmānuja that we read today are perhaps our main or our only source of information on his life, and we derive often uncritically the information from the hagiographical narratives without examining the nuanced textures of the texts. This work has attempted to demonstrate that the delineation of Rāmānuja in the early hagiographical texts of the Śrīvaiṣṇava community with all their multipart variations have completely been ignored in the modern biographies which, as a genre, claim a rational approach to the subject. One agrees that the biographies are a distinct literary category with their singular textual structure, yet often they replicate the hagiographies without analyzing the intricacies of the historical processes that shape and, in turn, get shaped by the narratives. For instance, compare the information about Rāmānuja and Śaṅkara, the important thinkers of the pre-colonial past, whom scholars and writers always compare as if they were contemporaries. This information is from the back cover of the famous comic book series the *Amar Chitra Katha:*

> *Ramanuja: a Great Vaishnava Saint*
> Ramanuja (AD 1017–1137) lived for 120 years, traversing the land from Tamil Nadu to Kashmir. People flocked to him to understand his unusual message: the path to ultimate bliss. High caste or low, wealthy or poor, Ramanuja turned no one away. The great Acharya who wrote scholarly commentaries on sacred texts like the Bhagvad Gita was first and foremost a simple-hearted devotee. He inspired the Bhakti movement that spread throughout the country.

For Śaṅkara the information is as follows:

> *Adi Shankara*
> Shankara's life may be compared to a brilliant flash of lightening that eradicated many areas of darkness in the life of man. He had an intellect that

> probed fearlessly, a mind that questioned constantly and a heart that felt deeply. Out of these god-given gifts, and thirty two years of tireless seeking, arose a great system of philosophy, Advaita, and an inspiring body of devotional literature. Shankara traveled throughout India, preaching that the Self or Brahman is one-undivided and imperishable. The rest is Maya or illusion. We are told of his historic debate with the sage, Mandana Mishra, when the latter withdrew and defeated. An even greater story tells us how Shankara, the learned Brahman, bowed to the superior wisdom of a lowly outcaste, accepting him as a Guru.

One recognizes that the biographical details of the individual religious leaders will be different. But it is the ideological frame within which these personalities are projected that becomes important. This also has ramifications for the kind of information chosen to depict the life of that great individual. Like all modern biographies and medieval hagiographies, even the innocent comic series of the *Amar Chitra Katha* is not value neutral and is clearly impressed with the modern understanding of both these personalities. Clearly, Śaṅkara appears to be more intellectual than Rāmānuja and Rāmānuja appears to be far more socially accessible than Śaṅkara. However, neither of these stereotypes have a historical base as the historical trajectory reveals a far more complex and multifaceted image. For instance, Rāmānuja's association with the *bhakti* movement as a register of his protest is to look at *bhakti* in an equally problematic monolithic fashion. The medieval notion of devotion was compounded and certainly Rāmānuja's school of thought was protesting, but not stridently against society and social hierarchies, but against the intellectually dominant school of thought, the Advaita. Both Śaṅkara and Rāmānuja, as their writings show, were clearly situating themselves within the Vedāntic tradition and engagement with social issues did not seem to be their preoccupation. It is the hagiographies that had combined the two—philosophy and social programme and, through their respective delineations, told us the life story of a 'saint'. These narratives have a power of their own that no rationality can shake. They represent the truth not only for their respective believers but also for those looking at the historical past for their contemporary concerns. Thus, as a part of life story genre, the hagiographies have been far more creative and influential in their individual tellings than the modern biographies.

Often accused of exaggerating historical facts and imparting a larger-than-life image to the protagonists, hagiographies have been accused of historical inaccuracies. However, it needs to be emphasized that this obsession with scientific history, historical precision, and textual accuracy has been a part of the modern history writing. It was a common practice to situate the work in an authoritative religious tradition and weave a narrative around the religious figure, the motivating principle being devotion and commitment to the community ideology. The hagiographies never intended to present an accurate account and were probably aware that they were exaggerating. The tropes and the language used in the narratives were a textual strategy to symbolically legitimize 'the religious ideals and institutions and the religious experiences associated with them' in order to inspire devotion and reaffirm the sacredness of the respective religious tradition.[1] It has been rightly pointed out that one sees 'no evidence that in traditional India any devotee ever felt guilty or anxious about his salvation as a result of repeating less-than-historically accurate anecdotes about a revered *ācārya* as long as these anecdotes were theologically correct and piously motivated'.[2]

Then the question arises: is it not possible to write a secular historical biography of religious leaders in which the author is not informed by any religious tradition? How does one write a biography when hardly any of these saints left any autobiographical accounts? Is it not possible to have the biographies of religious leaders as a theme of research like in the case of modern political and religious leaders and thinkers? Perhaps, the answer lies in weaving around the hagiographical narratives a web of historical contexts, which while may be independent, can be linked to each other and then to the protagonist in the centre to tell a story. In this connection, Richard Eaton's recent work is indeed a valuable contribution. Advocating the writing of biographies for understanding social histories, he provided the reason for such a work that was situated in the precolonial context:

> There was yet another reason for embarking on this approach. By foregrounding the biographies of some of India's precolonial figures, one could also reclaim for history subject matter that, having been largely abandoned by professional historians, has been eagerly appropriated by politically motivated myth makers.... There are, in short, compelling

1 Mumme (1997), 'Srīvaiṣṇava Hagiography', p. 167.

2 Ibid.

> reasons why responsible historians should restore biography and narrative to their craft.[3]

Focusing on the eight historical figures from different sections of the society and representing historical processes in the Deccan region between the fourteenth and the eighteenth centuries, Eaton remarked:

> Some might regard the recorded life of precolonial Indians as hagiographies and not biographies, on the ground that lives of such figures have been and continue to be popularly mythologized, even sanctified. But it would be wrong to neatly pigeon-hole the source material respecting the people in this volume as belonging to either category to the complete exclusion of the other. It is perhaps best to view biographies and hagiographies as genres occupying opposite ends of a continuum.[4]

One of the shortcomings of most of the modern works on Rāmānuja has been that his philosophy in general and philosophical works in particular have not informed his biographies. Since overwhelming number of works deal with various aspects of his ideas, in most of them, a biographical account usually forms the part of the Introduction or Chapter One, sitting uncomfortably with the main body of the text. Such an approach has also been because of two reasons. One, we hardly study the history of ideas, Indian philosophy and the historical context as a part of a single discourse, connecting the various threads from them into a cogent historical narrative. Our disciplinary training allows us to make only tenuous connections leaving, finally, each of these areas as discrete spheres of research and analysis. Two, there has been a failure to treat hagiographies as literary texts primarily due to their essentialization as religious, hence non-rational, texts. The ideological approaches of the nationalist movement, social reforms, and Dravidian movement pushed the hagiographies out of the domain of literary world into the exclusive world of religion and faith, as discussed in Chapter 5. It is perhaps for this reason that the modern works on Rāmānuja are characterized by emotions of devotion and reverence rather than a dispassionate objectivity that becomes important for writing a historical biography. Perhaps one can argue that since the life of Rāmānuja and other saints commenced on the basis of religious motivation, alternate ways of crafting their lives could never be thought

[3] Eaton (2005). *Eight Indian Lives: A Social History of the Deccan, 1300–1761*, p. 4.

[4] Ibid., p. 5.

of. They were always religious figures whose life stories would and could only inspire devotion to an average person. In this context, perhaps the beginning was made by Swami Ramamkrishnanda, the disciple of Swami Vivekananda in the end of the nineteenth century. Writing serially since February 1899 from the fourth issue of *Udbodhan*, the Bengali journal of the Ramakrishna Mission, his articles were compiled after eight years into a book called *Sri Ramanuja-charita.*[5] He mentions the reasons for writing on the life of Rāmānuja as:

> Few in Bengal know about Bhagavan Sri Ramanuja ... It is time that people of this part of the country knew what religious doctrine he preached and on the basis of what philosophical conclusions (Siddhanta); whether this doctrine was in vogue prior to his time; why his followers are known as Sri-Samparadayis; and whether there is any agrrement between his and Bhagvan Sri Sankaracharya's doctrine of non-duality.... It is more profitable to study the lives of great ones than to repeat parrot-wise hard and abstruse homilies. When the maxims—which being abstract, are difficult to grasp—find concrete expression in the lives of the great ones, they can be easily comprehended and followed by average people.[6]

Another trend that informed a large number of modern writings on Rāmānuja was the comparative analysis with Christianity and Western categories of philosophical thought. Though seen in the writings of the Orientalists, even the Indian scholars were not disengaged from such a methodology. Ālkondaville Gōvindāchārya was one of the few Indians who at the beginning of the twentieth century used such an analytical tool to highlight the superiority of Indian religious traditions. His *The Life of Rāmānujāchārya* (1906) carries long footnotes that explain the validity of Hindu traditions through the biography of Rāmānuja and counter the 'Christians' and their perception of Indian religion. A comparative analysis between Rāmānuja's ideas with Christianity continued and are now an important part of the discursive scholarly tradition. The two notable scholars in this category are John Braisted Carman and Julius J. Lipner, who presented us with a critical analysis of Rāmānuja's ideas. Carman clearly stated that he was approaching this study from the standpoint of 'a Western Christian Protestant'.[7] He further felt that

5 The Publisher (1959), 'Preface' in Swami Ramakrishnananda (1986), p. ii.

6 Swami Ramakrishnananda (1986), *Life of Sri Ramanuja*, pp. 1–2.

7 Carman (1981), *The Theology of Rāmānuja*, p. 1.

as a part of the 'interreligious understanding' (the sub topic in the title of his book), a phenomenological and historical approach to the study of religion was crucial. While exploring Rāmānuja's definitions and descriptions of the Divine nature (Chapter 4) and his understanding of the Supreme Being within the interpretative categories of the Vedanta (Chapters 5 to 14), Carman also provided an insightful analysis of Rāmānuja's life, his status as a Hindu theologian, and his relation to his successors in Chapters 2, 16, and 17 respectively. The theological and biographical analysis of Rāmānuja's ideas and personality by Carman inform till day the questions and analysis in several modern works on Rāmānuja. Similarly, Lipner, advocating an inter-religious dialogue between Hinduism and Christianity, argued for a long tradition of critical enquiry in Hindu theology, countering the common Western perception of Hinduism being dominated by mysticism and other worldly phenomenon. Arguing for 'theology' as an apt description for the substantial part of the intellectual traditions of the Hindus, Lipner also rightly pointed out that Śaṅkara was not the only representative of Vedānta.[8] There were other influential religious thinkers who have been ignored by scholars, and Rāmānuja is one of them. His book, like Carman's, focused on various aspects of Rāmānuja's ideas and their philosophical and theological relationship with each other and the Universe. Emphasizing the fact that the Vedāntins gave due importance to the study of the nature of sacred language, he provided a comparative analysis between Rāmānuja's ideas and those of his opponents belonging to the Pūrvamimāṅṣa and Advaita schools of thought.

There are several works that compare the Viśiṣṭādvaita school of thought as a theology within the Indian philosophical systems, especially that of the Advaita. But none of them connect ideas to Ramanuja's life or the historical context he was situated in. Most of the works written on his life have been hagiographical in nature with a focus on his social outlook as a reformer.

The literal acceptance of the hagiographical details of Rāmānuja's life in a monochromatic manner has entered the world of performance, in theatre and films. The theme of dissent and protest against the caste having its dramatic potential has been highlighted especially in these theatres

[8] Lipner (1986), *The Face of Truth: A Study of Meaning and Metaphysics in the Vedāntic Theology of Rāmānuja*, p. ix.

and films. Indira Parthasarathy's play *Ramanujar* presents the narratives on caste in a dramatic manner. Accompanied by a critical introduction by C. T. Indra, and translated into English as well as Hindi, this play has now acquired a near status of literary canon with the additional factor of Parthasarathy's fame as one of the foremost Tamil playwrights.

A recent work by the famous epigraphist R. Nagaswamy questions the veracity of such modern hagiographical-biographical accounts and qualifies the hagiographic narratives as myths and legends unsubstantiated by inscriptions and other historical evidence. According to him, 'Ramanuja was never the Srikaryam of the temple, was never a party to any administrative reforms nor was interested in any Social reforms but was a pure Vedantin and so by jettisoning these concocted stories propagated by these Pauranikas-myth makers, true greatness of Ramanuja as an outstanding intellectual would blossom'.[9] However, obsession with historical accuracy of these legends is to ignore the textual context in which they were composed, which was the hagiographical tradition. As stated before, the hagiographies had no intention of conveying historicity in the modern sense. They had their own sense of history and their main purpose was to eulogize their religious figures so that the Śrīvaiṣṇava community appeared exceptional and drew patronage and devotees, which was their main aim. Hence, accusation against the hagiographies for indulging in myth-making is based on fallacious understanding of the hagiographies and their respective contexts. R. Nagawsamy's views led to a heated debate which primarily appeared in newspapers and the Internet, the latter now being an important new public sphere of discursive exchange.

Thus, this work, attempting to analyse the nature of the hagiographies, presented the narratives on Rāmānuja to show that there was no single voice and a particular representation was invariably contested or reaffirmed within the framework of the hagiographies. The modern understanding has ignored this aspect and now the certain hagiographical accounts occupy the centre stage of religious and identity politics. It needs to be emphasized that this work in no way attempts to question the veracity of the accounts. That is not the concern here at all. Rather, the attempt has been to understand the logic of these hagiographical representations in their own terms, with different versions of similar

[9] Nagaswamy (2008), *Rāmānuja. Myth and Reality*, 'Preface'.

legends. The work argues that analyzing these hagiographical legends through the lens of modern worldviews often erases the multiple variants from the memory of the religious tradition and creates a homogeneous identity which marginalizes the space for competitive claims and dissenting voices.

REFERENCES

Aiyangar, S. Krishnaswami. 1909 [1985]. *The Yatirājavaibhavam of Āndhrapūrṇa* (*Life of Rāmānuja*), in Sir Richard Carnac Temple (ed.), *The Indian Antiquary, A Journal of Oriental Research*, vol. XXXVII, 1872–1933. Delhi: Swati Publication, pp. 129–44.

Annual Report on Indian Epigraphy. 1892, 1899, 1905, 1915, 1919, 1921, 1923, 1927, 1927–8, 1931–2, 1934–5, 1937–8. New Delhi: Archeological Survey of India.

Epigraphia Indica. (1981 [1905–06]) vol. VIII, E. Hultzch ed., pp. 290–306. New Delhi: Archeological Survey of India.

Epigraphia Carnatica, Vol. VII. 1979. Mandya District (Nagamangala, Manya, Madduru, Malavalli Taluks) Institute of Kannada Studies, University of Mysore.

Garuḍa Vāhana Paṇḍita. 1978. *Divyasūricaritam*. (Trans. from Hindi by Pandita Madhavacharya and ed. by T. A. Sampathakumaracharya and K.K.A. Venkatachari). Bombay: Ananthacharya Research Institute.

Havell, E. B. and A. E. Gough, trans. 1961 [1882]. *The Sarva-Darśana-Saṃgraha of Madhava Acharya. 'Review of the Different Systems of Hindu Philosophy'.* Varanasi: Chowkamba Sanskrit Series. (Originally Published by Trübner & CO., Lugate Hill: London)

Pandita, V. Krishnanacharya. 1979. *Vedāntasāra of Bhagvad Rāmānuja*. (Trans. from Sanskrit by M. B. Narasimha Ayyangar). Adyar: The Adyar Library and Research Centre.

Piṉbaḷagiya Perumāḷ Jīyar. 1968. *Āṟāyirappaṭi Guruparamparāprabhāvam*. (Ed. by Tiru Krishnaswami Ayyangar). Tirucci: Puttur Agraharam.

Rāmānuja. 1985. *The Gitābhāṣya* (Trans. from Sanskrit by M.R. Sampatkumaran). Bombay: Ananthacharya Research Institute.

———. 1994. *The Gadyatrayam with the Commentary of Periya Accān Piḷḷai.* (Trans. from Sanskrit by V.V. Ramanujan). Madras: Yatiraja Paduka.

———. 1959 *Śrībhāṣya* (Edited with a complete English Translation, Introduction, Notes and Appendices by Raghunath Damodar Karmakar). Poona: University of Poona Sanskrit and Prakrit Series. Volume I.

Rāmānuja Nuṟṟandādi. 'Ode to Rāmānuja of Tiruvaraṅgattamudanār', in *The Sacred Book of Four Thousand. Nalayīra Divya Prabandham.* (Rendered in English with Tamil Original. Based on the Commentaries of Purvacharyas by Srirama Bharati Selvamudaiyanpettai Araiyar.) 2000. pp. 741–61 Chennai: Sri Sadagopan Tirunarayanaswami Divya Prabandha Pathasala.

Rao, V.N. Hari (ed.). 1961. *Kōil Oḷugu. The Chronicle of the Śrīraṅgam Temple with Historical Notes.* Madras: Rockhouse and Sons.

Sekkizhaar. 1985. *Periya Puranam: A Tamil Classic on the Great Saiva Saints of South India.* (Condensed English version by G. Vanmikanathan and general editor Dr. N. Mahalingam) Madras: Sri Ramakrishna Math.

South Indian Inscriptions, vol. XXIV. 1982. *Inscriptions of the Ranganathsvami Temple, Srirangam.* New Delhi: Archaeological Survey of India.

Swami Adidevananda (trans.). 1950. *Stotraratna of Śrī Yāmunācharya.* Madras: Sri Ramakrishna Math.

The Sacred Book of Four Thousand. Nalayīra Divya Prabandham. 2000. (Rendered in English with Tamil Original. Based on the Commentaries of Purvacharyas by Srirama Bharati Selvamudaiyanpettai Araiyar.) Chennai: Sri Sadagopan Tirunarayanaswami Divya Prabandha Pathasala.

The Upadēśa-Ratna-Mālāi or Necklace of Precepts of Śrī Ramyajāmātri-Mahāmuni. (Edited with an English Introduction and Translation by M.T. Narasimhiengar). 1910. Madras: Ananda Press.

The Vedāntatattvasāra Ascribed to Rāmānujācharya (trans. from Sanskrit and with notes by Rev. J. J. John). 1898. Benares: Medical Hall Press.

Tirumala-Tirupati Devasthanam Epigraphical Series. Vol. I–II. 1933. (Trans. By S. Subrahmanyam Sastri and ed. by V. Vijayaragavacharya). Madras: Sri Mahants Devasthanam Press.

Tritīya Brahmatantra Svatantra Parkāla Svāmi. 1968. *Muāyirappaṭi Guruparamparāprabhāvam* (*Vaṭakalai*) Chennai: Lifco.

Varadachariar, V. (ed.). 1978. *Yatirāja-Vaibhava of Āndhrapūrṇa* (*Vaṭuka Nambi*). Madras: M.C. Krishnan.

Yatiraja Saptati of Vedāntadeśika. Based on Tamizh Commentary Rendered by H.H. Paramahamsetyadi Paravakottai Srimath Andavan Srimath Gopala Deshika Maha Deshikan. English Translation by C.G. Balaji, *Oppiliappan Koil Sri Varadachari Sathakopan.* www.sadagopan.org. http://www.ibiblio.org/sadagopan/ahobilavalli/yathiraja_saptati.pdf

Yatiraja Vimsati of Maṇavāḷamāmuṇi. (*An ode to the king of ascetics*) Sri S. Satyamurthi Iyengar. The Vedics Foundation: vedics.org/index.php?option=com_edocman&task=document

OTHER REFERENCES

Aggarwal, Puroshottam. 2011 [2010]. 'The Impact of Sectarian Lobbyism on Hindi Literary Historiography. The Fascinating Story of Bhagavacharya Ramanandi', in Hans Harder (ed.), *Literature and Nationalist Ideology*, pp. 209–58. New Delhi: Social Science Press.

Aiyengar, C.R. Srinivasa. 1908. *The Life and Teachings of Sri Ramanujacharya.* Madras: R. Venkateshwar & Co.

Aiyangar, S. Krishnaswami, Rajagopala Chariar, and M. Rangacharya. 1911. *Sri Ramanujacharya. A Sketch of His Life and Times.* Madras: G.A. Natesan & Co. Publishers.

Allchin, F. R. 1966. 'The Place of Tulsī Dās in North Indian Devotional Tradition', *Journal of the Royal Asiatic Society of Great Britain and Ireland*, 3 (4): 123–40.

Allchin, Raymond. 1971. 'The Attaining of the Void: A Review of Some Recent Contributions in English to the Study of Vīraśaivism', *Religious Studies*, 7 (4): 339–59.

Amin, Shahid. 2002. 'On Retelling the Muslim Conquest of North India', in Partha Chatterjee and Anjan Ghosh (eds), *History and The Present*, pp. 24–43. Delhi: Permanent Black.

Appadurai, Arjun. 1974. 'Right- and Left-Hand Castes in South India', *Indian Economic Social History Review*, 11 (2, 3): 216–59.

———. 1981. *Worship and Conflict under Colonial Rule.* Cambridge: Cambridge University Press.

Appadurai, Arjun and Carol A. Breckenridge. 1976. 'The South Indian Temple: Authority, Honour and Redistribution', *Contribution to Indian Sociology*, 10 (2): 187–212.

Apte, V. S. 1957–9. *The Practical Sanskrit–English Dictionary, 3 vols.* Poona: Prasad Prakashan.

Arnold, David and Stuart Blackburn (eds). 2004. *Telling Lives in India: Biography, Autobiography, and Life History.* Delhi: Permanent Black.

Asad, Talal. 2003. *Formations of the Secular: Christianity, Islam and Modernity.* Stanford: Stanford University Press.

Assmann, Jan. 1997. *Moses the Egyptian. The Memory of Egypt in Western Monotheism.* Cambridge, Massachusetts: Harvard University Press.

Auboyer, Jeannine. 1997. *Śrī Ranganāthasvāmi. A Temple of Vishnu in Śrīraṅgam.* A Srirangam Temple Publication. Third Edition.

Ayyangar, S. Krishnaswami. 1920. *Early History of Vaisnavism in South India*. Madras: Madras University Press.

———. 1923. *Some Contributions of South India to Indian Culture*. Calcutta: Calcutta University Readership Lectures.

———. 1941. 'The Contribution of Mysore to Vaishnavism in South India', *Quarterly Journal of the Mythic Society*, 31: 426–34.

Bader, Jonathan. 2000. *Conquest of the Four Quarters: Traditional Accounts of the Life of Śaṅkara*. New Delhi: Aditya Prakashan.

Bahuguna, Rameshwar Prasad. 2003. 'Symbols of Resistance: Non-Brahmanical Sants as Religious Heroes in Late Medieval India', in Biswamoy Pati, Bhairabi Prasad Sahu, and T.K. Venkatasubramanian (eds), *Negotiating India's Past: Essays in Memory of Partha Sarathi Gupta*, pp. 222–53. New Delhi: Tulika Books.

———. 2006. 'Conflict and Assimilation in Medieval North Indian Bhakti', *Occasional Papers, SAP—History Monograph—6*. New Delhi: Department of History and Culture, Jamia Millia Islamia.

Bailey, G.M. and I. Kesarcodi. 1992. *Bhakti Studies*. Bangalore: Sterling Publishers.

Balasubrahmaniam, R. 1976. *Some Problems in the Epistemology and Metaphysics of Ramanuja*. Madras: University of Madras.

Banerjee-Dube, Ishita and Saurabh Dube. 2009. *Ancient to Modern: Religion, Power and Community in India*. New Delhi: Oxford University Press.

Barth, A. (trans. from French by Rev. J. Wood). 1963. *The Religions of India*. New Delhi: Light & Life Publishers.

Barthes, Roland. 1977 [1968]. 'The Death of the Author', in *Image, Music, Text*, pp. 142–8. (trans. and ed. by Stephen Heath). New York: Hill & Wang.

Basham, A.L. 1975. *The Cultural History of India*. Oxford: Clarendon Press.

———. 1994. *The Wonder That Was India*. New Delhi: Rupa Publications.

Bayly, Susan. 1992. *Saints, Goddesses and Kings: Muslims and Christians in South Indian Society, 1700–1900*. Cambridge: Cambridge University Press.

Behl, Aditya. 2007. 'Presence and Absence in *Bhakti*: An Afterword', *International Journal of Hindu Studies*, 11 (3): 319–24.

Bhandarkar, R.G. 1965 [reprint]. *Vaisnavism, Saivism and Minor Religious Systems*. Varanasi: Indological Book House.

Bhargava, Rajeev (ed.). 1998. *Secularism and Its Critics*. New Delhi: Oxford University Press.

Breckenridge, Carol. 1985. 'Social Storage and Extension of Agriculture in South India, 1350 to 1750', in Anna Dalla Picola (ed.), *Vijayanagar—City and Empire: New Currents of Research*, pp. 41–68. Wiesbaden: Otto Harrosowitz.

Burghart, Richard. 2004 [1978]. 'The Founding of the Ramanandi Sect', in David Lorenzen (ed.), *Religious Movements in South Asia*, pp. 227–50. Delhi:

Oxford University Press. [Originally published in *Ethnohistory*, 25 (2), 1978: 121–39].

Carman, John Braisted. 1981. *The Theology of Rāmānuja: An Essay in Interreligious Understanding*. Bombay: Anantacharya Indological Research Institute.

——— and Vasudha Narayanan. 1989. *The Tamil Veda: Pillan's Interpretation of the Tiruvyamoli*. Chicago: University of Chicago Press.

Champakalakshmi, R. 1981. 'Peasant State and Society in Medieval South India: A Review Article', *Indian Economic and Social History Review*, 18 (3, 4): 411–26.

———. 1987. 'Urbanisation in South India: The Role of Ideology and Polity'. Presidential Address: Ancient Indian History. Srinagar: Indian History Congress, 47th Session.

———. 1989a. 'Religion and Social Change in Tamil Nadu, AD 600–1300', in N.N. Bhattacharya (ed.), *Medieval Bhakti Movements in India*, Sri Caitanya Quincentenary Commemoration Volume, pp. 162–73. New Delhi: Munshiram Manoharlal.

———. 1989b. 'The Study of Settlement Patterns in the Cola Period: Some Perspectives', *Man and Environment*, 14 (1): 91–101.

———. 1994. '*Patikama Patuvar*: Ritual Singing as a Means of Communication in Early Medieval South India', *Studies in Indian History*, 10 (2): 199–215. (Also published in R. Champakalakshmi 2012. *Religion, Tradition and Ideology: Pre-colonial South India* New Delhi: Oxford University Press: 213–34)

———. 1995. 'State and Economy: South India, Circa A.D. 400–1300', in Romila Thapar (ed.), *Recent Perspectives of Early Indian History*, pp. 275–317. New Delhi: Popular Prakashan.

———. 1996a. 'From Devotion and Dissent to Dominance: The *Bhakti* of the Tamil Āḻvārs and Nāyanārs', in R. Champakalakshmi and S. Gopal (eds), *Tradition, Dissent and Ideology: Essays in Honour of Romila Thapar*, pp. 135–63. New Delhi: Oxford University Press. (Also published in Champakalakshmi, R. 2012. *Religion, Tradition and Ideology:Pre-colonial South India*, pp. 53–86. New Delhi: Oxford University Press.)

———. 1996b. *Trade, Ideology and Urbanization: South India, 300 BC to AD 1300*. New Delhi: Oxford University Press.

———. 1997. *Re-Appraisal of a Brāhmaṇīcal Institution: The Brahmadeya and its Ramifications in Early Medieval South India*. Unpublished Paper.

———. 2000 [1955, 1958, 1966, 1975]. 'Introduction', in K. A. Nilakanta Sastri. *A History of South India. From Prehistoric Times to the Fall of Vijayanagar*, pp. xiii–xxiii. New Delhi: Oxford University Press.

———. 2010. 'The Making of a Religious Tradition: Perspectives from Pre-Colonial South India'. General Presidential Address. New Delhi: Indian History Congress.

———. 2012. *Religion, Tradition and Ideology. Pre-colonial South India*. New Delhi: Oxford University Press.

Chari, S. M. Srinivasa. 1994. *Vaiṣṇavism: Its Philosophy, Theology and Religious Discipline*. Delhi: Motilal Banarsidass.

———. 2004 [1961]. *Advaita and Viśiṣṭadvaita*. Delhi: Motilal Banarsidass.

———. 2004 [1988]. *Fundamenatals of Viśiṣṭadvaita Vedānta: A Study of Vedānta Deśika's Tattva-muktā-kalāpa*. Delhi: Motilal Banarasidass.

Chatterjee, Partha and Anjan Ghosh (eds). 2002. *History and The Present*. Delhi: Permanent Black.

Chattopadhyaya, B. D. 1998. *Representing the Other? Sanskrit Sources and the Muslims (Eighth to Fourteenth Century)*. Delhi: Manohar.

Chattopadhyaya, Debiprasad. 1975 [1964]. *Indian Philosophy. A Popular Introduction*. New Delhi: People's Publishing House.

Chaudhuri, Haridas. 1962. 'Existentialism and Vedānta', *Philosophy East and West*, 12 (1): 3–17.

Clooney, Francis X. 1988. '"I Created Land and Sea": A Tamil Case of God Consciousness and Its Śrīvaiṣṇava Interpretation', *Numen* 35, Fasc. 2: 238–59.

———. 1989. 'Finding One's Place in the Text: A Look at the Theological Treatment of Caste in Traditional India', *Journal of Religious Ethics*, 17 (1): 1–29.

———. 1991. 'Nammāḻvār's Glorious Tiruvallavāḻ: An Exploration in the Methods and Goals of Śrīvaiṣṇava Commentary', *Journal of the American Oriental Society*, 111 (2): 260–76.

———. 1992. 'Extending the Canon: Some Implications of a Hindu Argument about Scripture', *The Harvard Theological Review*, 85 (2): 197–215.

———. 1993. 'Śrīvaiṣṇava Studies Today: Writing in a Yet Richer Language', *Journal of Vaisnava Studies*, 2 (1): 171–81.

———. 1998. 'For Bhakti is Synonymous with Upāsana: Rāmānuja's Understanding of Upāsana Particularly as Exemplified in the Commentaries of Tiruvāymoḻi', *Journal of Vaisnava Studies*, 6 (1): 117–39.

———. 2002. 'Fierce Words: Repositionings of Caste and Devotion in Traditional Śrīvaiṣṇava Hindu Ethics', *Journal of Religious Ethics*, 30 (3): 399–419.

———. 2004. 'Śrīvaiṣṇavism in Dialogue, c. 1900: Alkondavilli Govindacharya as a Comparative Theologian', *Journal of Vaisnava Studies*, 13 (1): 103–24.

———. 2007. 'Exegesis, Theology, and Spirituality: Reading the Dvaya Mantra According to Vedānta Deśika', *International Journal of Hindu Studies*, 11 (1): 27–62.

Colebrooke, Henry Thomas. 1826. 'On the Philosophy of the Hindus. Part IV', *Transactions of the Royal Asiatic Society of Great Britain and Ireland*, 1 (2): 549–79.

———. 1826. 'On the Philosophy of the Hindus: Part V', *Transactions of the Royal Asiatic Society of Great Britain and Ireland*, 2 (1): 1–39.

Cutler, Norman. 1984. 'The Devotee's Experience of the Sacred Tamil Hymns', *History of Religions*, 24 (2): 91–112.

———. 1992. 'Interpreting Tirukkuṟaḷ: The Role of Commentary in the Creation of a Text', *Journal of the American Oriental Society*, 112 (4): 549–66.

Dalmia, Vasudha. 1993. *Orienting India: European Knowledge Formation in the Eighteenth and Nineteenth Century*. New Delhi: Three Essays Collective.

———. 1997. *The Nationalization of Hindu Traditions. Bhāratendu Hariśchandra and Nineteenth-Century Banaras*. New Delhi: Oxford University Press.

Dalmia, Vasudha, Angelika Malinar, and Martin Christof (eds). 2001. *Charisma and Canon: Essays on the Religious History of the Indian Subcontinent*. New Delhi: Oxford University Press.

——— and Heinrich von Stietencron (eds). 2007. *The Oxford India Hinduism Reader*. Delhi: Oxford University Press.

Dasgupta, Surendranath. 1975 (reprint). *A History of Indian Philosophy*. Vol. 3. Delhi: Motilal Banarasidass.

Deshpande, Prachi. 2007. *Creative Pasts: Historical Memory and Identity in Western India, 1700–1960*. New York: Columbia University Press.

Deshpande, Sharad. 2009. 'Philosophy in Colonial India'. Paper presented at the Indian Institute of Advanced Study, Shimla.

Dirks, Nicholas B. 1976. 'Political Authority and Structural Changes in Early South Indian History', *Indian Economic and Social History Review*, 13 (2): 125–57.

———. 1979. 'The Structure and Meaning of Political Relations in a South Indian Little Kingdom', *Contributions to Indian Sociology*, 13 (2): 169–204.

Durga, P., S. Kanaka, and Y.A. Sudhakar Reddy. 1993. 'Kings, Temples and Legitimation of Autochthonous Communities: A Case Study of a South Indian Temple', *Journal of the Economic and Social History of the Orient*, 35: 145–65.

Dutta, Ranjeeta. 2002. 'Imaging the Goddess: A Process in the Identity Formation of Śrīvaiṣṇava Community', in Neelima Chitgopekar (ed.), *Invoking Goddess: Gender Politics in Indian Religion*, pp. 112–39. New Delhi: Har-Anand Publications.

———. 2003. 'The Politics of Religious Identity: A Muslim Goddess in the Śrīvaiṣṇava Community of South India', *Studies in History*, 19 (2): 157–84.

———. 2004. *Community Identities and Sectarian Affiliations: The Śrīvaiṣṇavas of South India. (From Eleventh to Seventeenth Century AD)*. Unpublished

Doctoral Dissertation. New Delhi: Centre for Historical Studies, Jawaharlal Nehru University.

———. 2007. 'Texts, Tradition and Community Identity: The Srivaisnavas of South India', in *Social Scientist*, 35 (9–10): 22–42.

———. 2010. 'Pilgrimage as a Religious Process: Some Reflections on the Identities of the Srivaisnavas of South India', *Indian Historical Review*, 37 (1): 17–38.

———. 2014. 'Devotion and Dissent: The Biographical Process of Ramanuja in Shrivaishnava Tradition and History', in Vijaya Ramswamy (ed.), *Devotion and Dissent in Indian History*, pp. 54–77. New Delhi: Cambridge University Press, India under the imprint of Foundation Books.

Eaton, Richard M. 2000. 'The Articulation of Islamic Space in Medieval Deccan', in Richard M. Eaton (ed.), *Essays in Islam in Indian History*, pp. 159–75. Delhi: Oxford University Press.

———. 2005. *Eight Indian Lives: A Social History of the Deccan, 1300–1761*. Cambridge: Cambridge University Press.

Eliade, Mircea. (trans. from French by William R. Trask). 1957 (reprint). *The Sacred and the Profane: The Nature of Religion*. London: Harvest Books.

Farquhar, J. N. 1967 [1920]. *An Outline of the Religious History of India*. London: Oxford University Press.

Forsthoefel, Thomas A. and Patricia Y. Mumme. 1999. 'The Monkey-Cat Debate in Śrīvaiṣṇavism: Conceptualising Grace in Medieval India', *Journal of Vaisnava Studies*, 8 (1): 3–33.

Fost, Frederic F. 1998. 'Playful Illusion: The Making of Worlds in Advaita Vedānta', *Philosophy East and West*, 48 (3): 387–405.

Foucault, Michel. 1984 [1969]. 'What Is an Author?', in Paul Rabinow (ed.), *The Foucault Reader*, pp. 101–20. New York: Pantheon.

Ganeri, Jonardon. 1996. 'The Hindu Syllogism: Nineteenth-Century Perceptions of Indian Logical Thought', *Philosophy East and West*, 46 (1): 1–16.

———. 1999. 'Self-Intimation, Memory and Personal Identity', *Journal of Indian Philosophy*, 27 (5): 469–83.

———. 2008. 'Contextualism in the Study of Indian Intellectual Cultures', *Journal of Indian Philosophy*, 36 (5–6): 551–62.

Gohain, Hiren. 1987. 'The Labyrinth of Bhakti: On Some Questions of Medieval Indian History', *Economic and Political Weekly*, 22 (46): 1970–2.

Gonda, Jan. 1954. *Aspects of Early Vaisnavism*. Utrecht: Oosthek.

———. 1970. *Visnuism and Sivaism: A Comparison*. London: Athlone Press.

———. 1977. *Medieval Religious Literature in Sanskrit*. Wiesbaden: Otto Harrossowitz.

Gopal, B. R. 1983. *Sri Ramanuja in Karnataka: An Epigraphical Study*. Delhi: Sundeep Prakashan.

Gopinatha Rao, T. A. 1923. *Sir Subrahmanya Ayyar Lectures on the History of Śrī Vaiṣṇavas*. Madras: University of Madras, Government Press.

Gōvindāchārya, Ālkondaville. 1906. *The Life of Rāmānujāchārya. The Exponent of Viṣishṭādvāita Philosophy*. Madras: S. Murthy & Co.

Granoff, Phyllis. 1985. 'Scholars and Wonder-Workers: Some Remarks on the Role of the Supernatural in Philosophical Contests in Vedānta Hagiographies', *Journal of the American Oriental Society*, 105 (3): 459–67.

——— and Koichi Shinohara (eds). 1988. *Monks and Magicians: Religious Biographies in Asia*. Delhi: Motilal Banarasidass.

Grierson, George A. 1907. 'Bhakti Marga', in James Hastings (ed.), *Encyclopedia of Religion and Ethics*. Vol. 2, pp. 539–51. Edinburgh: T. & T. Clark.

Gunawardana, R. A. L. H. 1989. 'Anurādhapura: Ritual, Power and Resistance in a Pre-Colonial South Asian City', in Daniel Miller, Michael Rowlands, and Christopher Tilley (eds), *Domination and Resistance*, pp. 155–77. London: Unwin Hyman Ltd.

Gurukkal, Rajan. 1993. 'Towards the Voice of Dissent: Trajectory of Ideological Transformation in Early South India', *Social Scientist*, 21 (1, 2): 2–22.

———. 1995. 'The Beginnings of the Historic Period: The Tamil South', in Romila Thapar (ed.), *Recent Perspectives of Early Indian History*, pp. 246–74. New Delhi: Popular Prakashan.

Hacker, Paul. 2006. 'Dharma in Hinduism', *Journal of Indian Philosophy*, 34 (5): 479–96.

Halbfass, Wilhelm. 1985. 'India and the Comparative Method', *Philosophy East and West*, 35 (1): 3–15.

———. 1988. *India and Europe: An Essay in Understanding*. Albany: State University of New York Press.

———. 1991. *Tradition and Reflection: Explorations in Indian Thought*. Albany: State University of New York Press.

Hall, Kenneth (ed.). 2001. *Structure and Society in Early South India: Essays in Honour of Noboru Karashima*. New Delhi: Oxford University Press.

Hanusek, Denise Marie. 1997. 'How Should a Saint Act? An Examination of Two Stories Told of Rāmānuja and John of the Cross', *Journal of Vaisnava Studies*, 5 (2): 129–56.

Hardy, Friedhelm. 1974. 'Mādhavêndra Puri: A Link between Bengal Vaiṣṇavism and South Indian Bhakti', *Journal of Royal Asiatic Society*, 1: 23–41.

———. 1977. 'Ideology and Cultural Contents of the Śrī Vaiṣṇava Temple', *Indian Economic and Social History Review*, 14 (1): 119–51.

———. 1978. 'The Tamil Veda of a Śudra Saint: The Śrī Vaiṣṇava Interpretation of Nammāḻvār', in G. Krishna (ed.), *Contributions to South Asian Studies*, Vol. 1, pp. 42–114. Delhi: Oxford University Press.

———. 1983. *Viraha-Bhakti: The Early History of Kṛṣṇa Devotion in South India*. Delhi: Oxford University Press.

———. 1991. 'Tiruppāṇ-āḻvār: The Untouchable Who Rode Piggy-Back on the Brahmin', in Diana L. Eck and Françoise Mallison (eds), *Devotion Divine: Bhakti Traditions from the Regions of India; Studies in Honour of Charlotte Vaudeville*, pp. 129–51. Paris: École Française D' Extrême-Orient.

———. 1992. 'The Śrī Vaiṣṇava Hagiography of Parkāla', in Christopher Shackle and Rupert Snell (eds), *The Indian Narratives. Perspectives and Patterns*, pp. 81–116. Wiesbaden: Otto Harrassowitz.

———. 1995. *The Religious Culture of India: Power, Love and Wisdom*. Cambridge: Cambridge University Press.

———. 2001. 'The Formation of Śrīvaiṣṇavism', in Vasudha Dalmia, Angelika Malinar, and Martin Christof (eds), *Charisma and Canon: Essays on the Religious History of the Indian Subcontinent*, pp. 41–61. New Delhi: Oxford University Press.

———. 2007. 'A Radical Reassessment of the Vedic Heritage: The Ācāryahṛdayam and its Wider Implications', in Vasudha Dalmia and Heinrich von Stietencron (eds), *The Oxford India Hinduism Reader*, pp. 29–49. Delhi: Oxford University Press.

Hari Rao, V. N. 1967. *The History of Śrīraṅgam Temple: Art and Architecture*. Tirupati: The Sri Venkateswara University.

Hawley, John Stratton (ed.). 1987. *Saints and Virtues*. Berkeley and Los Angeles: University of California Press.

———. 1988. 'Author and Authority in the Bhakti Poetry of North India', *Journal of Asian Studies*, 47 (2): 269–90.

———. 2005. *Three Bhakti Voices: Mirabai, Surdas, and Kabir in Their Times and Ours*. New Delhi: Oxford University Press.

———. 2007. 'Introduction', *International Journal of Hindu Studies*, 11 (3): 209–25.

Heitzman, James. 1987. 'Temple Urbanism in Medieval South India', *Journal of Asian Studies*, 46 (4): 791–826.

———. 1997. *Gifts of Power: Lordship in an Early Indian State*. New Delhi: Oxford University Press.

———. 1999. 'Ritual Polity and Economy: The Transactional Network of an Imperial Temple in Medieval South India', *Journal of Economic and Social History of the Orient*, 34 (1, 2): 23–54.

———. 2001. 'Urbanisation and Political Economy in South India: Kāñcīpuram During the Cōḷa Period', in Kenneth Hall (ed.), *Structure and Society in Early South India: Essays in Honour of Noboru Karashima*, pp. 117–44. New Delhi: Oxford University Press.

Helfer, James S. 1964. 'The Body of Brahman According to Rāmānuja', *Journal of Bible and Religion*, 32 (1): 43–6.

Herman, A. L. 1971. 'Indian Theodicy: Śaṁkara and Rāmānuja on Brahma Sūtra II. 1. 32–36', *Philosophy East and West*, 21 (3): 265–81.

Hiltebeitel, Alf. 1999. *Rethinking India's Oral and Classical Epics: Draupadi among Rajputs, Muslims and Dalits*: Chicago: University of Chicago.

Hirst, Jacqueline Suthren. 1996. 'Strategies of Interpretation: Śaṃkara's Commentary on Bṛhadāraṇyakopaniṣad', *Journal of the American Oriental Society*, 116 (1): 58–75.

Hobsbawm, Eric. 1980. 'The Revival of Narratives: Some Comments', *Past and Present*, 86 (Feb.): 3–8.

——— and Terence Ranger (eds). 1983. *The Invention of Tradition*. Cambridge: Cambridge University Press.

Hopkins, Steven P. 2007. 'The Bell of Tirupati: Miracles, Love of God and a Touch of Politics in the Sacred Narratives of Vedāntadeśika', *Journal of Vaisnava Studies*, 5 (2): 207–20.

———. 2002a. 'Loving God in Three Languages: Vedas of Vedāntadeśika', *Journal of Vaisnava Studies*, 10 (2): 51–79.

———. 2002b. *Singing the Body of God: The Hymns of Vedāntadeśika in Their South Indian Tradition*. New York: Oxford University Press.

Houben, Jan E. M. and Sheldon Pollock. 2008. 'Theory and Method in Indian Intellectual History', *Journal of Indian Philosophy*, 36 (5–6): 531–2.

Hudson, Dennis. 1972. 'Hindu and Christian Theological Parallels in the Conversion of H. A. Kṛṣṇa Piḷḷai, 1857–1859', *Journal of the American Academy of Religion*, 40 (2): 191–206.

———. '1978. 'Siva, Minaksi, Visnu: Reflections on a Popular Myth in Madurai', in Burton Stein (ed.), *South Indian Temples An Analytical Reconsideration*, pp. 106–118, New Delhi: Vikas Publishers.

———. 1980. 'Bathing in Krishna: A Study in Vaiṣṇava Hindu Theology', *The Harvard Theological Review*, 73 (3/4): 539–66.

———. 1993. 'Vāsudeva Kṛṣṇa in Theology and Architecture: A Background to Śrīvaiṣṇavism', *Journal of Vaisnava Studies*, 2 (1):139–70.

———. 1995. 'The Śrīmad Bhāgavat Purāṇa in Stone: The Text as an 8th century Temple and its Implications', *Journal of Vaisnava Studies*, 3 (3): 137–82.

———. 1999. 'A New Year's Poem for Kṛṣṇa: The Tiruppallāṇṭu by Villiputtūr Viṣṇucittan ('Periyāḻvār')', *Journal of Vaisnava Studies*, 7 (2): 93–129.

———. 2001. 'Rādhā and Piṉṉai: Diverse Manifestations of the Same Goddess?', *Journal of Vaisnava Studies*, 10 (1): 115–53.

———. 2010. *Krishna's Mandala: Bhagavata Religion and Beyond*. New Delhi: Oxford University Press.

Iyengar, K.R. Srinivasa. 1939. 'The Notion of Dependence', *The Philosophical Review*, 48 (5): 506–24.

Jackson, William J. 1991. *Tyāgāraja: Life and Lyrics*. Delhi: Oxford University Press.

———. 1992. 'A Life Becomes a Legend: Srī Tyāgarāja as Exemplar', *Journal of the American Academy of Religion*, 60 (4): 717–36.

———. 1994. *Tyāgāraja and The Renewal of Tradition: Translations and Reflections*. Delhi: Motilal Banarsidass.

Jagadeesan, N. 1977. *History of Srivaishnavism in the Tamil Country (Post Ramanuja)*. Madurai: Koodal Publishers.

Jaiswal, Suvira. 1991. 'Varna Ideology and Social Change', *Social Scientist*, 19 (3/4): 41–8.

———. 1997. 'Caste: Ideology and Context', *Social Scientist*, 25 (5/6): 3–12.

———. 2000. 'Change and Continuity in Brahmanical Religion with Particular Reference to "Vaisnava Bhakti"' *Social Scientist*, 28 (5/6): 3–23.

Jha, D. N. 1981–2. 'Relevance of Peasant State and Society: Pallava-Cola Times', *Indian Historical Review*, 8 (1/2): 74–94.

Kapadia, Karen. 1995. *Siva and Her Sisters: Gender, Caste, and Class in Rural South India*. Boulder, CO: Westview Press.

Karashima, Noboru. 1984. *South India History and Society: Studies from Inscriptions, A.D. 850–1800*. New Delhi: Oxford University Press.

———. 1994. *Towards a New Formation: South Indian Society under Vijayanagar Rule*. New Delhi: Oxford University Press.

———. 2002. *A Concordance of Nāyakas: The Vijayanagar Inscriptions in South India*. New Delhi: Oxford University Press.

———. 2009. *South Indian Society in Transition: Ancient to Medieval*. New Delhi: Oxford University Press.

Kaylor, David R. 1976. 'The Concept of Grace in the Hymns of Nammāḻvār', *Journal of the American Academy of Religion*, 44 (4): 649–60.

Keene, Calvin J. 1953. 'Ramanuja: The Hindu Augustine', *Journal of Bible and Religion*, 21 (1): 3–8.

Keith, A. Berriedale. 1918. 'Ramanuja', in James Hastings (ed.), *Encyclopedia of Religion and Ethics*. Vol. 10, pp. 572–74. Edinburgh: T. & T. Clark.

Kosambi. D. D. 1962. *Myth and Reality*. Bombay: Popular Prakashan.

Kulke, Hermann. 1982. 'Fragmentation and Segmentation versus Integration? Reflections on the Concepts of Indian Feudalism and the Segmentary State in Indian History', *Studies in History*, 4 (2): 237–63.

———. 1993a. '"A Passage to India": Temples, Merchants and the Ocean', *Journal of Economic and Social History of the Orient*, 36 (2): 154–80.

———. 1993b. *Kings and Cults: State Formation and Legitimation in India and Southeast Asia*. New Delhi: Manohar.

Kulke, Hermann and G. D. Sontheimer. 1989. *Hinduism Reconsidered*. New Delhi: Manohar Publications.

Kumar, Prema Nanda. 2005. *The Hindu*: Friday, May 13. Entertainment Page.

Laine, James W. 2003. *Shivaji: Hindu King in Islamic India*. New Delhi: Oxford University Press.

Lakshamma, G. 1990. *The Impact of Rāmānuja's Teachings on Life and Conditions in Society*. Delhi: Sandeep Prakashan.

Leslie, Julia. 1998. 'Understanding Basava: History, Hagiography and a Modern Kannada Drama', *Bulletin of the School of Oriental and African Studies*, 61(2): 228–61.

Lester, Robert C. 1966. 'Rāmānuja and Śrī-Vaiṣŋavism: The Concept of Prapatti or Śaraṇāgati', *History of Religions*, 5 (2): 266–82.

———. 1994. 'The Śāttada Śrīvaiṣṇavas', *Journal of the American Oriental Society*, 114 (1): 39–53.

Lipner, Julius J. 1986. *The Face of Truth: A Study of Meaning and Metaphysics in the Vedāntic Theology of Rāmānuja*. Albany: State University of New York Press.

Lorenzen, David N. 1972. *The Kāpālikhas and Kālamukhas. Two Lost Śaivite Sects*. New Delhi: Thompson Press.

———. (ed.). 1996. *Bhakti Religion in North India: Community Identity and Political Action*. New Delhi: Manohar.

———. 2006. *Who Invented Hinduism? Essays on Religion in History*. New Delhi: Yoda Press.

Ludden, David. 1989. *Peasant History in South India*. Delhi: Oxford University Press.

Macdonell, Arthur Anthony. 1929. *A Practical Sanskrit Dictionary with Transliteration, Accentuation, and Etymological Analysis Throughout*. London: Oxford University Press.

Malik, S. C. (ed.). 1978. *Indian Movement: Some Aspects of Dissent, Protest and Reform*. Simla: Indian Institute of Advanced Studies.

Malkovsky, Bradley. 1997. 'The Personhood of Śaṁkara's "Para Brahman"', *The Journal of Religion*, 77 (4): 541–62.

Manring, Rebecca J. 2005. *Reconstructing Tradition: Advaita Ācārya and Gauḍiya Vaiṣṇavism at the Cusp of the Twentieth Century*. New York: Columbia University Press.

Miller, David. 1981. 'Sources of Hindu Ethical Studies: A Critical Review', *Journal of Religious Ethics*, 9 (2): 186–98.

Mines, Mattison. 1984. *The Warrior Merchants: Textiles, Trade and Territory in South India*. Cambridge: Cambridge University Press.

Mlecko, Joel D. 1982. 'The Guru in Hindu Tradition', *Numen* 29 (Fasc. 1): 33–61.

Monius, Anne E. 2004. 'Śiva as Heroic Father: Theology and Hagiography in Medieval South India', *The Harvard Theological Review*, 97 (2): 165–97.

Mumme, Patricia Y. 1988. *The Theology of Maṇavāḷamāmuṇi: Toward an Understanding of the Teṇkalai-Vaṭakalai Dispute in the Post-Rāmānuja Śrī Vaiṣṇavism*. Madras: New Era Publications.

———. 1993. 'Rules and Rhetorics: Caste Observance in Śrīvaiṣṇava Doctrine and Practise', *Journal of Vaisnava Studies*, 2 (1): 113–38.

———. 1997. 'Śrīvaiṣṇava Hagiography: Lessons from Biblical Scholarship', *Journal of Vaisnava Studies*, 5 (2): 157–200.

Nagaswamy, R. 2008. *Rāmānuja. Myth and Reality*. Chennai: Tamil Arts Academy.

Nair, Janaki. 2006. 'Beyond Exceptionalism. South India and the Modern Historical Imagination', *Indian Economic and Social History Review*, 43 (3): 323–47.

Nakamura, Hajime. 1962. 'Conflict between Traditionalism and Rationalism: A Problem with Śaṃkara', *Philosophy East and West*, 12 (2): 153–61.

Narasimhachary, M. 2007 [2004]. *Makers of Indian Literature. Sri Ramanuja*. New Delhi: Sahitya Akademi.

Narasimhiengar, M. T. and J. F. F. 1915. 'Ramanuja and Melukote', *Journal of the Royal Asiatic Society of Great Britain and Ireland*, 47 (1): 147–52.

Narayanan, Vasudha. 1993. 'The "Sacred Utterance" of the Silent Seer: Speech and Sight in the Revelation of the Tamil Veda', *Journal of Vaisnava Studies*, 2 (1): 79–111.

———. 1994a. 'Parāśara Bhaṭṭar's Commentary on the Viṣṇu Sahasranāma', *Journal of Vaisnava Studies*, 2 (2): 85–98.

———. 1994b. 'The Rāmāyaṇa in the Theology and Experience of the Śrīvaiṣṇava Community', *Journal of Vaisnava Studies*, 2 (4): 55–89.

———. 1995a. 'Realm of Play and the Sacred Stage', in William Sax (ed.), *The Gods at Play: Lila in South Asia*, pp. 177–203. New York: Oxford University Press.

———. 1995b. 'Tiruvenkatam in the Fifteenth Century', *Journal of Vaisnava Studies*, 3 (3): 91–108.

———. 1996. 'Music and the Divya Prabandham in the Śrīvaṣṇaiva Tradition', *Journal of Vaisnava Studies*, 4 (2): 37–56.

———. 1999. 'Śrī Vaiṣṇava Festivals and Festivals Celebrated by Śrī Vaiṣṇavas', *Journal of Vaisnava Studies*, 7 (2): 175–94.

———. 2007. '"With the Earth as a Lamp and the Sun as the Flame": Lighting Devotion in South India', *International Journal of Hindu Studies*, 11 (3): 227–53.

Nath, Vijay. 2001. 'From "Brahmanism" to "Hinduism": Negotiating the Myth of the Great Tradition', *Social Scientist*, 29 (3/4): 19–50.

Nayar, Nancy Ann. 1992. *Poetry as Theology: The Śrīvaiṣṇava Stotra in the Age of Rāmānuja*. Wiesbaden: Otto Harrosowitz.

———. 1993. 'The Śrīvaiṣṇava Stotra: Synthesizing the Tamil and Sanskrit Vedas', *Journal of Vaisnava Studies*, 2 (1): 55–76.

———. 1994. *Praise-Poems to Viṣṇu and Śrī: The Stotras of Rāmānuja's Immediate Disciples*. Bombay: Ananthacharya Research Institute.

———. 1995. 'The Bhagavad-Gītā and Śrīvaiṣṇavism: Multilevel Contextualization of an Ancient Hindu Text', *Journal of Vaisnava Studies*, 3 (2): 115–41.

———. 1997 'After the Āḻvārs: Kṛṣṇa and Gopī in the Śrīvaiṣṇava Tradition', *Journal of Vaisnava Studies*, 4 (5): 201–22.

———. 2003. 'Ālavandār's Catuhślokī with the Commentary by Periyavāccān Piḷḷai: An Introduction and Translation', *Journal of Vaisnava Studies*, 12 (1): 213–38.

Novetzke, Christian Lee. 2003. 'Divining an Author: The Idea of Authorship in an Indian Religious Tradition', *History of Religion*, 42 (3): 213–42.

———. 2007. 'Bhakti and Its Public', *International Journal of Hindu Studies*, 11 (3): 255–72.

———. 2008. *History, Bhakti and Public Memory: Namdev in Religious and Secular Tradition*. Ranikhet: Permanent Black.

Orr, Leslie. 1993. 'The Vaiṣṇava Community at Śrīraṅgam: The Testimony of Early Medieval Inscriptions', *Journal of Vaisnava Studies*, 3 (3): 109–36.

Padmanabhan, S. 1995. *Parasara Bhattar: His Contribution to Vishistadvaita*. Madras: Shri Vishistadvaita Research Centre.

Pai, Anant (ed.). 1974. *Adi Shankara. Vol. 656*. Mumbai: India Book House.

Pande, G. C. 1998 [1994]. *Life and Thought of Śaṅkarācārya*. Delhi: Motilal Banarsidass.

Parke, Catherine N. 2002. *Biography: Writing Lives*. New York: Routledge.

Parrinder, E. G. 1965. 'Recent Views of Indian Religion and Philosophy', *Religious Studies*, 1 (1): 109–18.

Parthasarathy, Indira. 2008. *Ramanujar: The Life and Ideas of Ramanuja*. (trans. from Tamil by T. Sriraman). Critical Introduction by C.T. Indra. New Delhi: Oxford University Press.

Peterson, Indira Vishwanathan. 1983. 'Lives of Wandering Singers: Pilgrimage and Poetry in Tamil Hagiography', *History of Religion*, 22 (3/4): 338–60.

———. 1991. *Poems to Śiva: The Hymns of the Tamil Saints*. Delhi: Motilal Banarsidass.

Pinch, Willam R. 1996a. 'Reinventing Ramanand: Caste and History in Gangetic India', *Modern Asian Studies*, 30 (3): 549–71.

———. 1996b. *Peasants and Monks in British India*. Berkeley/Los Angeles/London: University of California Press.

Pollock, Sheldon. 1985. 'The Theory of Practice and the Practice of Theory in Indian Intellectual History', *Journal of the American Oriental Society*, 105 (3): 499–519.

———. 2006. *The Language of Gods in the World of Men: Sanskrit, Culture, and Power in Pre-modern India*. Delhi and Ranikhet: Permanent Black and Himalayana.

———. 2008. 'Is there an Indian Intellectual History? Introduction to "Theory and Method in Indian Intellectual History"', *Journal of Indian Philosophy*, 36 (5–6) : 533–42.

Potter, Karl H. 1961. 'A Fresh Classification of India's Philosophical Systems', *Journal of Asian Studies*, 21:1 (Nov.): 25–32.

Pratt, James Bissett. 1933. 'Recent Developments in Indian Thought', *Journal of Indian Philosophy*, 30 (19): 505–17.

Preisendanz, Karen. 2008. 'Text, Commentary, Annotation: Some Reflections on the Philosophical Genre', *Journal of Indian Philosophy*, 36 (5–6): 599–618.

Prentiss, Karen Pechilis. 1999. *The Embodiment of Bhakti*. New York: Oxford University Press.

Raghavachar, S.S. 1957. *Introduction to the Vedārthasangraha of Śrī Rāmanujāchārya*. Mangalore: Mangalore Trading Association.

Raghavan, V. 1958. 'Methods of Popular Religious Instruction in South India', *Journal of American Folklore*, 71 (281): 336–44.

Rajagopalachariar, T. 1909. *The Vaishnavite Reformers of India: Critical Sketches of Their Lives and Writings*. Madras: G.A. Natesan and Company.

Raju, P. T. 1952. 'The Development of Indian Thought', *Journal of the History of Ideas*, 13 (4): 528–50.

———. 1964. 'The Existential and the Phenomenological Consciousness in the Philosophy of Rāmānuja (Svarūpajñāna and Dharmabhūtajñāna)', *Journal of the American Oriental Society*, 84 (4): 395–404.

Raman, K. V. 1975. *Sri Varadarajasvami Temple-Kanci: A Study of Its History, Art and Architecture*. New Delhi: Abhinav Publications.

Raman, Srilatha. 2007. *Self Surrender (Prapatti) to Gods in Śrīvaiṣṇavism. Tamil Cats and Sanskrit Monkeys*. New York: Routledge.

Ramanuja: A Great Vaishnava Saint. 1974. Mumbai: Amar Chitra Katha: Vol. 715.

Ramanujam, B. V. 1973. *History of Vaisnavism in South India upto Ramanuja*. Annamalainagar: Annamalai University.

Ramanujan, A. K. 1973. *Speaking of Siva*. Baltimore: Penguin Books.

———. 1992. 'Three Hundred *Rāmāyaṇas*: Five Examples and Three Thoughts on Translation', in Paula Richman (ed.), *Many Rāmāyaṇas: The Diversity of a Narrative Tradition in South Asia*, pp. 22–49. New Delhi: Oxford University Press.

———. 1993. *Hymns for the Drowning: Poems for Visnu by Nammalvar*. New Delhi: Penguin India.

———. 1999. 'Is there an Indian Way of Thinking? An Informal Essay', in Vinay Dharwadker (ed.), *The Collected Essays of A.K. Ramanujan*, pp. 34–51. New Delhi: Oxford University Press.

Ramaswamy, Vijaya. 1982. 'Peasant State and Society in Medieval South India: A Review Article', *Studies in History*, 4 (2): 307–19.

———. 1985a. 'The Genesis and Historical Role of the Master Weavers in South Indian Textile Production', *Journal of Economic and Social History of the Orient*, 28 (3): 294–325.

———. 2006 [1985]. *Textiles and Weavers in Medieval South India*. New Delhi: Oxford University Press.

Ramaswamy, Vijaya and Yogesh Sharma (eds). 2009. *Biography as History: Indian Perspectives*. Hyderabad: Orient Blackswan.

Rangachari, D.B.K. 1986. *The Sri Vaishnava Brahmans*. Delhi: Gian Publishing House.

Rangacharya, N. 1949. *The Origin and Growth of the Parakala Matha*. Bangalore: The Bangalore Press.

Rao, Velcheru Narayana, David Shulman, and Sanjay Subrahmanyam. 2001. *Textures of Time: Writing History in South India, 1600–1800*. Delhi: Permanent Black.

Regamey, Constantin. 1960–1. 'The Meaning and Significance of Spirituality in Europe and in India', *Philosophy East and West*, 10 (3/4): 105–33.

Reynolds, Frank E. and Donald Capps (eds). 1976. *The Biographical Process: Studies in the History and Psychology of Religion*. Hungary: Mouton.

Rice, L. 1915. 'The Hoysala King Bitti-Deva Vishnuvardhana', *Journal of the Royal Asiatic Society of Great Britain and Ireland*, 47 (3): 527–31.

Sastri, K.A. Nilakantha. 1937. *The Colas. 2 Vols*. The Madras University Historical Series, No. 10. Vol. II, Pt I. Madras: University of Madras.

———. 2000 [1975, 1955, 1958, 1966]. *A History of South India: From Prehistoric Times to the Fall of Vijayanagar*. Madras: Oxford University Press.

Sax, William S. 2000. 'Conquering the Quarters: Religion and Politics in Hinduism', *International Journal of Hindu Studies*, 14 (1): 39–60.

Schomer, Karen and W.H. McLeod. 1987. *The Sants: Studies in a Devotional Tradition of India*. Delhi: Motilal Banarsidass.

Sen, Amiya. 2007. 'The Idea of Social Reform and its Critique among Hindus of Nineteenth-Century India', in Sabyasachi Bhattacharya (ed.), *Development of Modern Indian Thought and the Social Sciences, History of Science, Philosophy and Culture in Indian Civilization, Vol. X, Part 5*, pp. 107–37. New Delhi: Oxford University Press.

———. (ed.). 2008 [2005, 2003]. *Social and Religious Reform. The Hindus of British India*. New Delhi: Oxford University Press.

Sen Gupta, Anima. 1959. 'Ramanuja on Causality', *Philosophy East and West*, 8 (3/4): 137–48.

———. 1962. 'The Meanings of "That Thou Art"', *Philosophy East and West*, 12 (2): 125–34.

Seshadri, Kandadai. 1996a. 'Ramanuja: Social Influence of His Life and Teaching', *Economic and Political Weekly*, 31 (5): 292–8.

———. 1996b. 'Ramanuja', *Economic and Political Weekly*, 31 (18): 1038.

———. 1998. *Srivaishnavism and Social Change*. Calcutta: K.P. Bagchi and Company.

Sharma, Krishna. 1987. *Bhakti and the Bhakti Movement: A New Perspective: A Study in the History of Ideas*. New Delhi: Munshiram Manoharlal.

———. 2004. 'Towards a New Perspective', in David N. Lorenzen (ed.), *Religious Movements in South Asia. 600–1800*, pp. 291–332. New Delhi: Oxford University Press. [Originally published in Krishna Sharma. 1987. *Bhakti and the Bhakti Movement: A New Perspective: A Study in the History of Ideas*, pp. 1–31. New Delhi: Munshiram Manoharlal.]

Sharma, V. 1996. 'Ramanuja', *Economic and Political Weekly*, 31 (8): 430.

Shrimali, Krishna Mohan. 1988. 'Religion, Ideology and Society', *Social Scientist*, 16 (12): 14–60.

Shukla, P. K. 2001. 'Pre-Colonial Cultural Legacy and Colonial Intervention: An Historical Appraisal', *Social Scientist*, 29 (3/4): 61–73.

Sinha, Jadunatha. 1972. *Philosophy of Ramanuja*. Calcutta: Sinha Publishing House.

Snell, Merwin-Marie. 1895. 'Evangelical Hinduism', *The Biblical World*, 6 (4): 270–7.

Spencer, George W. 1969. 'Religious Networks and Royal Influence in Eleventh-Century South India', *Journal of Economic and Social History of the Orient*, 12 (1): 42–56.

———. 1976. 'The Politics of Plunder: The Cholas in Eleventh-Century Ceylon', *Journal of Asian Studies*, 35 (3): 406–19.

Śrī Rāmānuja Vāṇī. 1979. *A Quarterly Journal of Viśiṣṭādvaita Vedānta*, 2 (3). Madras: Ramanuja Vedanta Centre.

Śrī Rāmānuja Vāṇī. 1985. *A Quarterly Journal of Viśiṣṭādvaita Vedānta*, 8 (4). Madras: Ramanuja Vedanta Centre.

Śrī Rāmānuja Vāṇī. 1979–85. *A Quarterly Journal of Viśiṣṭādvaita Vedānta*, Madras: Shri Ramanuja Vedanta Centre.

Stein, Burton. (ed.). 1978. *South Indian Temples: An Analytical Consideration*: New Delhi: Vikas Publishers.

———. 1980. *Peasant State and Society in Medieval South India*. Delhi: Oxford University Press.

———. 1989. *Vijayanagara*. The New Cambridge History of India. Cambridge: Cambridge University Press.

———. 2004. 'Social Mobility and Medieval South Indian Hindu Sects', in David Lorenzen (ed.), *Religious Movements in South Asia*, pp. 81–101. Delhi: Oxford University Press. [Originally published in James Silverberg (ed.). 1968. *Social Mobility and the Caste System in India: An Interdisciplinary Symposium*, pp. 78–94. Paris: Mouton].

Stevenson, J. 1843. 'An Account of the Bauddho-Vaishnavas, or Vitthal-Bhaktas of the Dakhan', *Journal of the Royal Asiatic Society of Great Britain and Ireland*, 7 (1): 64–73.

Stietencron, Heinrich von. 2001. 'Charisma and Canon: The Dynamics of Legtimization and Innovation in Indian Religion', in Vasudha Dalmia, Angelika Malinar and Martin Christof (eds). 2001. *Charisma and Canon: Essays on the Religious History of the Indian Subcontinent*, pp. 14–38. New Delhi: Oxford University Press.

Stoker, Valerie. 2004. 'Conceiving the Canon in Dvaita Vedānta: Mādhva's Doctrine of "All Sacred Lore"', *Numen*, 51 (1): 47–77.

Stone, Lawrence. 1979. 'The Revival of Narrative: Reflections on a New Old History', *Past and Present*, 85 (Nov.): 3–24.

Studies in Rāmānuja. 1980. Papers presented at the First All India Seminar on Sri Rāmānuja and His Social Philosophy at Śrīperumbūdur. Madras: Śrī Rāmānuja Vedānta Centre.

Subbarayulu, Y. 1973. *Political Geography of the Chola Country*. Madras: Government of Tamil Nadu, Department of Archeology.

Subramaniam, V. 1975. 'The Sage of Kanchi', *Economic and Political Weekly*, 10 (31): 1145–7.

Sundaresan, Vidya Shankar. 2000. 'Conflicting Hagiographies and History: The Place of Śaṅkaravijaya Texts in the Advaita Tradition', *International Journal of Hindu Studies*, 4 (2): 109–84.

Svāmin, A. Govindācārya. 1912. 'The Birthplace of Bhakti', *Journal of the Royal Asiatic Society of Great Britain and Ireland*, 44 (2): 481–3.

Svāmin, Govindacharya and G. A. G. 1912. 'Tengalai and Vadagalai', *Journal of the Royal Asiatic Society of Great Britain and Ireland*, 44 (3): 714–8.

Swami Ramakrishnananda (trans. from Bengali by Swami Budhananda). 1986. *Life of Sri Ramanuja*. Madras: Sri Ramakrishna Math.

Swamy, R. V. 2007. *Swamyin Ramanuja Vaibhavam*. Srirangam: Srirangam Karuthurai Mandapam

Talbot, Cynthia. 1987. 'Golaki Matha Inscriptions from Andhra: A Study of a Saiva Monastic Lineage', in Ajay Mitra Shastri and R. K. Sharma (eds), *Vajapeya: Essays on the Evolution of Indian Art and Culture*, pp. 130–46. Delhi: Agam Kala Prakashan.

———. 1991. 'Temples, Donors and Gifts: Patterns of Patronage in Thirteenth Century South India', *Journal of Asian Studies*, 50 (2): 308–40.

———. 1995. 'Inscribing the Other, Inscribing the Self: Hindu-Muslim Identities in Pre-colonial India', *Comparative Studies in Society and History*, 37 (4): 692–722.

———. 2001. *Precolonial India in Practice: Society, Region, and Identity in Medieval Andhra*. New Delhi: Oxford University Press.

Tambiah, Stanley Jeyaraja. 1984. *The Buddhist Saints of the Forest and the Cult of Amulets: A Study in Charisma, Hagiography, Sectarianism and Millennial Buddhism*. Cambridge: Cambridge University Press.

Taylor, McComas. 2008. 'What Enables Canonical Literature to Function as "True"? The Case of the Hindu Purāṇas', *International Journal of Hindu Studies*, 12 (3): 309–28.

Thapar, Romila. 1971. 'The Image of the Barbarian in Early India', *Comparative Studies in Society and History*, 13 (4): 408–36.

———. 1975. 'Ethics, Religion, and Social Protest in the First Millenium B. C. in Northern India', *Daedalus: Journal of the American Academy of Arts and Sciences*, 104 (2): 119–32.

———. 1992a. 'Imagined Religious Communities: Ancient History and the Modern Search for a Hindu Identity', in Romila Thapar, *Interpreting Early India*, pp. 60–88. Delhi: Oxford University Press.

———. 1992b. 'Society and Historical Consciousness: The Itihāsa-Purāṇa Tradition', in Romila Thapar, *Interpreting Early India*, pp. 137–73. New Delhi: Oxford University Press.

———. 1999. *Śakuntalā. Texts, Readings, Histories*. New Delhi: Kali/Zubaan.

Trautmann, T. R. 1981. *Dravidian Kinship*. Cambridge: Cambridge University Press.

The American Historical Review. 2009. 114: June (3). USA: Oxford University Press.

Timm, Jeffrey R. 1991. *Texts in Contexts: Traditional Hermeneutics in South Asia*. New York: State University of New York.

Uberoi, Patricia (ed.). 1993. *Family, Kinship and Marriage in India*. Delhi: Oxford University Press.

Vaali, Kavingnar. 2008. *Rāmānuja Kaviyam*. Chennai: Vaanathi Pathipagam.

Vaidyanathan, T. G. 1989. 'Authority and Identity in India', *Daedalus: Journal of the American Academy of Arts and Sciences*, 118 (4): 147–69.

Van der Veer, Peter. 1987. 'Taming the Ascetic: Devotionalism in a Hindu Monastic Order', *Man*, 22 (4): 680–95.

Vasantha, R. 1973. 'The Cholas and the Introduction of Shrivaisnavism into Karnataka', *Quarterly Journal of the Mythic Society*, 44 (1–4): 32–6.

———. 1991. *The Narayanasvami Temple at Melkote*. Mysore: Directorate of Archaeology and Museums.

Vaudeville, Charlotte. 1962. 'Evolution of Love-Symbolism in Bhagavatism', *Journal of the American Oriental Society*, 82 (1): 31–40.

———. 1980. 'The Govardhana Myth in Northern India', *Indo-Iranian Journal*, 22 (1): 1–45.

———. 1991. *Myths, Saints and Legends in Medieval India*. New Delhi: Oxford University Press.

———. 1993. *A Weaver Named Kabir*. New Delhi: Oxford University Press.

Veliath, S. J. Cyril. 1993. *The Mysticism of Ramanuja*. New Delhi: Munshiram Manoharlal.

Veluthat, Kesavan. 1993a. 'Religious Symbols in Political Legitimation: The Case of Early Medieval South India', *Social Scientist*, 21 (1/2): 23–33.

———. 1993b. *Political Structure of Early Medieval South India*. Delhi: Orient Longman.

Venkatachalapathy, A. R. 2006. *In Those Days There Was No Coffee. Writings in Cultural History*. New Delhi: Yoda Press.

———. 2012. *The Province of the Book. Scholars, Scribes, and Scribblers in Colonial Tamilnadu*. Ranikhet: Permanent Black.

Venkatachari, K. K. A. 1978. *The Manipravala Literature of the Srivaisnava Acaryas*. Bombay: Anantacarya Indological Institute.

Venkatesan, Archana. 2007. 'The Gift of a Garland: The Āṇṭāl Story in the Guruparamaparā Prabhāvam 6000 and in the Śrī Villiputtār Sthala Purāṇa', *Journal of Vaisnava Studies*, 15 (2): 189–205.

Vidyarthi, P. B. 1977. *Śrī Rāmānuja's Philosophy and Religion: A Critical Exposition of Viśiṣṭadvaita*. Madras: Prof. M. Rangacharya Memorial Trust.

———. 1978. *Knowledge, Self and God in Ramanuja*. New Delhi: Oriental Publishers and Distributors.

Vries, Hent de and Lawrence E. Suvillan. 2007. *Political Theologies: Public Religions in a Post-Secular World* [abridged edition]. New Delhi: Social Science Press and Orient Longman.

Wadia, A. R. 1995. 'Can Indian and Western Philosophy Be Synthesized?' *Philosophy East and West*, 4 (4): 291–3.

Wagoner, Philip B. 1996. '"Sultan Among the Hindu Kings": Dress, Titles and Islamicization of Hindu Culture at Vijayanagar', *The Journal of Asian Studies*, 55 (4): 851–80.

———. 2000. 'Harihara, Bukka and the Sultan: The Delhi Sultanate in the Political Imagination of Vijayanagar', in David Gilmartin and Bruce B. Lawrence (eds), *Beyond Turk and Hindu: Rethinking Religious Identities in Islamicate South Asia*, pp. 300–26. Gainesville: Florida.

Wilson, J. G. 1970. 'Sankara, Ramanuja, and the Function of Religious Language', *Religious Studies*, 6 (1): 57–68.

Younger, Paul. 1982. 'Singing the Tamiḻ Hymnbook in the Tradition of Rāmānuja: The "Adyayanōtsava" Festival in Srīraṅkam', *History of Religions*, 21 (3): 272–93.

http://www.itsdiff.com/ Its Different KZSU Stanford 90.1 FM. 'An Interview with Indira Parthasarathy', by Balalji. Part I and II. Interview held on April 9, 2006.

INDEX

ABOUT THE AUTHOR

Ranjeeta Dutta teaches at the Department of History and Culture, Jamia Millia Islamia, New Delhi. With a focus on the peninsular region, she primarily works on religion and society, and the relationship between the text, narrative, context, and the history of ideas in the pre-colonial period of Medieval Indian History. Her research also includes concepts such as heritage monuments, conservation, and history in the public sphere.